Under the Magnolias

A Tasteful Tour of Athens

Athens Academy Parent Service Organization
Athens, Georgia

Athens Academy's Parent Service Organization sponsors *Under the Magnolias: A Tasteful Tour of Athens* in celebration of the richness of our community. Just as Athens blends past and present, *Under the Magnolias* incorporates old and new recipes which treat the tastes of a variety of people while maintaining our hometown flavor.

Athens Academy
1281 Spartan Lane
Athens, GA 30606

First printing   November 1999   5,000 copies
Second printing   March 2001   10,000 copies

Printed in the USA by
WIMMER
The Wimmer Companies
Memphis
1-800-548-2537

Introduction

There are few things more Southern than the magnolia. Over the years, it has become symbolic of a lifestyle we enjoy in the South: one of beauty, graciousness and hospitality. Southerners like their children to be polite, their homes to be inviting, and their tables to overflow. Whenever and wherever Southerners gather, food is certain to be center stage. We plan meetings around breakfast, take lunch to our sick, and arrange dinners for our needy. We welcome new ministers with a "pounding," new neighbors with a pound cake, and newly marrieds with a party. In short, food — with all its intrinsic meanings — is what being Southern is all about. Here, in the Classic City, we are blessed with beautiful homes old and new, beautiful vistas inside and out, wonderful restaurants in all parts of town, and too many good cooks to count. In this book, we have endeavored to acquaint you with our home through a tasteful tour of Athens. We hope you enjoy your journey and will visit with us often. We can promise you a warm welcome, a cold glass of iced tea (sweetened, of course), and a nice long visit under the magnolias. Y'all come back soon.

Claire Callaway
Editor

Linda Childers
Editor

A Taste of Athens History

To savour Athens' history is to understand that here is a town turning 200 years old with a tasteful blend of past and present. Athens is the home of the first chartered, state-supported university in the nation; indeed it was here that the notion of public education began. The Georgia General Assembly drafted a charter establishing the University of Georgia in 1785. In 1801 the legislature appointed a committee to ride out into the farthest frontier to select a healthful site on which to build the "college or seminary of learning." The committee agreed upon 633 wilderness acres on a hill above Cedar Shoals on the Oconee River as the site. Committee man John Milledge made the purchase himself and donated the parcel to the trustees of the university. The trustees named the place Athens after the Greek center of culture.

In the earliest years the town grew slowly on lots adjacent to the fledgling Franklin College (as the university was originally called), land sold by the trustees in order to fund the building of the first structures on the small campus. From a tiny village in the wilderness, Athens thrives today as a college town that has grown into a university city.

Preserved today are houses and sites that reflect the rich culture of the town. The town is blessed with a significant inventory of Greek Revival and Italiante houses that offer a taste of the life of aristocrats, merchants, planters and industrialists who built fine town homes in an era when cotton was king, and Athens was a center for cotton manufacture powered by the Oconee River. Athens is nationally known as the site of the first Garden Club of America, founded in 1891.

Athens is a quintessential Southern town with patches of urban forest that include copious magnolia, dogwood and other hardwood trees. Fortunately, Union troops did not burn or destroy property in Athens during the Civil War. No major battles took place here; the only altercation was a brief skirmish at Mitchell's Bridge just south of town (on today's route 441 to Watkinsville halfway between Milledge Avenue and the turn at Spartan Lane to Athens Academy). Here the Home Guard placed the Athens-manufactured, double-barreled cannon (now standing on the lawn of City Hall) and defended the town against fragments of Stoneman's raiders.

From a rapid post-Civil War recovery through the turn of the Twentieth Century, town and gown have prospered and grown to encompass vast tracts of surrounding farmland, changing much of the rural landscape. Athens Academy itself sits on former farmland on which much of the historic prosperity of the town and counties of Clarke and Oconee (once part of Clarke County) rest.

Today Athens is the site of the State Botanical Garden, the Georgia Museum of Art, the Classic Center with its magnificent theater and meeting areas, the University Performing Arts Center, a world class and vast university, historic districts, hundreds of sites listed on the National Register of Historic Places, and much more. Its historic and charming downtown sets the stage for music and visual arts that attracts people from all over the country. Athens is today multi-cultural and eclectic. It treats the tastes of a great variety of people and cultures while still maintaining a hometown flavor. Come taste and enjoy.

Athens Academy History

Athens Academy is a coeducational, independent, college preparatory day school which seeks students from diverse social, economic, religious and racial backgrounds who can benefit from a rigorous academic program led by a highly qualified and enthusiastic faculty. Founded in 1967, the school moved from its original site in the Cabaniss House near downtown Athens to a 105-acre campus just outside Athens in Oconee county.

Based on the ethic of the Judeo-Christian tradition, the school stresses respect for the beliefs of others and shares with families concern for the intellectual, moral, spiritual, emotional and physical development of the child. In a safe and caring environment, Athens Academy values a spirit of cooperation and individual achievement. The hallmark of Athens Academy is its quest for a high quality educational and personal experience for each of its students. Its motto "Excellence with Honor" epitomizes that quest.

Today's student body comes from 14 counties surrounding Athens. Graduates regularly earn admission to prestigious colleges and universities, compile outstanding records in Advanced Placement, and score high on nationally normed examinations.

5

Original Cookbook Committee

Claire Callaway, *Editor*   Linda Childers, *Editor*

Gayle Felchlin   Kathy Lober
1997–1998, Chairman   *1997–1998, Co-Chairman*

Carolyn Adams	Deena Eberhardt	Juli Howell	Beth Mills
Natalia Alexeev	Marie Eisenberg	Patsy Huban	Beth Milner
Nancy Allen	Sheri Eldridge	Lisa Huggins	Susan Moore
Jeane Argo	Gigi Elkabbani	Donna Hulsey	Frances Morang
Kim Arnold	Betsy Ellison	Zanne Hunt	Laura Morang
Susan Barrett	Marsha Elsberry	Darcy Iams	Elise Nadler
Sally Barnes	Sissy Erwin-Toro	Helen Irving	Pam NeSmith
Kim Barton	Julie Finlayson	Kay Isley	Anne Nielson
Kay Bennett	Jennifer Fitzgerald	Sandy Jarrett	Robin O'Rear
Kelley Blanton	Valerie Franklin	Melanie Jattuso	Claudia O'Steen
Chris Blount	Kathy Frary	Anne Jones	Omayma Obeidin
Cindy Boerma	Vicki Gaines	Holly Kaplan	Toni Parr
Nina Borremans	Karen Gardner	Patricia Kardon	Jean Petrovs
Tina Boswell	Carolyn Garrard	Karen Kimbaris	Alice Pruitt
Sherry Brackett	Tina Gaskins	Sheryl Kimbrough	Lisa Ransom
Jenny Broadnax	Em Gibson	Teresa Kittle	Caroline Ridlehuber
Jan Brooks	Rosalind Gilbert	Brenda Klein	Eileen Robb
Alice Bullock	DeDe Guest	Carol Kohl	Lili Rogers
Betsy Canfield	Sallie Hale	Ginger Lamb	Monie Salloum
Candy Carrillo	Julie Harris	Angelyn Lewis	Mamata Shetty
Stephanie Cartwright	Cindy Haygood	Mary Ann Lewis	Mary Simpson
Alice Ann Colley	Ginger Heery	Margaret Liedberg	Leslie Sinyard
Linda Cook	Eva Henson	Katie Lloyd	Judy Smith
Amy Cowsert	Nina Herrington	Lee Lyons	Robin Stewart
Elizabeth Dalton	Diane Hodson	Beth Mahoney	Jerri Stracener
Anne Dattilo	Terry Hastings	Rosemary Malone	Kelley Tison
Betty DeVore	Suzette Hodge	Kim Mansfield	Patsy Tripp
Laurie Douglas	Jana Hollingsworth	Julie Maynard	Marlo Wiggans
Meg Downs	Jane Horn	Sheri McLeod	Sue Williams
Anna Dyer	Bett Houser	Karen Middendorf	

2000-2001 Cookbook Committee

Tootise Adams, *Chairman*   Jan Solomon, *Co-Chairman*

Nina Borremans	Jeannie Green	Tammy Lindsay	Beverly Sligh
Stephanie Cartwright	Kim Griffith	Gail Lopes	Linda Smith
Jane Crawshaw	Nancy Hunter	Wendy Marbut	Gayle Spears
Ellen Cunningham	Kay Isley	Beth Milner	Angi Thompson
Angela Duvoisin	Teresa Kittle	Lisa Moore	Linda Ward
Jane Fleming	Cary Leonard	Gwen Payton	

Table of Contents

About the Artists

Bett Houser

The cover artist, Bett Houser, has created a watercolor depicting Athens and Athens Academy. Bett lives in Athens with her family and is the former director of the fine arts program at Athens Academy. She has studied art at the Savannah College of Art and Design. Her son attends Athens Academy.

Alice Pruitt

The pen and ink drawings found throughout *Under the Magnolias* have been reproduced from original drawings done by Alice Pruitt. Alice is an Athens artist whose children attend Athens Academy. She studied architecture at Tulane University and art education at the University of Georgia. Alice has taught in an elementary school for 16 years.

Cabaniss Rogers House

Sautéed Dusted Oysters
with Tabasco Butter Sauce

Sauce

2	shallots, minced		1	cup clam juice
1	tablespoon oil		½	tablespoon fresh thyme leaves, stems
7	tablespoons butter, divided, chilled			removed
¼	cup all-purpose flour		1	tablespoon Tabasco
1	cup white wine			

Oysters

	All-purpose flour		24-30	shucked oysters
	Salt and pepper			Fresh chives, chopped
½	cup oil			

Sauté shallots in oil over medium heat until tender. Add 2 tablespoons butter and flour and cook, stirring constantly with a whisk, over low heat for 2 minutes. Add wine, clam juice and thyme. Bring to a simmer and reduce heat for 3 minutes, stirring occasionally. Sauce will thicken as it cooks. Remove from heat. Stir in Tabasco and remaining 5 tablespoons butter. Set aside and keep warm.

To prepare oysters, season flour with salt and pepper. Heat oil in a large skillet over medium heat to about 350°. Dredge oysters heavily in seasoned flour. Cook in oil until golden brown on both sides. To serve, drizzle sauce on serving plates. Place oysters on top of sauce. Garnish with chives.

Yield: 4 servings

The Basil Press

*Contemporary cuisine
in an intimate bistro with a
bird's-eye view of downtown Athens.*

Dixie Sugared Nuts

*No Southern wedding reception would be complete
without sugared nuts, pulled mints and tea sandwiches.*

Preheat oven to 300°.

½ **(6-ounce) can frozen orange juice concentrate, thawed**	¾ **teaspoon salt**
2 **egg whites**	2 **(12-ounce) cans salted cashews**
1¾ **cup sugar**	1 **(6-ounce) can pecan halves**
5 **teaspoons ground cinnamon**	1 **(4½-ounce) can whole blanched almonds**
2¼ **teaspoons allspice**	

In a large bowl, beat orange juice concentrate and egg whites with a fork until blended. In a shallow bowl, combine sugar, cinnamon, allspice and salt. Stir cashews, pecan halves and almonds into orange juice mixture. Using a slotted spoon, remove nut mixture, about ½ cup at a time, and dip into sugar mixture. Toss well to coat. Spread sugar-coated nuts in 2 jelly-roll pans. Bake, stirring occasionally, for 30 to 35 minutes or until nuts are golden. Cool nuts slightly in pan, then transfer to wax paper to cool completely. Store in a tightly covered container for up to 2 weeks.

Yield: 10 cups

Sugared Peanuts

It's Southern, after all!

Preheat oven to 300°.

2 cups sugar	**4 cups raw peanuts**
Dash of cinnamon (optional)	**1 cup water**
Dash of nutmeg (optional)	

Season sugar with cinnamon and nutmeg, if using. Combine sugar mixture, peanuts and water in a saucepan. Bring to a rolling boil. Reduce heat to low. Cook until liquid evaporates. Spread peanuts on a baking sheet. Bake for 20 to 30 minutes. Use a knife or spatula to loosen peanuts and break apart when cool.

Someone once said that hospitality is a gift: the gift of oneself, the opening of one's home to create a place where family, friends and even total strangers may feel at ease. Hospitality comes from the heart. It's a genuine desire to make others feel warm and welcomed. When it comes to hospitality, no one does it better than the South. Southerners love to entertain and to be entertained - be it a backyard cookout, an afternoon tea or a black tie fundraiser. It's all the same to us. All we ask is for good food (and lots of it), something cold to drink and good friends to enjoy it with.

Pizza Dip

Teenagers love this.

Preheat oven to 350°.

1 **(8-ounce) package cream cheese**	1 **(6-ounce) can black olives, drained and chopped**
1 **(14-ounce) jar pizza sauce**	2 **ounces pepperoni, finely chopped**
⅓ **cup chopped onions**	**Corn chips**
1½ **cups grated mozzarella cheese**	

Press cream cheese into the bottom of a 9-inch pie pan. Spread pizza sauce over the top. Layer onions, mozzarella cheese, olives and pepperoni in order listed. Bake for 25 minutes. Serve with chips.

Yield: 8 to 10 servings

Vidalia Onion Dip

It's Southern, after all!

Preheat oven to 325°.

2 **cups chopped Vidalia onions**	2 **dashes Tabasco sauce**
2 **cups mayonnaise**	**Parmesan cheese**
2 **cups grated Swiss cheese**	

Combine onions, mayonnaise, Swiss cheese and Tabasco sauce. Pour into a 9-inch baking dish. Sprinkle with Parmesan cheese. Bake for 20 minutes. Serve with crackers.

Yield: 8 to 10 servings

Roasted peanuts (we call them "parched" in the South) are a favorite snack at fall football games and other sporting events. They are even served as appetizers in some restaurants. Anytime the craving hits, they can easily be "parched" at home. Spread peanuts onto a jelly-roll pan and bake at 300° for 30 to 45 minutes if in the shell or 20 to 30 minutes if shelled. Turn frequently to avoid scorching.

~

Boiled Peanuts

A trip to the mountains is sure to turn up at least a half dozen roadside stands selling boiled peanuts hot out of an old black kettle. They are so good, it's hard to know when to stop eating them. Like "parched" peanuts, boiled peanuts can easily be prepared at home. Simply add green peanuts in the shell to boiling salted water, using 1 tablespoon salt for each quart of water. Boil for 2½ to 3 hours. Serve hot or cold.

Hot Dip in a Hat

Great dip for those nippy fall parties

Preheat oven to 325°.

½ cup finely chopped onions	2 (8-ounce) packages cream cheese, softened
5 green onions, chopped	1 cup mayonnaise
½ cup finely chopped bell peppers	¾ cup chopped pecans
1 tablespoon butter	1 (5-ounce) jar dried beef, chopped
1 tablespoon Worcestershire sauce	1 large round loaf of bread
½ teaspoon garlic salt	

Sauté onions and bell peppers in butter over low heat for 5 minutes or until softened but not browned. Transfer to a large mixing bowl. Add Worcestershire sauce, garlic salt and cream cheese. Mix well. Add mayonnaise, pecans and beef. Mix thoroughly. Cut a slice off the top of the loaf of bread, reserving the slice. Hollow out enough of inside of bread to hold the cream cheese mixture. Spoon mixture into cavity and replace top slice of bread as a lid. Wrap loaf tightly with foil and place on a baking sheet. Bake for 60 minutes. Serve with large corn chips or crackers.

Yield: 8 to 10 servings

Dried beef can be used in many different ways. For an easy hors d'oeuvre, wrap sweet gherkin pickles with slices of dried beef, and skewer with toothpicks.

For a different break-fast idea, sauté a jar of dried beef in 4 tablespoons butter or margarine until crisp. Drain and crumble. Add to a basic white sauce and serve over buttered toast points.

~

"As soon as Stuart was able to sit on a stool by himself, we started going to Add's to eat. He had a grilled cheese and fries every day of his life! He still eats there and he is 18 years old. We love Add's!"

Linda Jerkins, referring to the lunch counter in Add Drug Store in Five Points. Stuart is a 1998 graduate of Athens Academy.

Hot Crab and Almond Dip

Perfect when you need something wonderful in a hurry

Preheat oven to 350°.

¼ cup sliced almonds	1 (7¾-ounce) can crabmeat,
1 (8-ounce) package cream cheese	undrained
1 tablespoon lemon juice	½ teaspoon curry powder

Spread almonds in a shallow pan. Bake for 4 minutes. Set aside. Beat cream cheese, lemon juice, undrained crabmeat and curry powder until well blended. Stir in half of the almonds and pour into a baking dish. Sprinkle remaining almonds on top. Bake for 20 minutes. Serve hot with raw vegetables or crackers.

Yield: 2 cups

Tomato Poppers

2 pints
cherry tomatoes
¼ cup mayonnaise
¼ cup cream cheese,
softened
2 teaspoons fresh
chopped parsley, plus
extra for topping
1 cup cooked and
crumbled bacon, plus
extra for topping

Using a small knife, core tomatoes. Combine mayonnaise, cream cheese, parsley and bacon. Mix well. Stuff tomatoes with mixture. Sprinkle with extra parsley and bacon.

Yield: 60 to 70 tomatoes

If tomatoes tend to roll, slice a thin layer from the bottom.

~

To cook large quantities of bacon at one time, place strips on the rack of a broiler pan. Bake at 400° until crisp. No need to turn while cooking.

BLT Dip

A crowd-pleaser every time

2 pounds bacon	4-5 tomatoes, seeded and finely
1 cup mayonnaise	diced
1 cup sour cream	Bagel chips, thin wheat
Lettuce leaves	crackers or crackers of choice

Cook bacon until very crisp. Drain and blot on paper towels; crumble. Combine bacon, mayonnaise and sour cream and refrigerate several hours or overnight. Line a serving dish with lettuce leaves. Shape bacon mixture into a ball or mound and center on top of lettuce. Cover bacon mixture completely with tomatoes. Serve with bagel chips or crackers.

Yield: 8 to 10 servings

Note: If doubling recipe, use 3 pounds bacon.

Blue Cheese, Apple and Walnut Spread

A unique blend of flavors

2 teaspoons raisins	1 tablespoon finely chopped walnuts
1 tablespoon sweet sherry	
4 ounces blue cheese	1 tablespoon chopped pine nuts
1 tablespoon cream	
2 tablespoons finely chopped apples	⅛ teaspoon dried thyme

Soak raisins in sherry for 20 minutes. Drain raisins, reserving sherry. In a bowl, mash together cheese, cream and reserved sherry until smooth. Stir in raisins, apples, walnuts, pine nuts and thyme. Serve at room temperature as a spread for crackers. Store in an airtight container in refrigerator for 1 to 2 days.

Yield: 16 canapés, 4 servings

Canapé: (KAN uh pay, KAN uh pee) Small, decorative pieces of bread topped with a savory garnish or spread and served as an appetizer.

Crunchy Apple Dip

A pleasant change from chips and dip

1 (8-ounce) package cream cheese, softened	1 cup chopped dates
	½ cup chopped pecans
1 tablespoon mayonnaise	2 apples, unpeeled and cut into thin wedges
1 (8-ounce) can crushed pineapple, drained	

Combine cream cheese and mayonnaise. Beat well. Stir in pineapple, dates and pecans. Cover and chill. Serve with apple wedges.

Yield: 2 cups, 6 to 8 servings

Variation: For a festive variation at Christmas, form the dip mixture into a ring. Press sliced almonds onto surface, overlapping each slice to form a "pine cone wreath". Curl an apple peel for the bow, and surround with alternating red and green apple slices.

Banana Balls

Ripe bananas
Sour cream
Flaked coconut

Cut bananas into 1-inch chunks. Dip in sour cream to completely cover. Roll in coconut. Place on a cookie sheet and freeze. Remove 20 minutes before serving to partially thaw. To serve, mound in a deep bowl with toothpicks on the side.

Fresh Strawberries with Brown Sugar

½ cup brown sugar or to taste
1 (16-ounce) container sour cream
1 quart fresh strawberries

Mix together brown sugar and sour cream. Place mixture in a hollowed out pineapple or a crystal bowl. Surround with strawberries.

~

To keep apples from turning brown after cutting, marinate in a small amount of lemon-lime carbonated beverage.

Pesto

Good to have on hand

4 ounces fresh basil	¼ cup Parmesan cheese
1 ounce fresh parsley	¼ cup pine nuts
2 cloves garlic, chopped	Salt and pepper to taste
¼ cup olive oil	

Combine basil, parsley, garlic, oil and cheese in a blender or food processor. Blend until well mixed. Add pine nuts and blend for a few seconds. Season with salt and pepper. Cover and store in the refrigerator.

Yield: ½-¾ cup

> Pesto comes from the Italian word "Pestare" which means to pound or bruise. The classic way to make pesto is with a mortar and pestle, but today it is easier to use a blender or food processor. Ingredients can include a variety of herbs, garlic, nuts, salt, olive oil and cheese, along with black and red beans and sun-dried tomatoes. Pesto can be kept in the refrigerator and used as a dip or to enhance sauces, soups or stews.

Sun-Dried Tomato Pesto

An earthy flavored pesto

2½ tablespoons extra virgin olive oil	1 cup coarsely chopped oil-packed sun-dried tomatoes, oil drained and reserved
4 cloves garlic, minced	½ teaspoon salt
1 (28-ounce) can Italian plum tomatoes in purée	½ teaspoon black pepper

Heat olive oil and garlic in a saucepan. Cook gently for 3 minutes, being careful not to let garlic brown. Using the back of a large spoon, crush plum tomatoes slightly, then add with purée to saucepan. Simmer, uncovered, over low heat for 60 minutes or until mixture forms a very thick sauce. Remove from heat and add sun-dried tomatoes. Let stand 5 minutes. Transfer mixture to a food processor. Process until smooth, adding ¼ cup of reserved tomato oil through the feed tube. Stir in salt and pepper. Store in an airtight container in the refrigerator for up to 4 days.

Yield: 2½ cups

Note: This makes a wonderful spread for toasted crostini, or mix with mayonnaise and serve with grilled fish. Also good added to tomato soup.

Pesto Palmiers

Serve as an appetizer or with your favorite soup for a quick, easy meal.

Preheat oven to 400°.

1 **sheet puff pastry, thawed**	3 **tablespoons Parmesan or**
3 **tablespoons pesto**	**pecorino cheese**

Working quickly, unfold pastry on a lightly floured board. Roll out to form a rectangle. Spread pesto over dough and sprinkle evenly with cheese. Starting at the long sides, roll up the dough from both sides, meeting in the middle. Dip fingers in water and lightly dampen the center seam of the pastry between the 2 rolls. Press the seam together to make a long rectangle. Cut into ½-inch thick slices and place, cut-side down, on an ungreased baking sheet. Bake for 20 minutes or until puffed and golden. Pastries will be heart-shaped.

Yield: 18 pastries, 8 to 10 servings

Puff Pastry: A rich, delicate multi-layered pastry used in baking.

Black Bean Pesto

A hot and spicy spread

8 **ounces dried black beans, rinsed**	2 **jalapeño peppers, seeded**
1 **quart water**	2 **cloves garlic**
1 **bay leaf**	1 **bunch cilantro, stems only**
1 **ham hock**	**Salt and pepper to taste**

Combine beans, water, bay leaf, ham hock, jalapeño peppers, garlic and cilantro stems in a large saucepan. Bring to a boil. Reduce heat and simmer, uncovered, for 1 hour, 30 minutes. Discard ham hock and bay leaf. Drain and reserve cooking liquid. Transfer bean mixture, in batches, to a food processor. Blend, adding reserved cooking liquid as needed, to form a smooth, thick paste. Season with salt and pepper. Store in an airtight container in the refrigerator for up to 2 to 3 days.

Yield: 3 cups

Note: Good on fajitas or nachos, in layered Mexican dips, or served as a side dish garnished with sour cream and cilantro.

Pesto can be frozen in ice cube trays, then transferred to plastic bags and stored in the freezer. Use thawed pesto squares to:

Add zip to a sandwich or spread

Spread on pizza or nachos as a basic sauce

Top a baked potato

Spread under the skin of chicken before baking

Blend with butter and serve with grilled fish

~

Pesto Wheels

1 sheet puff pastry, thawed
Pesto (homemade or store-bought)
Roasted red bell peppers

Place pastry sheet on a lightly floured surface. Spread with pesto. Top with red peppers. Roll up pastry. Cut into thin slices and place on a baking sheet. Bake in preheated 425° oven for 10 minutes.

Lemon Hummus

Great served as a dip with pita crisps and fresh vegetables

3 cups drained chickpeas	1 cup tahini
2-3 cloves garlic	1¼ cups lemon juice

Place all ingredients in a blender. Blend thoroughly. Refrigerate at least 4 hours before serving.

Yield: 10 to 12 servings

Tahini: A smooth paste made of ground sesame seeds.

Hummus: (HOOM uhs) A thick Middle Eastern sauce made from mashed chickpeas seasoned with lemon juice, garlic and olive or sesame oil. Usually served as a dip with pita bread or as a sauce.

Asparagus Rollups

Wonderful in spring when fresh asparagus is abundant

Preheat oven to 400°.

1 large bunch asparagus, trimmed	½ (8-ounce) package cream cheese, softened
2 sheets frozen puff pastry, thawed	1 egg
¼ cup sweet hot mustard	1 tablespoon water
	Poppy seeds

Steam asparagus for 3 minutes or until just tender. Immerse immediately in cold water to stop cooking process. Drain and set aside. On a lightly floured surface, roll out a sheet of pastry to form a 12-inch square. Cut pastry in half. Combine mustard and cream cheese. Spread a fourth of mustard mixture over each half. Lay 6 or 7 asparagus spears at the narrow end of each pastry piece. Roll up, jelly roll style, as tightly as possible. Repeat with remaining pastry sheet. Place rolls on a greased baking sheet, seam side down. Beat together egg and water for an egg wash. Brush rolls with egg wash and sprinkle with poppy seeds. Bake for 15 minutes.

Yield: 8 to 10 servings

Pita Crisps

For a great tasting, low fat alternative to purchased chips, cut pita bread rounds in half horizontally, then cut each half into 6 to 8 wedges. Place wedges in a single layer on an ungreased baking sheet. Bake in a preheated 350° oven for 10 to 12 minutes or until crisp.

~

Homemade Taco Chips

12 corn tortillas
Non-stick cooking spray
Salt to taste

Cut tortillas into quarters. Place in a single layer on a baking sheet sprayed with non-stick cooking spray. Bake in preheated 350° oven for 12 to 15 minutes or until crisp.

Salsa Al Fresco

Also good as a relish for grilled chicken or fish

6-8 tomatoes, seeded and chopped
¼ cup seeded and chopped cucumbers
¼ cup chopped bell peppers
2 cloves garlic, crushed
½ teaspoon salt
¼ teaspoon black pepper

2-4 tablespoons minced fresh cilantro or parsley
2 tablespoons olive oil
Juice of ½ lemon or lime
½ teaspoon ground cumin
½ teaspoon chili powder
Tortilla chips

Combine all ingredients except tortilla chips. Cover and chill several hours before serving. Serve with tortilla chips.

Yield: 10 to 12 servings

Salsa: A spicy sauce made up of tomatoes, onions and hot peppers.

Black Bean Salsa

Chunky, spicy and low in fat

1 (16-ounce) can black beans, rinsed and drained
2 tomatoes, chopped
4 green onions, sliced
1 clove garlic, crushed
3 tablespoons fresh cilantro

2½ tablespoons vegetable oil
2 tablespoons lime juice
¼ teaspoon ground cumin
¼ teaspoon salt
¼ teaspoon black pepper
Tortilla chips

Combine all ingredients except tortilla chips. Cover and refrigerate 8 hours. Drain and discard liquid. Serve with tortilla chips.

Yield: 3 cups

"It was truly an honor to be asked to become a member of the first faculty at Athens Academy. I never regretted it, and my 22 years as a fourth grade teacher were my happiest teaching years. Now after retirement, I come in contact with so many of my students and am so proud of having a small part in forming their lives."

Mrs. Flora Faircloth, a retired teacher

Piroshki

Serve as an hors d'oeuvre or as an accompaniment to soups or salads.

> Caps are the key to choosing mushrooms. Look for caps that are closed around the stem. Caps that are wide open are a sign of age. Color depends on the variety. White, off white and tan are the most common colors. Because they are highly perishable, purchase mushrooms only as needed. If necessary, they may be stored loosely wrapped in the refrigerator for 1 to 2 days.

Pastry

2 cups all-purpose flour	4 tablespoons butter, softened
½ teaspoon baking powder	1 egg, beaten
½ teaspoon salt	½ cup sour cream

Filling

½ cup finely chopped fresh mushrooms	⅛ teaspoon black pepper
3 green onions, sliced	1 teaspoon fresh dill or ½ teaspoon dried
1 tablespoon butter	⅓ cup sour cream
2 teaspoons all-purpose flour	1 egg yolk
¼ teaspoon salt	1 teaspoon water

Combine all pastry ingredients in a food processor. Process 1 to 2 minutes or until dough forms a ball. Chill 1 hour.

Meanwhile, prepare filling by sautéing mushrooms and green onions in butter until tender. Remove from heat and stir in flour, salt, pepper and dill. Cool. Stir in sour cream. Prepare an egg wash by beating egg yolk and water together. Set aside.

Roll pastry to ⅛-inch thickness on a lightly floured surface. Cut into 2½-inch circles. Place 1 teaspoon of filling in center of each circle. Brush edge of pastries with egg wash. Fold each pastry in half and press edges to seal. Place on a lightly greased baking sheet. Brush pastry tops with egg wash. Bake in preheated 375° oven for 30 minutes.

Yield: 3 dozen

Piroski: (pih ROSH kee) A small Russian turnover consisting of pastry wrapped around various fillings.

Hot Cheese Pastries

Good for a morning coffee

Preheat oven to 400°.

Filling

2   (8-ounce) packages cream
     cheese
8   ounces feta cheese, crumbled

1   egg
3   tablespoons butter, melted

Pastry

1   (17.3-ounce) package puff
     pastry

2   sticks butter, melted

Combine all filling ingredients in a small bowl. Beat at medium speed until well blended and smooth. Set aside.

To prepare pastry, place 2 sheets of pastry on a board. Brush with melted butter. Cut lengthwise into 2-inch wide strips. Place 1 teaspoon of filling at one end of each strip. Fold over a corner of each strip to the opposite side, making a triangle. Continue folding, keeping triangle shape, to the end of the strip. Repeat with remaining sheets of pastry. Bake for 20 minutes or until golden brown.

Yield: 7 dozen pastries

Note: Pastries can be made ahead and frozen. Arrange unbaked pastries in a single layer on a baking sheet. Freeze until solid. Transfer to an airtight container and store in freezer until ready to bake. Adjust baking time if not thawed when baked.

To use frozen phyllo dough, thaw while still wrapped. Once sheets are removed from the box and unwrapped, they quickly dry out and become unusable. Keep unwrapped sheets covered with plastic wrap or a slightly dampened paper towel. Rewrap unused sheets of dough and return to freezer.

Greek Pizza Bites

Careful - they're addictive!

Preheat oven to 400°.

The preparation of garlic for cooking purposes depends upon the intensity of flavor desired. Garlic has a high oil content; the fresher the bulb the more oil it contains and the stronger the flavor. For the most intense flavor, finely chop or mash cloves to release more of the oils. For a milder taste, cloves may be used whole, often unpeeled, and removed prior to serving. Cloves that are peeled and halved provide a stronger but less pungent flavor.

1 cup chopped onions	Juice of ½ large lemon
3 large cloves garlic, crushed	1 stick butter, melted
6 tablespoons olive oil, divided	8 ounces phyllo dough
½ teaspoon basil	1½ cups crumbled feta cheese
½ teaspoon oregano	4 cups grated mozzarella cheese, divided
1 pound fresh spinach, rinsed and chopped, stems discarded	2 medium tomatoes, thinly sliced
¼ teaspoon salt	1 cup breadcrumbs
Black pepper to taste	

Sauté onions and garlic in 2 tablespoons olive oil until tender. Add basil, oregano, spinach, salt, pepper and lemon juice. Cook until spinach is wilted and the mixture is almost dry. Combine remaining 4 tablespoons olive oil and butter. Layer phyllo dough on a greased baking sheet, brushing each layer with butter mixture. Using a slotted spoon, transfer spinach mixture to top of dough layers, leaving a ½-inch edge. Sprinkle with feta cheese and 2 cups mozzarella cheese. Coat both sides of tomato slices with breadcrumbs. Arrange slices on top of cheeses. Sprinkle with remaining 2 cups mozzarella. Bake for 25 to 30 minutes or until pizza is golden brown. Cool. Cut into small squares.

Yield: 16 servings

Phyllo dough: (FEE loh) A Greek pastry made from a mixture of flour and water that has been rolled or stretched paper-thin and then cut into sheets. It can usually be found in the frozen foods section of the grocery store.

Pizza Squares Continental

A new twist on an old favorite

Preheat oven to 425°.

2 tablespoons olive oil
2 large onions, thinly sliced
1 (10-ounce) can refrigerated pizza crust dough
6 ounces sliced provolone cheese

1 (7.25-ounce) jar roasted red bell peppers, drained and diced
2 ounces Montrachet or other goat cheese, crumbled
2 tablespoons pine nuts

Heat oil in a large skillet over medium heat until hot. Add onions and cook 10 to 12 minutes or until light golden brown, stirring occasionally. Unroll dough and press into a greased 12-inch pizza pan or a 9x13-inch baking pan. Arrange provolone cheese over dough. Spoon onions over cheese. Top with bell peppers and Montrachet cheese. Bake for 16 to 21 minutes or until crust is golden brown. Sprinkle with pine nuts. Cut into squares or wedges.

Yield: 8 to 10 servings

Montrachet cheese: (mohn truh SHAY) A white goat cheese with a soft, moist and creamy texture and a mild tangy flavor.

You don't have to be a gourmet chef to cook and entertain creatively. In fact, some of the most successful hosts and hostesses are those that know how to turn the ordinary into the extraordinary. Spend some time in the grocery store or deli to see the variety of ready-made products that are available. For many, all that's needed is a more attractive container and a little dressing up, what chefs refer to as "presentation." For example, purchase a commercial cheese spread, either sweet or savory. Serve sweet spreads in a hollowed out apple. Rub cut surfaces of the apple with lemon juice to prevent browning. For savory spreads, slice away the top of a bell pepper and remove seeds. Spoon in spread or pipe in using a large fluted pastry tube. Serve on a platter surrounded by assorted crackers.

Calzone with Noena's Basic Sauce

A traditional post-game feast at Athens Academy

Bruschetta

3 large
ripe tomatoes,
seeded and chopped
½ large red onion, diced
1 cucumber, peeled,
seeded and diced
1 cup shredded fresh
basil
¼ cup olive oil
1 tablespoon red wine
vinegar

Combine all ingredients in a bowl. Serve on slices of toasted Italian or French bread that have been rubbed with garlic and drizzled with olive oil.

Noena's Basic Sauce

2 (28-ounce) cans whole tomatoes
1 small sweet onion, finely chopped
5 cloves garlic, crushed
1 tablespoon extra virgin olive oil

2 (6-ounce) cans tomato paste
3 tablespoons chopped fresh basil, or 2 tablespoons dried
1 teaspoon dried Italian seasoning, crushed
½ cup wine

Calzone

1 (3-pound) package frozen bread dough rolls
2 pints part-skim or non-fat ricotta cheese

1 (8-ounce) package grated part-skim or non-fat mozzarella cheese
1 egg, or ¼ cup egg substitute
2 tablespoons parsley flakes

To make sauce, drain tomatoes through a sieve over a mixing bowl, reserving the juice. Remove and discard core and seeds from tomatoes. (The seeds and core make the sauce bitter and chunkier. You can add ½ teaspoon sugar to the sauce and skip this step, but the flavor is better if you take the time to remove the seeds and core.) Shred the tomatoes by hand and add to bowl with tomato juice. Sauté onions and garlic in oil until golden. Add tomato paste and cook over very low heat, stirring constantly, for about 5 minutes. Add tomatoes and juice mixture. Stir in basil, Italian seasoning and wine. Simmer slowly for 2 to 3 hours. The sauce ages very well. It is best to make it a day or two ahead to give the flavors time to blend.

To make calzone, place rolls on a greased baking sheet to thaw and rise a little. Mix together cheeses, egg and parsley. Refrigerate until dough thaws. Using floured hands and work surface, flatten each dough ball into a 4-inch circle. Place a heaping tablespoon of cheese mixture in the center of each circle. Fold over to make a half-circle. Press the edges together and seal using fingertips. Place on a greased baking sheet to rise. Bake in preheated 400° oven for 15 to 20 minutes or until golden. Serve with Noena's Basic Sauce for dipping.

Yield: 36 calzones

Calzone: (kal ZOH-nay, kahl SOH-neh) A stuffed pizza resembling a large turnover.

Red Hot Fried Jalapeños

Guaranteed to set the night on fire

15 medium raw jalapeño peppers	1 egg
	Salt and pepper to taste
1 (8-ounce) package cream cheese, softened	½ cup all-purpose flour
	2 cups breadcrumbs
1 cup milk	Oil for frying

Blanch jalapeño peppers in boiling water for 3 minutes. Cool in ice water. Slice through top and lengthwise down one side of each pepper. Gently scrape out seeds and membranes. (Gloves are suggested for this step.) Place seeds in a small bowl. Add cream cheese to seeds and mix well. Stuff peppers with cheese mixture and freeze 30 to 45 minutes. In a shallow bowl, beat together milk, egg, salt and pepper. Place flour and breadcrumbs each in a separate shallow bowl or plate. Roll frozen peppers in flour. Dip in milk mixture and then roll in breadcrumbs. Dip in milk again and then roll in breadcrumbs. Press mixture firmly around peppers. Freeze. When ready to serve, carefully lower frozen peppers into 325° oil and fry 2 to 3 minutes or until crispy and brown. Serve hot with salsa or ranch dressing.

Yield: 15 peppers

Jalapeño: A small, plump, dark green hot pepper.

Increasing or decreasing the amount of seeds added to the cheese in this recipe greatly influences the "heat" of the peppers. For crispy peppers heated throughout, make sure the oil is really hot; use a candy thermometer to check the temperature.

Olivita Crostini

Tasty little toasts

1	(4.25-ounce) can chopped black olives	1	tablespoon extra virgin olive oil
½	cup pimento-stuffed green olives, chopped	2	cloves garlic, minced
½	cup Parmesan cheese	¾	cup grated Monterey Jack cheese
4	tablespoons unsalted butter, softened	¼	cup minced fresh Italian parsley
		1	crusty French baguette, cut into 24 thin slices

In a medium bowl, combine olives, Parmesan cheese, butter, oil and garlic. Blend well. Stir in Monterey Jack cheese and parsley. Arrange bread on a baking sheet. Spread bread slices with olive mixture. Broil 3 to 4 minutes or until toasted and bubbly. Serve immediately.

Yield: 10 to 12 servings

Crostini: (kroh STEE nee) Translated means little toasts. Slices of bread are brushed with olive oil and toasted.

Olive oils are graded according to the amount of acid they contain. The lower the acid, the better the oil. Cold-pressed extra virgin olive oil has the finest and fruitiest flavor. The deeper the color, the more intense the flavor. Light olive oil is not lighter in calories, but lighter in flavor. It should be used in recipes where a strong olive oil taste is not desirable. It has a higher smoking point than other olive oils, so it should be used for high heat frying.

Black Eyed Susans

A good take along snack for away games and road trips

Preheat oven to 300°.

2	sticks unsalted butter, softened		Cayenne pepper to taste
1	pound cheddar cheese, grated	1	(8-ounce) box pitted dates, halved lengthwise
2	cups all-purpose flour		Sugar for topping

Blend butter and cheese. Add flour and cayenne pepper to form a dough. Chill if dough is sticky. Wrap about ½ tablespoon of dough around each date half. Place on a nonstick baking sheet. Bake for about 30 minutes. Sprinkle with a little sugar while hot and serve warm or at room temperature.

Yield: 4 to 5 dozen

Note: To freeze, place unbaked dough-wrapped dates on a pan. Freeze until solid. Transfer to a zip-top bag and store in freezer until ready to serve.

Feta Cheese Crisps

*A Middle Eastern snack treat and a nice change
from the more traditional cheese wafers*

Preheat oven to 350°.

½ **cup vegetable oil**	½ **cup crumbled feta cheese**
½ **cup water**	1¾ **cups all-purpose flour**
½ **cup Parmesan cheese, plus**	
extra for topping	

Combine oil, water and cheeses in a bowl. Gradually stir in flour to make a moist dough. Form dough into ¾-inch balls. On a greased baking sheet, flatten balls into about ¼-inch thick circles, 1½-inches in diameter. Sprinkle wafers with extra Parmesan cheese. Bake on the bottom oven rack for 10 minutes. Move to upper rack and bake 10 minutes longer or until golden, checking frequently to avoid burning.

Yield: 70 crisps

Feta: (FEHT-uh) A traditional cheese made from goat's milk.

Apricot Stuffed Dates

Perfect for teas and open houses

½ **cup dried apricots**	1 **tablespoon orange juice**
⅓ **cup flaked coconut**	1 **(8-ounce) package pitted**
¼ **cup chopped pecans**	**dates**
	Powdered sugar

Steam apricots for 5 minutes. Combine apricots, coconut and pecans in a food processor. Blend until mixture appears ground. Add orange juice and mix well. Make a lengthwise slit down one side of each date. Stuff with apricot mixture. Dust with sugar.

Yield: 4 dozen

Steam: A method of cooking in which food is placed on a rack or in a steamer basket over boiling water.

---

*Tour
Weekend
Patron's Party
at the
Classic Center*

The Tour of Homes weekend, signaling the beginning of the holiday season, is a long-standing tradition in Athens and always begins with the Patron's Party on Friday night.

~

MENU

Buffet Tenderloin

Assorted Breads

Easy Horseradish Sauce

Tropical Chicken Bites with Chutney Sauce

Shrimp Salad in Miniature Pastry Shells

Asparagus Roll-Ups

Brie Cheese Dip with Assorted Fruits

Banana Balls

Almond Cream Confections

Forgotten Cookies

Dixie Sugared Nuts

Orange Blossom Champagne Punch

Brie Cheese Dip

Great with fruit

8 ounces ripe Brie cheese, rind removed, softened	½ cup plain yogurt
1 (8-ounce) package cream cheese, softened	¼ cup honey
	⅛ teaspoon cinnamon

Combine all ingredients in a food processor. Process until smooth. If mixture is too thick, add extra yogurt. Chill. Serve with sliced red and yellow apples, pears and nectarines.

Yield: 1½ cups

Ripe Brie cheese should feel soft to the touch, especially in the middle, when at room temperature. An ammonia-like smell indicates over-ripeness. To hasten the ripening process, leave at room temperature overnight or until it feels very soft in the center.

~

Low-fat cream cheese may be substituted for regular cream cheese in hot dishes without changing the texture. Fat-free cream cheese may be substituted in cold recipes, but tends to separate in hot recipes.

Sherry Cheese Pâté

Simple but sophisticated - a great combination of flavors

2 (3-ounce) packages cream cheese, softened	½ teaspoon curry powder
1 cup grated sharp cheddar cheese	¼ teaspoon salt
4 teaspoons dry sherry	1 (8-ounce) jar chutney
	3-4 green onions with tops, chopped

Combine cream cheese, cheddar cheese, sherry, curry and salt. Spread to ½-inch thick on a serving platter. Chill 30 minutes. Spread chutney over top and sprinkle with onions. Serve with wheat or sesame crackers.

Yield: 8 servings

Pâté: (pah TAY) Generally refers to a thick spread of finely chopped or puréed seasoned meat.

Zesty Blue Cheese Dip

Serve in a hollowed-out red cabbage for a unique presentation

1 (8-ounce) package cream cheese, softened	¼ cup grated carrots
½ cup sour cream	¼ cup finely chopped green onion tops
½ cup crumbled blue cheese	2 tablespoons chopped pimento
1 teaspoon lemon juice	2 tablespoons chopped parsley
½ teaspoon prepared horseradish	6 slices bacon, cooked and crumbled

Place cream cheese, sour cream and blue cheese in a food processor. Process until smooth. Stir in lemon juice, horseradish, carrots, onions, pimento, parsley and bacon. Mix well and chill thoroughly. Serve with fresh vegetables.

Yield: 2½ cups

Mango Chutney Torta

Deliciously different

1 cup 1% cottage cheese	1 cup golden raisins
2 (8-ounce) packages cream cheese, softened	1 (9-ounce) jar mango chutney, divided
1 teaspoon curry powder	Sliced green onions, chopped peanuts, and toasted coconut for garnish
1 cup dry roasted peanuts	
1 cup sliced green onions	

Process cottage cheese in a food processor until smooth, stopping once to scrape down sides. Add cream cheese and curry. Process until smooth. Add peanuts, onions, raisins and ¼ cup chutney. Pulse 3 or 4 times or until coarsely chopped. Spread half of mixture into a 9x5-inch loaf pan lined with plastic wrap. Spread ½ cup chutney over top. Spoon remaining mixture over chutney. Top with remaining chutney. Cover and chill 8 hours. Invert onto a serving plate and garnish with sliced green onions, chopped peanuts and toasted coconut.

Yield: 25 appetizers

Chutney: A spicy condiment containing fruit, vinegar, sugar and spices. May be sweet or hot.

Watermelon Rind Chutney

Spiced Vinegar
- 2 cups cider vinegar, heated
- 5 tablespoons whole all spice
- 2 sticks cinnamon
- 5 tablespoons whole cloves

Chutney
- 2 quarts watermelon rind, white part only, cut into ⅛-inch chunks
- 1 bell pepper, chopped
- 2 large onions, chopped
- 2 cloves garlic, chopped
- 2 tablespoons salt
- 2 cups fresh lime juice
- 1 pound light brown sugar
- 3½ cups granulated sugar
- 2 tablespoons white mustard seed
- 3½ teaspoons ground ginger
- 1 (15-ounce) package raisins
- Zest of 5 limes
- Spiced Vinegar, strained

Combine all spiced vinegar ingredients in a saucepan. Heat, but do not boil. Remove from heat and refrigerate 1 week before using.

To make chutney, combine first 5 ingredients. Let stand 1 hour. Drain. Combine remaining ingredients. Cook over low heat to desired consistency. Refrigerate.

Yield: 8 cups

Pesto and Sun-Dried Tomato Torte

Destined to be a classic

Dried tomatoes,
commonly called
sun-dried tomatoes,
add a zesty flavor to
many dishes. Vine-
ripened tomatoes are
cut in half, often
salted, and then dried.
The result is a chewy,
meaty tomato with
concentrated flavor.

~

Dried tomatoes may
be purchased dry or
packed in oil. To
rehydrate the dry
version, cover with
boiling water and let
stand 2 minutes, then
drain. Oil packed
tomatoes should be
removed from the oil
and patted dry with
paper towels.

~

The dry form of
tomatoes can be stored
up to 1 year in an
airtight container out
of direct light, or in a
refrigerator or freezer
for up to 1 year. Oil
packed tomatoes, once
opened, can be stored
in the refrigerator for
up to 6 months if the
oil covers the tomatoes.

4	ounces provolone cheese, thinly sliced	¼	cup pesto
2	(8-ounce) packages cream cheese, softened	½	cup sun-dried tomatoes in oil, drained and chopped, plus extra for topping
2	cloves garlic, minced	¼	cup roasted pine nuts (optional)
1½	teaspoons dried thyme		

Line a 9x5-inch loaf pan with plastic wrap, leaving several inches hang-ing over on all sides. Layer provolone cheese on the bottom of the pan and part way up the sides. Combine cream cheese, garlic and thyme in a food processor. Process until smooth. Spread a third of mixture over provolone cheese. Cover with pesto. Spread with another third of cream cheese mixture. Cover with tomatoes. Spread remaining cream cheese mixture over top. Cover with overhanging plastic wrap and pat down firmly. Chill overnight or up to 2 days. Invert onto a serving dish and sprinkle with extra tomatoes and pine nuts. Serve with crackers.

Yield: 12 to 15 servings

Note: Drained and chopped roasted red bell peppers may be substituted for the sun-dried tomatoes.

Smoked Oyster Spread

If you like oysters, you'll love this.

2	(8-ounce) packages cream cheese		Dash of hot pepper sauce
¼	cup evaporated milk		Salt to taste
1	tablespoon lemon juice	2	(6-ounce) cans smoked oysters or clams, minced
2	tablespoons mayonnaise		Parsley and paprika for
1	tablespoon Worcestershire sauce		garnish

Combine all ingredients except parsley and paprika. Mix well. Spoon into a mold lined with plastic wrap. Chill. Unmold onto a serving dish and remove plastic wrap. Garnish with parsley and paprika. Serve with crackers.

Yield: 10 to 12 servings

Boursin

A garlic lover's delight

8	ounces whipped butter, softened	¼	teaspoon basil
2	(8-ounce) packages cream cheese, softened	¼	teaspoon dill weed
		¼	teaspoon marjoram
½	teaspoon oregano	¼	teaspoon black pepper
		¼	teaspoon thyme
		2	cloves garlic, crushed

Combine all ingredients in a food processor. Process until smooth. Chill several hours to allow flavors to blend. Serve with English table wafers.

Yield: 10 to 12 servings

Boursin cheese: (boor SAHN) A smooth, white cheese with a buttery texture that is often flavored with herbs, garlic or cracked pepper.

Cool Gazpacho Spread

Refreshing taste

1	(8-ounce) package cream cheese, softened	1	clove garlic, pressed
¼	cup sour cream	1	small tomato, seeded and chopped
½	cup grated cheddar cheese	2	green onions, sliced
2	tablespoons minced fresh cilantro	⅓	cup chopped cucumbers

Combine cream cheese and sour cream. Mix well. Stir in cheddar cheese, cilantro and garlic. Cover and chill several hours to allow flavors to blend. When ready to serve, mound cream cheese mixture onto a serving dish. Top with tomatoes, onions and cucumbers. Serve with bagel chips or baked pita chips.

Yield: 4 to 6 servings

Gazpacho: (gahz PAH choh) A cold, uncooked soup made from puréed tomatoes, bell peppers, onions, celery, cucumbers, breadcrumbs, garlic, olive oil, vinegar and lemon juice.

Boursin can be used for more than simply a spread or dip. It makes a delicious topping for broiled tomatoes, or mix with a little milk and toss with hot pasta. Smear Boursin onto thick slices of French bread and grill for fabulous garlic toast. Spread some under the skin of chicken before baking, or add to a potato mixture to give twice baked potatoes a new twist. For a quick and easy hors d'oeuvre, spoon into mushroom caps and serve hot or cold, or pipe a small amount onto crinkle cut cucumber slices.

Shrimp Salad in Miniature Pastry Shells

Scrumptious and so pretty on a silver tray

2 cups water	3 tablespoons chopped sweet
½ pound unpeeled raw shrimp	pickles
3 tablespoons finely chopped	6 tablespoons bottled Italian
celery	salad dressing
2 tablespoons finely chopped	42 miniature pastry shells
bell peppers	Alfalfa sprouts

Bring water to a boil. Add shrimp and cook 3 to 5 minutes. Drain well and rinse with cold water. Chill shrimp. Peel, devein and coarsely chop. Combine shrimp, celery, peppers, pickles and dressing. Toss well and chill 8 hours. Line each pastry shell with alfalfa sprouts. Drain chilled shrimp salad well. Spoon about 1 teaspoon of salad mixture into each shell.

Yield: 24 servings

The dainty tea sandwich has been a mainstay of the Southern hostess for generations. It can be found at afternoon teas, morning coffees, church receptions and even at cocktail parties. Part of its appeal comes from the unique ways the bread is cut, the color contrast of the breads and fillings and the creative ways it may be garnished, not to mention the many delightful spreads that can be used as fillings.

~

Ham Spread

1 (5-ounce) can ham
1 (8-ounce) can crushed pineapple, drained
1 (8-ounce) package cream cheese
¼ cup finely chopped pecans
2 tablespoons mayonnaise

Combine all ingredients and mix well. Use extra mayonnaise if needed to make mixture a spreading consistency. Chill.

Shrimp Butter

Big look - little effort

2½ cups water	¼ cup chopped onions
¾ pound unpeeled raw shrimp	¼ cup mayonnaise
1 egg, hard cooked and	1 clove garlic
coarsely chopped	⅛ teaspoon salt
1 (3-ounce) package cream	⅛ teaspoon black pepper
cheese, softened	⅛ teaspoon Worcestershire
1 stick butter, softened	sauce

Bring water to a boil. Add shrimp and cook 3 to 5 minutes. Drain well and rinse in cold water. Chill shrimp. Peel, devein and coarsely chop. Combine shrimp and remaining ingredients in a food processor. Process until smooth. Line a 2-cup mold or bowl with plastic wrap, allowing 2 inches of wrap to hang over sides. Spoon shrimp mixture into mold. Cover with overhanging plastic and chill at least 4 hours. When ready to serve, uncover and invert mold onto a serving plate. Peel plastic wrap off and let stand 20 to 30 minutes. Serve with crackers.

Yield: 1⅔ cups

Mandarin Shrimp Sticks
with Warm Curry Sauce

Try it. You'll like it!

2	teaspoons curry powder	1	teaspoon instant chicken broth
2	tablespoons butter or margarine	1	cup water
1	tablespoon all-purpose flour	1	teaspoon lemon juice
2	teaspoons dry minced onions	1	pound shrimp, cooked, peeled and deveined
½	teaspoon parsley-garlic salt	1	(11-ounce) can mandarin oranges, drained
½	teaspoon sugar		

Heat curry and butter in a small saucepan for 1 minute. Stir in flour, onions, garlic salt, sugar and instant chicken broth. Cook, stirring constantly, until bubbly. Stir in water. Continue to cook and stir until sauce thickens. Boil 1 minute. Remove from heat. Stir in lemon juice and keep warm. Thread wooden skewers or picks with a shrimp and an orange segment. Serve with warm curry sauce.

Yield: 10 to 12 servings

Curry Powder: A pulverized blend of up to 20 spices; used in East Indian cooking.

Olive and Pecan Spread

2 (3-ounce) packages cream cheese

½ cup finely chopped pecans

1 cup finely chopped green olives

2 tablespoons olive juice

½ cup mayonnaise

Dash of black pepper

Combine all ingredients and mix well. Chill.

~

Cucumber Spread

1 (8-ounce) package cream cheese

½ cup sour cream

2-3 tablespoons mayonnaise

1 tablespoon dried onion flakes

1½ tablespoons grated onions

1½ cups grated cucumbers, drained if needed

Combine cream cheese, sour cream, mayonnaise, onion flakes and grated onions. Mix well. Stir in cucumbers. Chill.

Little Shrimp Surprises

Fool your guests with these little wonders.

1	pound shrimp, cooked, peeled, deveined and chilled	¼ cup finely chopped celery
1	teaspoon Worcestershire sauce	1 egg, hard cooked and chopped
3	tablespoons cream cheese	1 tablespoon grated onions
1	tablespoon chili sauce	1 cup plus 1 tablespoon finely chopped parsley, divided
2	teaspoons horseradish	¾ teaspoon salt
		⅛ teaspoon black pepper

Finely chop shrimp and place in a mixing bowl. Add Worcestershire sauce, cream cheese, chili sauce, horseradish, celery, egg, onions, 1 tablespoon parsley, salt and pepper. Mix well. Form mixture into 30 small balls. Roll in remaining 1 cup parsley. Chill at least 4 hours before serving.

Yield: 30 balls

Sidebar

For a tea sandwich that is sure to get attention, try this unusual but delicious flavor combination. You'll need 2 loaves of sandwich bread, one light colored and one dark. Trim crusts off slices. Take a slice of one color and spread with a pimento cheese mixture. Cover with a slice of the second color. Spread second slice with a mixture of peanut butter and grape jam. Top with the same bread as used for the bottom. (Alternate sequence for some of the sandwiches so some have 2 lights, 1 dark and some have 2 darks, 1 light.) Cut into finger sandwiches. Your guests won't believe it when you tell them how they're made. They're delightful!

Crabmeat Remick

This makes an elegant first course. Serve with a crusty bread to soak up extra sauce.

Preheat oven to 450°.

1	pound fresh lump crabmeat, picked over	1 teaspoon tarragon vinegar
8-12	slices (2 slices per serving) bacon, cooked crisp	½ teaspoon Tabasco sauce
½	cup mayonnaise	1 teaspoon dry mustard
½	cup chili sauce	½ teaspoon paprika
		½ teaspoon celery salt

Divide crabmeat into 4 to 6 individual ramekins. Crumble bacon over top and set aside. Combine mayonnaise, chili sauce, vinegar, Tabasco, mustard, paprika and celery salt. Stir until smooth. Place ramekins on a baking sheet. Pour sauce over crabmeat mixture. Bake until sauce starts to bubble.

Yield: 4 to 6 servings

Poached Salmon A La Elegant

Impressive!

Salmon

2½-3	pounds whole salmon	1	small white onion, finely chopped
½	cup white wine		
1	cup water	1	medium carrot, thinly sliced

Sauce

½	cup mayonnaise	1	teaspoon fresh basil, finely chopped
½	cup sour cream		
½	cup heavy cream	1	teaspoon dill weed
2	tablespoons poaching liquid or red wine vinegar	1	teaspoon Worcestershire sauce
1	small onion, minced		Salt and pepper to taste

Place salmon in a long poaching pan or steamer. Combine wine, water, onions and carrots and pour over salmon. Cover and cook until salmon flakes easily with a fork. Remove from heat and cool. When ready to serve, carefully transfer salmon from pan to a serving platter.

Combine all sauce ingredients and mix well. Spread sauce over top of salmon. Surround salmon with crackers and garnish with chopped olives, parsley sprigs and carrot curls.

Yield: 15 to 20 servings

Variation: After salmon is cooked and cooled, flake into a bowl. Add sauce and mix well. Spoon into a mold and refrigerate several hours. Unmold onto a serving plate and surround with crackers.

Poach: To cook gently in liquid just below the boiling point.

Poached salmon can be served as an entrée for a spring or summer dinner with fresh asparagus and new potatoes.

~

Candles should only be used after sundown, when the light dims outside, or on a dark, gloomy day. If used on a table, they should be lighted. Never use candles without a charred wick, not even in a decorative arrangement.

Lilah's Salmon Mousse

A buffet showstopper

For a truly impressive presentation, mold salmon mousse in a fish mold, or shape chilled mousse by hand into a fish shape. Unmold and use chopped pecans to cover the head portion of the fish. Separate the head from the body with thin strips of pimento. Cover the body with chopped parsley. Place slices of egg white so as to resemble fish fins. Use half of a pimento-stuffed olive as an eye and another small strip of pimento for a mouth.

2 envelopes unflavored gelatin	2 green onions, chopped
¾ cup clam juice	Juice of ½ lemon
2 (7-ounce) cans red sockeye salmon	1 tablespoon chopped fresh dill
6 flat anchovy fillets	8 drops hot pepper sauce
2 tablespoons capers	¾ cup sour cream
	Fresh dill for garnish

Dissolve gelatin in clam juice in a saucepan over low heat. Transfer to a food processor. Add salmon, anchovy fillets, capers, onions, clam juice, dill and hot pepper sauce. Process until smooth. Fold in sour cream. Pour into a mold sprayed with cooking spray. Chill until set. Unmold onto a serving platter and garnish with fresh dill. Serve with crackers.

Yield: 20 servings

Mousse: (MOOS) A rich, airy dish that can be either sweet or savory, hot or cold. The fluffiness is due to the addition of whipped cream or beaten egg whites, and is often fortified with gelatin.

Sally Ann's Tangy Wings

A specialty of Athens caterer, Sally Ann Cauthen, owner of Delightful Bitefuls (and it is dee-lite-ful!)

⅓ cup soy sauce	½ teaspoon ground ginger
¼ cup honey	¼ teaspoon garlic powder
2 tablespoons vegetable oil	¼ teaspoon cayenne pepper
2 tablespoons chili sauce	3 pounds chicken wings
1 teaspoon salt	

Combine all ingredients except chicken wings in a large zip-top plastic bag. Add chicken wings, seal and place in a large bowl. Refrigerate 8 hours, turning occasionally. Remove wings, reserving marinade. Place wings in an ungreased 15x10-inch jelly-roll pan. Bake, uncovered, in preheated 325° oven for 60 minutes or until done. Baste frequently with reserved marinade. Serve warm.

Yield: 8 to 10 servings

Waikiki Chicken Bites with Chutney Sauce

Combines a Southern favorite with an Island flavor

4	boneless, skinless chicken breast halves	½	cup finely chopped macadamia nuts
¼	cup lemon juice	½	cup fine dry breadcrumbs
¼	cup dry sherry	½	cup all-purpose flour
3	tablespoons Worcestershire sauce	2	eggs, beaten
			Chutney Sauce (see sidebar)

Cut chicken into 1-inch pieces and place in a zip-top bag. Combine juice, sherry and Worcestershire sauce. Pour mixture over chicken. Close bag tightly and toss to coat chicken. Marinate in refrigerator for 30 minutes or more. Combine macadamia nuts and breadcrumbs. Remove chicken from marinade and dredge in flour. Dip in eggs and roll in breadcrumb mixture. Place on a lightly greased 15x10-inch jelly-roll pan. Bake in pre-heated 350° oven for 25 to 30 minutes or until done. Serve warm with Chutney Sauce.

Yield: 4½ dozen bites

Macadamia Nut: (mak uh DAY mee uh) A marble-sized, buttery-rich and slightly sweet nut, widely used in many sweet and savory dishes.

Chicken Pâté Log

Easy enough for even the most inexperienced cook

2	(8-ounce) packages cream cheese, softened	1½	cups minced cooked chicken
1	tablespoon steak sauce	⅓	cup finely chopped celery
½	teaspoon curry powder	2	tablespoons minced parsley
		½	cup chopped toasted almonds

Combine cream cheese, steak sauce and curry in a mixing bowl. Beat with an electric mixer until smooth. Stir in chicken, celery and parsley. Shape mixture into a 9-inch log. Wrap in wax paper and chill 4 to 5 hours. Uncover and roll log in almonds. Place on a serving plate surrounded with assorted crackers.

Yield: about 4 cups

Chutney Sauce

¾ cup mayonnaise

¼ cup prepared mustard

3 tablespoons chutney, finely chopped

Combine all ingredients. Stir well, cover and chill.

Yield: 1 cup

Also good with beef or pork tenderloin.

~

How many appetizers do you need for a party? Plan on serving 4 bites per person if dinner is to follow hors d'oeuvres or 10 bites for a cocktail party. For an affair with no dinner afterwards, like a wedding reception, plan on 10 to 15 bites per person.

Spicy Chicken Nachos

A Southwestern sensation

Preheat oven to 375°.

1½ (8-ounce) packages cream cheese, softened

1½ cup grated Monterey Jack cheese

1 whole skinless chicken breast, cooked and diced

½ red bell pepper, chopped

4 jalapeño peppers, seeded and minced

⅓ cup minced red onions

¼ cup chopped fresh cilantro (optional)

2 cloves garlic, minced

1 teaspoon cumin

1 teaspoon chili powder

Salt and pepper to taste

6 pita bread, sliced horizontally into 12 rounds

Paprika

Combine cheeses and mix well. Fold in chicken, bell peppers, jalapeño peppers, onions, cilantro, garlic, cumin and chili powder. Season with salt and pepper. Mix well. Mixture will be very thick. Spread each pita round with a generous amount of filling. Cut each into 8 wedges. Place on a baking sheet and bake for 10 minutes. Sprinkle with paprika and serve.

Yield: 8 dozen

Note: Filled wedges can be placed on a baking sheet and frozen until hard. Transfer to a plastic bag and freeze until ready to bake.

Cilantro: (sih LAHN troh) An herb in the parsley family also known as coriander leaves or Chinese parsley. A typical ingredient in Mexican, Caribbean, Indian and Asian dishes.

"Athenians we are, not by birth; but graciously gathered into the 'Classic' embrace of the community's demeanor of acceptance."

Jon and Virginia Appleton

Dr. Appleton retired as pastor of the First Baptist Church for 23 years in April 1999.

Easy Beef Pinwheels

No cooking required

1 (8-ounce) container cream cheese with chives and onion	2 (4¼-ounce) cans chopped black olives
6 medium flour tortillas	1 pound thinly sliced deli roast beef
1½ cups finely chopped and seeded cucumbers	

Spread cream cheese over one side of each tortilla. Top with cucumbers and olives. Layer slices of roast beef over top, leaving a ½-inch border around the edge. Roll up tightly and chill. To serve, trim ends and cut into 8 slices.

Yield: 10 to 12 servings

Buffet Tenderloin

Always memorable served warm, cold or at room temperature

4½-5 pounds trimmed beef tenderloin	¾ cup soy sauce
Black pepper	2 tablespoons Worcestershire sauce
¼ cup browning sauce	

Rub tenderloin with black pepper and place in a plastic zip-top bag. Combine browning sauce, soy sauce and Worcestershire sauce and pour over meat. Close bag and place in refrigerator to marinate 24 hours, turning bag occasionally. When ready to cook, place meat and some of marinade in a baking pan. Bake, uncovered, in preheated 450° oven for 25 minutes. Turn off heat and leave meat in oven for 15 minutes; do not open oven door. Remove from oven, cool and slice very thin. Serve with biscuits or rolls and your favorite sauce.

Yield: 20 to 25 servings

Note: If you prefer meat more "done," increase initial cooking time in small increments.

Easy Horseradish Sauce

1 cup sour cream
¼ cup prepared horseradish, drained
1 tablespoon white vinegar
1 teaspoon sugar
½ teaspoon salt

Combine all ingredients. Serve with beef.

Yield: 1¼ cups

~

Mustard Sauce

2 teaspoons grated onion
1 tablespoon Dijon mustard
1½ teaspoons sugar
1-2 tablespoons vegetable oil

Combine all ingredients and mix well. Serve with beef.

Yield: ¼ cup

Mini Reuben Pastries

Attention all Reuben lovers

Preheat oven to 400°.

1	sheet puff pastry	6	thin slices corned beef
¼	cup Dijon mustard, plus extra for dipping	1	egg, beaten
6	thin slices Swiss cheese	1	tablespoon caraway seeds

Thaw pastry according to package directions. Roll dough to a 12x10-inch rectangle. Spread mustard evenly over dough. Top with cheese and beef. Cut in half, crosswise, to form 2 rectangles. Roll up each rectangle from narrow end. Pinch seams to seal. Cut into ¼-inch thick slices. Place slices on a greased baking sheet. Brush with egg and sprinkle with caraway seeds. Bake for 10 to 12 minutes or until golden. Serve warm with additional mustard on the side.

Yield: 8 to 10 servings

Variation: Ham and honey mustard may be substituted for the beef and Dijon mustard. Omit caraway seeds.

Corned Beef: Beef cured in a seasoned brine.

South of the Border Meatballs

Men can't get enough of these.

Preheat oven to 350°.

1½	pounds ground beef	½	teaspoon salt
2	cups crumbled cornbread	1	(8-ounce) can tomato sauce
1	(10½-ounce) can mild enchilada sauce, divided	½	cup grated Monterey Jack cheese

Combine beef, cornbread, ½ cup enchilada sauce and salt. Mix well and form into 1-inch meatballs. Place meatballs on a 15x10-inch jelly-roll pan. Bake for 18 to 20 minutes or until thoroughly cooked. Drain on paper towels. Place in a chafing dish. In a small saucepan, combine remaining enchilada sauce and tomato sauce. Cook over low heat until heated. Pour sauce over meatballs and sprinkle with cheese. Serve with toothpicks.

Yield: 7 dozen meatballs

Delectable Tuna Cakes with Rémoulade Sauce

So versatile it can also be used as a main dish

Rémoulade Sauce

1 cup mayonnaise
2 tablespoons Dijon mustard
2 tablespoons finely chopped gherkins
2 tablespoons finely chopped capers

1 tablespoon finely chopped fresh parsley
1 teaspoon finely chopped tarragon
½ teaspoon lemon zest
½ teaspoon black pepper
Salt to taste

Tuna Cakes

3 tablespoons butter
½ cup finely chopped celery
¼ cup finely chopped green onions
¼ cup finely chopped red bell peppers
3 eggs, beaten
1 tablespoon Dijon mustard
½ cup half-and-half

4 cups breadcrumbs, divided
2 tablespoons finely chopped parsley
1 (12-ounce) can tuna, drained and flaked
Salt and pepper to taste
Olive oil and butter for cooking

Combine all sauce ingredients. Mix until smooth. Chill several hours.

To make tuna cakes, melt 3 tablespoons butter in a small saucepan. Add celery, onions and bell peppers, and sauté until tender. In a large bowl, combine eggs, mustard, half-and-half and sautéed vegetables. Mix well. Stir in 3½ cups breadcrumbs, parsley, tuna, salt and pepper. Shape into small balls and roll in remaining breadcrumbs. Slightly flatten each ball. In a large, heavy skillet, heat oil and butter over medium heat until hot. Sauté tuna cakes until golden on each side. Remove from skillet and serve immediately with chilled rémoulade sauce.

Yield: 2 dozen

Note: Rémoulade sauce is also delicious served over crab claws, crab cakes, scallops or shrimp.

Rémoulade: (rah muh LAHD) A classic sauce made by combining mayonnaise, mustard, capers, chopped gherkins, herbs and anchovies. Served chilled.

Fruited Cream Cheese Cookies

Spread any flavor fruited cream cheese onto ginger cookies. Top each with a matching fruit - a strawberry on strawberry cream cheese or a mandarin orange segment on orange flavored cream cheese.

~

Neufchâtel Cheese Balls

Pinch off small pieces of Neufchâtel cheese and roll into small bite-size balls. Do not soften cheese. Roll each ball in chopped nuts and chill.

~

Mozzarella Pinwheels

Place a 1-ounce round slice of room temperature salami on a work surface. Top with a thin round slice of room temperature mozzarella cheese. Roll up jelly roll fashion. Slice into 1-inch pieces and secure with decorative picks.

Iced Lemonade Tea
It's Southern, after all!

8 regular tea bags	1 quart homemade or mixed
1 quart cold tap water	lemonade, chilled
	Sugar to taste

Remove tags from tea bags and add to cold water. Cover and let stand 6 hours or overnight. Remove bags, squeezing gently. Combine tea water and lemonade in a 2-quart pitcher. Sweeten with sugar to taste.

Yield: 2 quarts

Note: Makes a cool and refreshing "no-cloud" tea! Great for a hot summer day.

Fruited Iced Tea
A fruity take on an old favorite

2 cups sugar	2 quarts cold water
2 cups water	2 cups orange juice
1 quart hot water	¾ cup lemon juice
8 regular tea bags	Mint sprigs for garnish

Boil sugar and 2 cups water for 5 minutes. Add hot water and tea bags. Steep 5 minutes. Discard bags. Add 2 quarts cold water and juices, mixing thoroughly. Serve over ice. Garnish with mint.

Yield: 1 gallon

Lime Cooler
A refreshing alternative to lemonade

Juice of 6 limes	2½ cups cold water
¾ cup sugar	1 (2-liter) bottle ginger ale
1½ cups strong tea	

Combine lime juice, sugar, tea and cold water. Add ginger ale and chill. Serve over ice.

Yield: 16 to 20 servings

Summer days in the South can be long, hot and muggy. A tall glass of cold iced tea has long offered a welcome respite to the sometimes oppressing heat. It is brewed fresh each day and served at both the noon and evening meals, and usually at some point in-between. Drop-in company is offered a glass before they even have a chance to sit down. Why, you might expect to see it on the table at the most lavish dinner party or fancy restaurant without even one eyebrow raised. It is such a traditional part of Southern home life that failure to offer iced tea at meals is considered downright inconsiderate, the mark of someone who was obviously "not raised in the South".

Everybody's Favorite Fruit Punch

A great punch for your next shower or tea

6	cups sugar	2	(12-ounce) cans frozen pineapple juice concentrate
4	cups boiling water	1	gallon water
4	(3-ounce) packages lemon gelatin	1½	ounces almond extract
1	(6-ounce) can frozen lemon juice concentrate		Orange and lemon slices for garnish
1	(6-ounce) can frozen orange juice concentrate		

Mix sugar with boiling water to make a syrup. While still hot, add gelatin and mix well. Cool. Add juices, water and almond extract. Mix well. Chill thoroughly. When ready to serve, garnish with orange and lemon slices.

Yield: 2 gallons

Mock Champagne Punch

Good for all ages

2	(25.4-ounce) bottles non-alcoholic sparkling grape juice, chilled	1	(6-ounce) can frozen lemonade concentrate, thawed
2	(2-liter) bottles ginger ale, chilled		Ice ring made of ginger ale and lemon and lime slices
1	(32-ounce) bottle white grape juice, chilled		

In a punch bowl, combine all ingredients except ice ring. Float ice ring on top and serve.

Yield: 6½ quarts

Cranberry Orange Blush

1 (6-ounce) can frozen orange juice concentrate, thawed
1 cup cranberry juice
¼ cup sugar
2 cups sparkling water or club soda

Combine juices and sugar. Chill thoroughly. When ready to serve, stir in sparkling water. Pour over ice in old-fashioned glasses.

Yield: 6 servings

~

Frosty Orange Slush

1 (16-ounce) can frozen orange juice concentrate
½ cup sugar
1 cup milk
1 cup water
1 teaspoon vanilla
12 ice cubes

Place all ingredients in a blender. Blend until smooth. Serve immediately or freeze 1 to 2 hours.

Yield: 6 servings

Orange Blossom Champagne Punch

Perfect for a summer wedding reception under the magnolias

A frozen ice ring may be used in a punch bowl to keep the contents cold. It can be as simple as freezing water, club soda or ginger ale in a mold, or it can be made from a mixture of juices and/or lemon lime carbonated beverage. Use food coloring to color clear liquids. Assorted fruits cut into rings or small pieces can also be added when the ring is partially frozen. Edible flowers can be added to carry out a party theme. After fruits or flowers are added, return to freezer until solid. To unmold, dip quickly into hot water or wrap in a hot wet towel.

4 (25.4-ounce) bottles California Sauternes or other white table wine, chilled	Several strips lemon peel
8 cups orange juice	4 (25.4-ounce) bottles California champagne, chilled
1½ cups lemon juice	Ice ring
2 cups Cointreau	Orange blossoms or other edible flowers for garnish
4 cups sugar	

Combine Sauternes, juices, Cointreau and sugar in a punch bowl. Stir to dissolve sugar. Twist each strip of lemon peel and drop into punch bowl. Just prior to serving, stir in champagne. Float ice ring and orange blossoms on top.

Yield: 100 (3-ounce) servings

Sauternes: An elegant sweet wine known as a dessert wine.

Luscious Piña Coladas

Cool, creamy and refreshing

1 (8-ounce) can crushed pineapple, undrained	¼ cup water
	¼ cup light rum
1 (8½-ounce) can cream of coconut	1 teaspoon lemon juice
	1 tablespoon sugar
1 large banana, sliced	15 ice cubes
½ cup nonfat dry milk powder	Flaked coconut for garnish (optional)

Combine all ingredients except coconut in a blender. Process until ice is finely crushed. Pour into glasses and sprinkle with coconut. Serve immediately.

Yield: 4 servings

Cream of Coconut: Not to be confused with coconut cream, this sweetened liquid is used primarily in desserts and mixed drinks.

Minted Wine Cooler

Fruity and so good

1¼ cups water	1	tablespoon lemon zest
1 cup sugar	¾	cup coarsely chopped fresh mint
¼ cup pineapple juice	5	cups Chablis or other dry white wine, chilled
¼ cup fresh lime juice	2½	cups club soda, chilled
¼ cup fresh orange juice		Orange, lemon and lime slices for garnish
¼ cup fresh lemon juice		
2 tablespoons orange zest		

Combine water and sugar in a medium saucepan. Bring to a boil and stir until sugar dissolves. Pour mixture into a medium mixing bowl. Add juices, zests and mint. Stir well and cover. Let stand at room temperature for 4 hours. Strain, discarding zests and mint. To serve, pour into a large bowl or pitcher. Add wine and club soda. Garnish with citrus slices and serve immediately.

Yield: 2 quarts

Note: Mixture can be made ahead and frozen up to 3 months. Strain mixture into an airtight container and freeze. To serve, thaw until slushy and add wine and club soda.

Quick and Easy Party Punch

Great for children's parties

1 (46-ounce) can unsweetened pineapple juice, chilled

1 (46-ounce) can apple juice, chilled

2 (28-ounce) bottles lemon-lime carbonated beverage, chilled

Combine all ingredients in a container such as a sand bucket, a plastic wheelbarrow, a watermelon basket or a hollowed out pumpkin.

Yield: 30 cups

Of all the herbs, mint is probably the most familiar to Southerners. In the old days, every yard or garden had a patch. You could smell it wafting through open windows from flower gardens below. One Southern lady recalls being sent out to the yard before each meal to collect a few leaves for iced tea. And of course, there is the proverbial mint julep — the drink usually associated with the old Southern aristocracy.

~

"One of the great things about life in the South is sweet tea. Everyone in Widespread Panic loves Southern sweet tea. In fact, when the band travels up north or out west, we fax ahead directions for making it to the production staffs so that when we roll into town, we are assured of getting our recommended daily allowance of sweet tea."

Michael Houser, Athens resident and member of the Widespread Panic band.

Hot Buttered Brandy

A wonderful way to warm up on a cold winter night

2 sticks butter, softened	1 pint vanilla ice cream,
½ cup brown sugar	softened
½ cup sifted powdered sugar	Brandy
1 teaspoon nutmeg	Whipped cream (optional)
1 teaspoon cinnamon	Cinnamon sticks (optional)

Cream butter, sugars, nutmeg and cinnamon until light and fluffy. Stir in ice cream until blended. Spoon into a 2-quart freezer container and freeze. To serve, thaw slightly. Place 3 tablespoons of mixture into a large mug. Add 1 ounce of brandy and fill with boiling water, stirring well. Top with whipped cream and serve with a cinnamon stick. Any remaining butter mixture can be refrozen.

Yield: 12 to 15 servings

Brandy Milk Punch

Rich and delicious!

1½ ounces brandy	1 ounce crème de cacao
1 tablespoon sugar or 1 packet	1 cup milk
sugar substitute	Ice
Drop of vanilla	Freshly grated nutmeg

Combine all ingredients except nutmeg in a blender. Process to desired consistency. Pour into 4-ounce glasses and sprinkle with nutmeg.

Yield: 2 or 3 servings

Gluhwein

A welcome treat after a day of Christmas shopping

1	cup water	2	cinnamon sticks
1	thick slice of lemon	2	cups red wine
4	cloves		Sugar to taste

Bring water to a boil. Add lemon slice, cloves and cinnamon sticks. Boil 5 minutes. Add wine and sugar and reheat, but do not boil. Serve warm in mugs.

Yield: 4 servings

Gluhwein: (GLUE vine) A traditional German hot spicy wine.

Raspberry Kiss

An excellent after dinner drink

1½ ounces Kahlúa	**3 ounces half-and-half**
1½ ounces Chambord (raspberry liquor)	**½ cup ice**

Combine all ingredients in a cocktail shaker. Shake until well mixed. Strain into liqueur glasses or very small cocktail glasses.

Yield: 2 servings

Kahlúa: (kah LOO ah) A coffee flavored liqueur from Mexico.

If you entertain often, it's a good idea to invest in your own cocktail glasses. They can be bought inexpensively at discount stores and outlet malls and stored in empty liquor cartons. For a party of 50, plan on about 3 dozen high ball and 3 dozen old fashioned glasses. Have lots and lots of cocktail napkins on hand. Never serve a drink without one.

~

For a refreshing flavored water, add lemon, lime, orange and cucumber slices along with fresh mint to a pitcher of cold water. Chill thoroughly and strain.

Cafe Vienna

⅓ cup instant coffee
⅔ cup sugar

⅔ cup dry milk powder
½ teaspoon cinnamon

Combine all ingredients. To serve, place 3 to 4 teaspoons of mixture into a cup and fill with hot water.

Yield: 2 cups dry mix, about 20 servings

Beverage mixes make wonderful Christmas gifts when bagged in plastic and packed in decorative containers or mugs. Keep extras on hand for those times when you need "just a little something" for unexpected guests or a hostess gift. For an added touch, include the recipe with each container.

~

Hot Chocolate Mix

1 (25.6-ounce) box nonfat dry milk powder

1 (32-ounce) box instant hot chocolate mix

2 cups sugar

1 (30-ounce) container nonfat dairy creamer

Combine all ingredients and store in an airtight container. Use ¼ cup of mixture or to taste per 1 cup hot water.

Cappuccino Coffee Mix

1   cup instant coffee
2¼ cups nonfat dry milk powder
1½ cups sugar

½   cup instant hot chocolate mix
2   teaspoons cinnamon
1½ teaspoons ground orange zest

Combine all ingredients. Store in a tightly sealed glass jar. To serve, place 2 teaspoons of mixture in a teacup. Fill with boiling water.

Yield: 6½ cups dry mix

Variation: A splash of brandy and a dollop of whipped cream may be added if desired.

Suisse Mocha

½ cup instant coffee
½ cup sugar

1 cup nonfat dry milk powder
2 tablespoons unsweetened cocoa

Combine all ingredients. Place 3 to 4 teaspoons of mixture in a cup and add hot water.

Yield: 2 cups dry mix, about 20 servings

BREADS

Athens/Clarke County City Hall

Cornbread Dressing with Giblet Gravy

Preheat oven to 350°.

31 cornmeal muffins (see recipe, page 55)
25 slices bread
5 (14½-ounce) cans chicken broth
4 teaspoons sage
2 teaspoons poultry seasoning

1 stick margarine, melted
1 stick butter, melted
1 large onion, chopped
4 eggs, beaten
½ bunch celery, chopped

Tear muffins and bread into small pieces or grind. Combine muffin and bread pieces with remaining ingredients. Transfer to a greased baking pan. Bake for 60 minutes.

Yield: 35 servings

Giblet Gravy

Gizzards and liver of 1 large turkey
3 cups water
2 cups turkey broth
5 tablespoons all-purpose flour

2 eggs, hard-cooked and chopped
1 tablespoon salt
1 teaspoon black pepper

Cook gizzards and liver, cut into medium slices, and place in a saucepan. Add water and broth. Mix ½ cup of liquid into flour in a separate container. Stir until smooth, removing any lumps that will not dissolve. Stir flour mixture into liquid in saucepan until smooth. Cook until thickened. Stir in eggs and season with salt and pepper.

Yield: about 20 servings

Weaver D's

Down home cooking from the originator of the world famous phrase "Automatic for the People" and made popular by the Athens-based band REM.

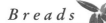

Cloud Biscuits

It's Southern, after all!

Preheat oven to 450°.

2¼ cups self-rising flour	1 egg, beaten
1 tablespoon sugar	⅔ cup milk
½ cup butter flavored shortening	1 tablespoon butter, melted

Mix flour and sugar in a large bowl. Cut in shortening. Combine egg and milk and stir into flour mixture. Mix until dough leaves sides of bowl. Turn dough out onto a lightly floured surface. Knead gently. Roll dough to ½-inch thick. Cut with a biscuit cutter, being careful not to twist cutter. Place biscuits on an ungreased baking sheet. Bake for 10 to 12 minutes. Brush with melted butter.

Yield: 12 (2-inch) biscuits

Cut In: To mix a solid fat, such as butter or shortening, with dry ingredients until mixture resembles cornmeal.

Angel Biscuits

A delightful refrigerator biscuit made with yeast

Preheat oven to 425°.

5 cups sifted all-purpose flour	1 cup shortening
¼ cup sugar	1 package dry yeast
1 tablespoon baking powder	2 tablespoons warm water
1 teaspoon baking soda	2 cups buttermilk
1 teaspoon salt	

Sift flour to measure. Sift again into a large bowl with sugar, baking powder, baking soda and salt. Cut in shortening. Dissolve yeast in warm water. Add yeast and buttermilk to flour mixture. Mix well. Pat or roll out on floured wax paper. Cut into biscuits and place on a greased baking sheet. Bake for 15 minutes.

Yield: 20 to 24 biscuits

Note: Dough does not need to rise. It will keep several days in the refrigerator.

Southern women have always taken great pride in their biscuits. In some circles, a woman's reputation as a cook was determined by the biscuits she made. If they were good, her standing was assured. If they fell short, her fate was sealed. To pass muster, good biscuits had to be fluffy and flaky on the outside, tender and white in the middle. Much of our success in the South is actually due to the flour we use. We bake with a soft wheat flour that has less gluten or protein than the harder flours found in the North and West. But good biscuits can be made from any number and combination of ingredients, be it shortening or lard, regular milk or buttermilk, all-purpose flour or self-rising. The fact is, you only need a few basics to make good biscuits — a good recipe, fresh ingredients, a little know how and a whole lot of practice.

Cheese Biscuits

*Compare these to the ones served at Red Lobster.
Bet you can't tell the difference.*

Preheat oven to 450°.

2 cups baking mix	½ stick butter, melted
½ cup cold water	1 teaspoon dried parsley
¾ cup grated sharp cheddar cheese	½ teaspoon garlic powder
	½ teaspoon Italian seasoning

Stir together baking mix, water and cheese. Drop by large spoonfuls onto a greased baking sheet. Bake for 8 to 10 minutes. Combine butter, parsley, garlic powder and Italian seasoning. Brush mixture over biscuits while still hot.

Yield: 12 biscuits

Raspberry-Filled Almond Muffins

Perfect choice for a luncheon

Preheat oven to 400°.

2 cups all-purpose flour	1 teaspoon vanilla
⅔ cup sugar	½ teaspoon almond extract
2 teaspoons baking powder	5 tablespoons raspberry preserves
½ teaspoon salt	42 whole almonds, blanched and toasted
1 cup milk	Sugar for topping
1 stick butter, melted	
1 egg, lightly beaten	

In a large bowl, combine flour, ⅔ cup sugar, baking powder and salt. Mix well. Add milk, butter, egg, vanilla and almond extract. Stir until dry ingredients are moistened. Spoon batter into greased (3½-inch diameter) muffin tins, filling half full. Spoon 1 teaspoon preserves into the center of batter. Top with remaining batter, filling tins three-fourths full. Top each muffin with 3 almonds. Sprinkle sugar lightly over the top. Bake for 15 to 20 minutes or until golden.

Yield: 14 muffins

Oatmeal Raisin Muffins

Good for lunch or dinner—healthy, too!

Preheat oven to 400°.

1¼ cups rolled oats	1 cup all-purpose flour
1¼ cups buttermilk	1¼ teaspoons baking powder
2 eggs, lightly beaten	½ teaspoon salt
¾ cup brown sugar	½ teaspoon baking soda
1 stick butter, melted and cooled	½ cup raisins

Combine oats and buttermilk in a mixing bowl. Let stand 1 hour. Add eggs, brown sugar and butter. Beat with an electric mixer 30 seconds, scraping down sides of bowl. Combine flour, baking powder, salt and baking soda. Add dry ingredients and raisins to oats mixture. Mix on low speed for 15 seconds or until dry ingredients are just moistened. Do not overmix. Spoon batter into greased muffin tins, filling half full. Bake for 15 to 20 minutes.

Yield: 12 servings

Note: Enhance the flavor of rolled oats by roasting in a dry skillet over medium-high heat until lightly browned.

Banana Muffins

If you like banana bread, you'll love these!

Preheat oven to 350°.

½ cup shortening	2 eggs, lightly beaten
1 cup sugar	2½ cups all-purpose flour
1 cup mashed bananas	2½ teaspoons baking soda
	½ teaspoon salt

Cream shortening and sugar. Add bananas and eggs and mix well. Sift together flour, baking soda and salt. Stir dry ingredients into banana mixture until moistened. Spoon into greased muffin tins. Bake for 20 to 25 minutes.

Yield: 12 muffins

To reduce fat, applesauce can be substituted for up to half the oil, margarine or butter in many recipes for muffins, quick breads and cakes. Eliminating all the fat, however, can result in an overly dry baked product.

~

Don't throw overripe bananas away. They are great in breads, muffins, pancakes, waffles, milkshakes and fruit salad dressings. They may also be frozen for use later.

Muffins were known to the English as "tea cakes", but we prefer serving them at breakfast with lots of butter and jam. Though muffins are typically thought of as being sweet, there are so many variations these days that they are just as appropriate for lunch and even dinner.

Lemon Yogurt Muffins

Great idea for gift baskets

Preheat oven to 375°.

Muffins

2 cups all-purpose flour	2 eggs, room temperature
1 teaspoon baking soda	1¼ cups plain or lemon yogurt
1 teaspoon baking powder	½ stick butter, melted and cooled
¼ teaspoon salt	1 tablespoon lemon zest
¼ cup sugar	
2 tablespoons honey	

Syrup

⅓ cup fresh lemon juice	3 tablespoons water
⅓ cup sugar	

Combine flour, baking soda, baking powder and salt. Set aside. In a large bowl, mix together sugar, honey, eggs, yogurt, butter and zest. Stir in dry ingredients until just combined. Spoon into muffin tins. Bake for 15 to 20 minutes or until pale golden brown and a toothpick inserted in the center comes out clean.

While muffins bake, prepare syrup by combining lemon juice, sugar and water in a heavy saucepan. Bring to a boil and cook 1 minute. When done, take muffins from oven and pierce tops gently 2 to 3 times with a fork. Drizzle 2 to 3 teaspoons of syrup over each muffin. Cool for 3 minutes, then turn out onto a rack to cool.

Yield: 12 muffins

Note: To obtain the most juice from a lemon or lime, microwave it for 20 seconds, then cut and squeeze.

Sleepover Cinnamon Muffins

A big hit at weekend sleepovers

Preheat oven to 350°.

1½ sticks butter, softened	1 tablespoon baking powder
1½ cups sugar	Pinch of salt
3 eggs	1 tablespoon cinnamon
2¼ cups all-purpose flour	¾ cup milk
	¾ cup raisins (optional)

Cream butter and sugar. Beat in eggs, one at a time. Sift together flour, baking powder, salt and cinnamon. Add dry ingredients alternately with milk, mixing well after each addition. Stir in raisins. Spoon into greased muffin tins. Bake for 20 to 25 minutes.

Yield: 20 muffins

Variation: Bake in mini muffin tins. When done, dip in melted butter and roll in a mixture of cinnamon and sugar.

Cream: To beat an ingredient or combination of ingredients until mixture is smooth and creamy.

Weaver D's Cornmeal Muffins

The Best!

Preheat oven to 425°.

1⅓ cups self-rising white cornmeal	1 egg, slightly beaten
1 tablespoon sugar	1⅓ cups buttermilk
	4 tablespoons butter, melted

Combine cornmeal and sugar in a mixing bowl; make a well in the center. Combine egg, buttermilk and butter; add to dry ingredients and stir until smooth. Spoon into greased muffin tins, filling two-thirds full. Bake 20 minutes or until golden.

Yield: 12 muffins

To have fresh muffins without last minute fuss, prepare batter ahead of time. Spoon into nonstick muffin tins or paper muffin cups and freeze. Bake frozen muffins as needed, adding 10 minutes on to baking time.

~

Substituting 2 egg whites for 1 whole egg lightens a recipe by 3 grams of fat and 213 milligrams of cholesterol.

Granny's Buttermilk Cornbread

It's Southern, after all!

Preheat oven to 475°.

¼	cup vegetable oil	1	teaspoon salt
2	cups cornmeal	2	cups buttermilk
½	teaspoon baking powder	2	eggs, lightly beaten
1	teaspoon baking soda		

Pour oil into a 10-inch iron skillet and place in a 475° oven to heat. Meanwhile, combine cornmeal, baking powder, baking soda and salt in a large bowl. Mix together buttermilk and eggs and add to dry ingredients. Stir until just moistened. Remove skillet from oven and swirl to coat bottom and sides. Pour hot oil from pan into batter and stir. Pour batter into skillet and bake for 25 minutes or until golden brown. Serve hot.

Yield: 6 to 8 servings

Note: "Real" Southern cornbread does not contain flour or sugar.

Francine's Sour Cream Cornbread

Rich and moist!

Preheat oven to 350°.

1½	cups self-rising cornmeal	2	eggs, beaten
½	teaspoon chili powder (optional)	1	cup grated cheddar cheese, divided
¼	cup oil	1	cup creamed corn
1	cup sour cream	2	tablespoons butter, melted

Combine cornmeal, chili powder, oil, sour cream, eggs, ¾ cup cheese and creamed corn. Spoon into a greased 8-inch square pan. Sprinkle remaining cheese on top. Bake for 35 minutes. Remove from oven and brush with butter.

Yield: 6 servings

Variation: May add chopped onions or jalapeño peppers if desired.

"Even today as I travel the state, especially north to south, I always make it a point to stop and see my mother because she continues to cook good food like butter beans, corn and greens, just as she did when I was growing up. I guess one of the best dishes that I keep coming back to is her thin cornbread. Cornbread is so good, but only if it's thin and crusty, and my mother's is just right. As a matter of fact, everything she does, she does well and her food is a basic presentation...nothing with excessive trimmings. Just good down-home cooking. As I've gotten older, I find that I don't really enjoy eating heavy meals at night, but when you put farm vegetables on the table before me, I can't get my fill. Best of all is going back home to middle Georgia and enjoying a meal with my mother."

Loran Smith, Color Commentator, UGA Football, Secretary of Bulldog Club

Creekside Hushpuppies
It's Southern, after all!

1½ cups yellow cornmeal	¾ cup milk
½ cup all-purpose flour	¼ cup minced onions
2 teaspoons baking powder	1 bunch green onion tops,
1 teaspoon sugar	finely minced
½ teaspoon salt	Vegetable oil for frying
1 egg, beaten	

Combine cornmeal, flour, baking powder, sugar and salt in a bowl. Stir in egg, milk, onions and green onion tops. Drop by rounded teaspoonfuls into 365° oil. Fry until golden brown. Drain well and serve immediately.

Yield: 4 to 6 servings

Shredded Wheat Bread
A healthy alternative to white bread

4 large shredded wheat biscuits, crushed	2 tablespoons salt
¼ cup brown sugar	4 cups boiling water
¼ cup sorghum syrup or molasses	2 packages yeast
2 tablespoons butter or margarine, melted	½ cup warm water
	9 cups all-purpose flour

Combine shredded wheat, brown sugar, syrup, butter and salt in a large bowl. Pour boiling water over all and stir. Cool. Dissolve yeast in warm water until foamy. Add yeast to shredded wheat mixture. Gradually stir in flour until dough is no longer sticky. Turn out onto a lightly floured surface and knead until elastic. Cover and put in a warm place. Let rise 60 minutes or until dough is doubled. Punch down and divide into quarters. Shape each quarter and place in 3½x7½-inch greased loaf pans. Let rise 30 minutes. Bake in preheated 350° oven for 35 minutes.

Yield: 4 loaves

Note: Most cereals or wheat bran can be substituted for shredded wheat. This is a good way to use cereal that is no longer fresh.

Yeast: A commercially available product used to make breads rise.

The Original Hushpuppy

"Around 1929, Uncle Charlie began cooking for friends and family at Pinecrest Lodge in Athens, Georgia. Since the only air conditioning in the Lodge was an occasional cool breeze off the lake, the kitchen was located out back.

The smells coming from the kitchen caused every hunting dog within miles to make a run for the back door. Now, it didn't take long for Uncle Charlie to figure out that he needed to create a diversion.

Some extra cornbread batter was sitting on the counter. Uncle Charlie heated up the skillet where he'd just fried the fish and dropped some batter into the hot oil.

Now, the dogs outside were getting real excited, so Uncle Charlie opened the screen door and tossed the cornbread bites just a little out of their reach. Then he uttered the two most famous words in the Southern language, 'Hush Puppy!'

Of course, the guests at the Lodge had been getting a whiff of those same delicious smells. They were waiting just inside the door with their tongues practically hanging out. That's when Uncle Charlie decided he'd better add hush puppies to his dinner menu."

Charlie Williams' Pinecrest Lodge

Sour Dough Starter and Bread

Gets better as starter ages

Rich in iron, molasses also improves the "keeping" qualities of breads and cakes.

Soft Molasses Gingerbread

1 cup molasses

5 tablespoons butter or margarine

1¾ teaspoons baking soda

½ cup sour milk

1 egg, well beaten

2 cups all-purpose flour

2 teaspoons ground ginger

½ teaspoon salt

Bring molasses and butter to a boil in a saucepan. Remove from heat and vigorously beat in baking soda. Stir in milk, egg, flour, ginger and salt. Pour into a greased 8-inch square pan and bake in preheated 350° oven for 20 minutes or until firm.

Starter

2 packages dry yeast

1½ cups warm water, divided

⅔ cup sugar

Food for starter

¾ cup sugar

3 tablespoons instant potato flakes

1 cup hot water

Bread

1 cup starter

⅓ cup sugar

½ cup canola oil

1 tablespoon salt

1½ cups hot water

6 cups bread flour

Melted butter

To prepare starter, dissolve yeast in ½ cup warm water. Stir in remaining 1 cup warm water and ⅔ cup sugar. Let mixture sit on counter for 12 hours. Feed starter by adding ¾ cup sugar, potato flakes and hot water. Refrigerate 3 to 5 days before making bread.

To make bread, combine 1 cup of starter with sugar, oil, salt, hot water and flour. Lightly cover and let rise in a warm place for 8 to 12 hours. Punch down and divide among 3 greased loaf pans. Lightly cover and let rise another 8 to 12 hours. Bake in preheated 375° oven for 30 minutes. Brush butter over hot bread. After you have removed a cup of starter, feed the starter again and let sit on counter for 12 hours, then refrigerate. If you do not make bread one week, you must remove and discard a cup of starter and repeat the feeding process with the remaining starter.

Yield: 3 loaves

Sourdough Bread: A bread with a slightly sour, tangy flavor created by using a yeast starter as the leavening.

Dill Bread

Tried and true

1 package yeast	¼ teaspoon baking soda
¼ cup warm water	1 tablespoon instant onion
1 cup 2% cottage cheese	flakes
1 tablespoon butter or	2 teaspoons dried dill weed
margarine	1 egg, lightly beaten
2 tablespoons sugar	2½ cups sifted all-purpose flour
1 teaspoon salt	

Dissolve yeast in warm water. Heat cottage cheese and butter in a microwave until warm. Combine sugar, salt, baking soda, onion flakes and dill in a large bowl. Add cheese mixture and egg. Mix well. Slowly stir in flour until completely blended. Cover and let rise in a warm, draft-free place for 60 minutes or until doubled in bulk. Punch down and transfer to a greased 9x5x3-inch loaf pan. Let rise 30 to 45 minutes or until almost doubled in size. Bake in preheated 350° oven for 50 minutes or until golden brown on top. Serve warm with butter.

Yield: 1 loaf

Pepperoni Cheese Bread

Also good as an appetizer

4½ cups all-purpose flour	2 (3½-ounce) packages
¼ cup sugar	pepperoni, divided
1 teaspoon salt	1 (8-ounce) package grated
1 package yeast	Monterey Jack cheese
4 tablespoons butter, melted,	1 (8-ounce) package grated
plus extra for topping	mozzarella cheese
1½ cups warm water	

Combine flour, sugar, salt and yeast in a large bowl. Add butter and water and stir until flour is completely moistened. Turn dough out onto a floured surface and knead about 10 minutes. Place in a greased bowl, turning greased side of dough up. Cover and let rise 20 minutes. Punch down and divide in half. Roll each into a rectangular shape. Using one package, place a layer of pepperoni on the dough. Sprinkle with cheeses. Top with a second layer of pepperoni, using remaining package. Roll up dough. Bake in preheated 375° oven for 20 to 25 minutes. Brush hot bread with melted butter. Cool slightly before cutting.

Yield: 8 servings

Flavored butters make a good bread even better. Almost any herb or ingredient can be used. Use your imagination to see what you can come up with.

Cheese Herb Butter

Add 2 teaspoons minced fresh parsley, ½ teaspoon oregano, 2 tablespoons Parmesan cheese and ⅛ teaspoon garlic salt to ½ cup softened butter.

~

Cinnamon Butter

Cream ½ cup brown sugar, ½ cup softened butter and 1 tablespoon cinnamon until light and fluffy.

~

Strawberry Butter

In a blender, combine a 10-ounce package thawed strawberries, 1 cup softened butter and 1 cup powdered sugar. Blend until smooth.

Cinnamon Bread

The smell will bring them running to the kitchen.

7-8 cups bread flour, divided
½ cup sugar
1 tablespoon yeast
1 tablespoon salt
2½ cups warm water

½ cup shortening
1 egg
1½ cups cinnamon sugar, divided

Combine 3 cups flour, sugar, yeast and salt in a large mixing bowl. Add warm water and shortening. Mix with an electric mixer on low for 1 minute. Increase to medium speed and mix 2 minutes. Add egg and 1 cup flour. Mix 2 minutes on medium speed. Add 1 cup flour and mix well. If using the dough hook on the mixer, start using it now to incorporate the additional 2 to 3 cups flour; otherwise, turn the batter onto 1 cup of flour spread on the counter and knead in the additional 1 to 2 cups flour. Place well-kneaded bread in a greased bowl large enough to allow for doubling. Cover and let rise in a warm place for about 60 minutes or until doubled in size. Divide dough into thirds. Roll out one portion into a 9x18-inch rectangle. Sprinkle with ½ cup of cinnamon sugar. Roll up, jelly-roll style, starting at the narrow end. Seal the edges by squeezing the dough together. Place in a greased loaf pan. Repeat with remaining portions of dough. Let rise about 1 hour, 30 minutes. Place in a cold oven and set the temperature to 350° for 15 minutes. Reduce temperature to 325° without opening the oven door. Bake 25 minutes. Remove loaves from pan and cool on a wire rack at least 20 minutes before cutting.

Yield: 3 loaves

Bread Flour: This flour contains more gluten than all-purpose or cake flours making it ideally suited for yeast breads.

Mother's Day Lunch at the State Botanical Garden of Georgia Conservatory

Imagine dining amidst lush tropical splendor in a beautiful three-story glass structure overlooking three acres of international gardens. You may never want to leave.

~

Menu

Mock Champagne Punch

Chilled Strawberry Soup

Chicken Breast Saute with Wild Rice

Green Bean Bundles

Carrot Souffle

Crunchy Romaine Toss

Cheese Biscuits

Frozen Almond Cream with Rich Almond Sauce

Iced Tea

Coffee

Mother's Refrigerator Yeast Rolls

"Ladies in my mother's garden club always asked her to
prepare these yeast rolls for them on special holidays."

¼ cup shortening	1¼ cup warm water, divided
⅓ cup sugar	4 cups all-purpose flour
1 egg, beaten	1 teaspoon salt
1 package yeast	

Cream shortening and sugar. Add egg. Dissolve yeast in ¼ cup warm water and stir into creamed mixture. Combine flour and salt. Add dry ingredients to creamed mixture alternately with remaining 1 cup water. Turn dough out onto a lightly floured board and knead until smooth and elastic, about 5 minutes. Place in a well-greased bowl, turning to grease top. Cover and let rise 2 hours, 30 minutes. Punch down, cover, and refrigerate until doubled in bulk or until needed. To use, punch down and turn out onto a lightly floured board. Roll out to ½-inch thickness and cut out or shape as desired. Let rise on a baking sheet at room temperature. Bake in preheated 375° oven for about 20 minutes.

Yield: 3 dozen

Rock Eagle Bran Yeast Rolls

Generations have enjoyed them

2 packages yeast	1½ teaspoons salt
1 cup warm water	1 cup boiling water
1 cup shortening	2 eggs, well beaten
½ cup sugar	5 cups all-purpose flour
1 cup wheat bran cereal	

Dissolve yeast in warm water. Combine shortening, sugar, cereal and salt in a large mixing bowl. Add boiling water and stir until shortening is melted. Let stand until mixture is lukewarm. Stir in eggs and yeast mixture. Add flour and beat well, using extra flour if necessary. Let rise until doubled in size, or refrigerate overnight. Form into rolls and let rise 2 hours. Bake in preheated 400° oven for 15 minutes or until brown.

Yield: 3 dozen

When dissolving yeast for bread making, adding a small amount of sugar to the liquid will cause the yeast to activate quicker. Liquids should be between 105° and 115°. Any cooler or warmer and the yeast will not work. Always check the expiration date on the yeast package to be sure it has not expired.

~

Rock Eagle is the 4-H Club Center operated by the University of Georgia near Eatonton, Georgia. It has served over 2 million children and adults since its beginning in 1955. These bran rolls have been a favorite of several generations of Georgia families.

Homemade Pretzels

Great for a snack anytime

Preheat oven to 400°.

1 tablespoon yeast	5¼ cups bread flour
2¼ cups warm water	1 egg, beaten (optional)
3¾ teaspoons sugar	1 teaspoon Kosher salt
1½ teaspoons salt	(optional)

Dissolve yeast in warm water in a large bowl. Let stand 5 minutes. Stir in sugar and salt until dissolved. Add flour and stir until smooth. Turn dough out onto a lightly floured surface and knead 5 to 10 minutes or until smooth. Divide dough into 12 to 16 equal portions. Roll each portion on a lightly floured surface into a 9-inch rope. Shape each as desired and place on a greased baking sheet. If a golden color is desired, brush pretzels with egg. Sprinkle with salt. Bake for 10 to 12 minutes or until golden brown.

Yield: 12 to 16 pretzels

Kosher Salt: An additive free coarse-grained salt enjoyed for its texture and flavor.

Sour Cream Coffee Cake

A classic for the Classic City

Preheat oven to 350°.

Cake

2 sticks butter, softened	½ teaspoon vanilla
2 cups granulated sugar	2 cups cake flour
2 eggs	½ teaspoon salt
1 cup sour cream	1 teaspoon baking powder

Topping

⅔ cup chopped pecans	¼ cup brown sugar
2 teaspoons cinnamon	

Cream butter and sugar in a large bowl. Add eggs, one at a time, beating well after each addition. Fold in sour cream and vanilla. Sift together flour, salt and baking powder. Stir dry ingredients into batter. Pour half the batter into a greased and floured 10-inch tube pan.

Combine all topping ingredients. Sprinkle half of topping mixture over batter in pan. Add remaining batter and sprinkle with remaining topping mixture. Bake for 55 to 60 minutes. Cool thoroughly for about 60 minutes before removing from pan. Sprinkle with powdered sugar.

Yield: 16 servings

Pretzels are a delicious, low fat treat. For special occasions, offer one or more of the following for dipping.

Peanut Butter Dip

⅔ cup creamy peanut butter
⅔ cup honey
¼ cup lemon juice

Combine all ingredients in a small bowl. Beat at low speed with an electric mixer until smooth.

Yield: 1⅓ cups

~

Honey Mustard Dip

¾ cup Dijon mustard
2 tablespoons cider vinegar
2 tablespoons honey
Hot pepper sauce to taste

Whisk together all ingredients in a small bowl.

Yield: 1 cup

~

Cheese Dip

Pour pasteurized processed cheese spread into a microwave-safe dish. Heat until hot.

Toffee Bar Coffee Cake

Unusual and absolutely delightful

Preheat oven to 350°.

1	stick butter, softened	1	egg
2	cups all-purpose flour	1	teaspoon vanilla
1	cup brown sugar	6	chocolate-covered toffee
½	cup granulated sugar		candy bars, finely crushed
1	cup buttermilk	¼	cup chopped pecans
1	teaspoon baking soda		

Combine butter, flour and sugars and blend well. Reserve ½ cup of mixture. Add buttermilk, baking soda, egg and vanilla to remaining mixture. Blend well. Pour into a greased and floured 9x13x2-inch baking pan. Combine candy, pecans and reserved sugar mixture. Sprinkle over batter. Bake for 30 minutes.

Yield: 16 to 20 servings

Pecan Breakfast Loaf

So easy even children can make it

Preheat oven to 375°.

Bread

2	(8-ounce) cans refrigerated	½	cup sugar
	crescent rolls	2	teaspoons cinnamon
2	tablespoons butter, softened	¼	cup chopped pecans

Topping

2	tablespoons honey	1	teaspoon vanilla
¼	cup powdered sugar	¼	cup pecan halves
2	tablespoons butter		

Unroll crescent dough and separate into 16 triangles. Spread with butter. Combine sugar, cinnamon and pecans and sprinkle over the top. Roll up each triangle, starting at the wide end and rolling to the opposite point. Place rolls, point side down, in a greased 9x5-inch loaf pan, forming 2 layers of 8 rolls each. Bake for 35 to 40 minutes or until golden brown and center is done.

Meanwhile, prepare topping by combining honey, sugar, butter and vanilla in a saucepan. Bring to a boil, stirring constantly. Stir in pecan halves; cool slightly. When done baking, remove bread from pan and drizzle with topping.

Yield: 1 loaf

Out of buttermilk? Don't despair. Simply add 2 tablespoons white vinegar to 1 cup milk and stir to thicken.

~

For homemade baking powder, add 2 teaspoons cream of tartar, 1 teaspoon baking soda and ½ teaspoon salt for each cup of flour in a recipe.

~

Measure honey in a greased measuring spoon so honey will slip out easily. If recipe calls for oil, measure the oil first, then measure honey in the same utensil.

Lemon-Frosted Breakfast Ring

Bread

2 (8-ounce) cans refrigerated crescent rolls

3 tablespoons butter, melted

1 teaspoon lemon juice

¼ cup sugar

1 teaspoon cinnamon

½ teaspoon mace

1 teaspoon lemon zest

Topping

2 tablespoons plus 1 teaspoon lemon juice

1 tablespoon lemon zest

1½ cups powdered sugar

¼ cup chopped nuts

Unroll dough and separate into triangles. Combine butter and lemon juice and brush over triangles. Combine sugar, cinnamon, mace and zest. Sprinkle 1 teaspoon of mixture over each triangle. Roll triangles into crescent shapes. Place in a greased tube pan. Bake in preheated 350° oven for 30 minutes.

Meanwhile, make topping by combining lemon juice, zest and sugar. Drizzle topping over hot baked bread. Sprinkle with nuts.

Christmas Morning Coffee Cake

A delicious, no fuss breakfast for Christmas morning

1	(3-pound) package frozen bread dough rolls, partially thawed	½	cup brown sugar
		2½	teaspoons cinnamon
		½	cup chopped nuts
1	(3-ounce) package butterscotch pudding mix (not instant)	1	stick butter or margarine

Divide each roll into 3 pieces. Combine pudding mix, brown sugar, cinnamon and nuts; mix well. Cut butter into pieces. Place a single layer of dough pieces in a greased and floured Bundt or tube pan. Sprinkle with pudding mixture and dot with butter pieces. Repeat layers until all ingredients are used. Cover with greased wax paper. Let rise on counter 8 to 10 hours or overnight. Bake in preheated 350° oven for 35 minutes. Serve warm.

Yield: 12 to 16 servings

Note: Vanilla pudding mix may be substituted for butterscotch.

Apple Bread

A new use for canned pie filling

Preheat oven to 350°.

1	cup vegetable oil	½	teaspoon allspice
2	cups sugar	1	teaspoon salt
3	eggs	1	teaspoon baking soda
1	teaspoon vanilla	1	(21-ounce) can apple pie filling
3	cups all-purpose flour		
1	teaspoon cinnamon	½	cup chopped pecans

Beat oil, sugar and eggs together. Add vanilla and blend. Combine flour, cinnamon, allspice, salt and baking soda. Stir dry ingredients into sugar mixture. Chop apples in pie filling into small pieces and stir into batter. Add pecans and spoon into 2 greased and floured 9x5x3-inch loaf pans. Bake for 55 to 60 minutes.

Yield: 2 loaves

Holiday Cranberry Coffee Cake

Always a hit at holiday time

Preheat oven to 350°.

Coffee Cake

1	stick butter, softened	½	teaspoon salt
1	cup sugar	1	(8-ounce) container sour cream
2	eggs	1	teaspoon almond extract
2	cups all-purpose flour	1	(16-ounce) can whole berry
1	teaspoon baking powder		cranberry sauce
1	teaspoon baking soda	½	cup chopped pecans

Glaze

¾	cup powdered sugar	1	tablespoon warm water
½	teaspoon almond extract		

Cream butter and sugar until light and fluffy. Add eggs, one at a time, beating well after each addition. Combine flour, baking powder, baking soda and salt. Add dry ingredients to creamed mixture alternately with sour cream, beating well after each addition. Add almond extract and mix well. Spoon a third of batter into a greased and floured 10-inch tube pan. Spread a third of cranberry sauce over batter. Repeat layers twice, ending with cranberry sauce. Sprinkle pecans over the top. Bake for 60 minutes or until a toothpick inserted in the center comes out clean. Cool 5 minutes before removing from pan.

Meanwhile stir together all glaze ingredients. Drizzle glaze over warm cake.

Yield: 12 to 16 servings

Glaze: A thin mixture that is spread or poured over baked goods while still warm; typically a sweet mixture.

"I moved to Athens at 15 after the death of my father. The only thing my father left me was two female bird dogs. I worked my way through high school and college by waiting tables and breeding high pedigreed bird dogs. During the depression, I sold the puppies for fifty dollars apiece — a huge amount for those days. At that time room and board at the university was eighteen dollars a month."

Hon. Paul Broun,
Georgia State Senator

Poppy Seed Tea Loaf

A must for your files

Preheat oven to 350°.

Poppy seeds are the small, dried, blue-gray seeds of the poppy plant. They are so small that it takes about 900,000 of them to equal one pound! Poppy seeds are used to give texture and a nutty flavor to many dishes, especially those originating in Central Europe, the Middle East and Asia. Because they are high in oil, poppy seeds become rancid quickly. They can be stored in an airtight container in the refrigerator for up to 6 months.

Bread

3   cups all-purpose flour
2½ cups sugar
1½ teaspoons salt
1½ teaspoons baking powder
3   eggs
1½ cups milk

1   cup plus 2 tablespoons
    vegetable oil
1½ tablespoons poppy seeds
1½ teaspoons vanilla
1½ teaspoons almond extract
1½ teaspoons butter extract

Glaze

¾ cup sugar
¼ cup orange juice
½ teaspoon vanilla

½ teaspoon butter extract
½ teaspoon almond extract

Combine all bread ingredients in a bowl and beat 2 minutes. Pour into two 9x5x3-inch greased loaf pans. Bake for 60 minutes.

To make glaze, combine all ingredients. Pour over hot baked bread. Cool before slicing.

Yield: 2 large loaves

Oven Baked French Toast
with Apple Sausage Filling

Very rich; fabulous for brunch

Preheat oven to 425°.

½	pound bulk pork sausage	6	tablespoons sugar
½	cup applesauce	⅔-1	cup milk
6	eggs, separated	12	slices bread, crusts removed
1	teaspoon salt	1	cup apple jelly, melted

Brown sausage and drain. Stir in applesauce and keep warm. Beat egg whites with salt until fluffy. Gradually add sugar until stiff but not dry. Beat egg yolks until thick and lemon colored. Stir milk into yolk. Fold yolk mixture into egg whites. Dip bread into egg mixture and place on a baking sheet. Bake for 10 minutes. Turn and bake 5 minutes longer or until brown and puffy. To serve, spread sausage mixture on one slice of bread. Top with a second slice. Pour melted jelly over top.

Yield: 6 servings

French Toast: A breakfast dish made by dipping bread into a milk-egg mixture, then frying until golden brown on both sides.

"What was Athens like fifty years ago when the Holders were new in town? University students tended to be very serious about their studies, being mostly veterans of the recent war, many with families. Ladies wore heels and hose to football games, which was hazardous considering the splinters in the bleachers. A major event each year was the Art Auction, when student and faculty work was available. Randolph Holder was an auctioneer, and if you were lucky, you could acquire a Lamar Dodd painting."

—Clementi Holder
Clementi and
Randolph Holder
are longtime Athens
residents who are
active in many
community
organizations.

Caramel-Soaked French Toast

Your guests will be so impressed!

Preheat oven to 350°.

1½ cups brown sugar
1½ sticks butter or margarine
¼ cup plus 2 tablespoons light corn syrup
10 (1¾-inch thick) French bread slices
4 eggs, beaten

2½ cups milk or half-and-half
1 tablespoon vanilla
¼ teaspoon salt
3 tablespoons granulated sugar
1½ teaspoons cinnamon
¼ cup melted butter or margarine

Combine brown sugar, butter and corn syrup in a medium saucepan. Cook over medium heat, stirring constantly for 5 minutes or until bubbly. Pour syrup evenly into a lightly greased 9x13-inch baking dish. Arrange bread slices over syrup. Combine eggs, milk, vanilla and salt. Stir well and slowly pour over bread. Cover and refrigerate at least 8 hours. Combine granulated sugar and cinnamon. Sprinkle evenly over soaked bread. Drizzle ¼ cup melted butter over top. Bake, uncovered, for 45 to 50 minutes or until golden and bubbly.

Yield: 10 servings

Breakfast Muesli

Better known as granola

½ cup raisins
½ cup rolled oats
1½ cups quick oats
⅓ cup brown sugar

¼-½ teaspoon cinnamon
2 cups milk
Fresh fruit
Walnuts or pecans

Combine raisins, oats, sugar, cinnamon and milk. Refrigerate overnight or up to 5 days. Stir well before serving. Serve with fresh fruit and nuts.

Yield: 4 servings

"Athens has always been a wonderful place. Although I was born and grew up in Atlanta, I always tell people I had sense enough to leave."

Robert G. Stephens, Jr., former representative and congressman from Georgia

SOUPS & SALADS

Athens Street Scene

Chunky Corn Chowder

Yum yum!

A bowl of soup is the ultimate comfort food. It's what we crave on cold, rainy nights. It's what we feed our children when they have a miserable winter cold. It's what we order out when nothing else seems right. The best thing about making soup is that you can't go wrong. Use what you like in the amounts you prefer. Make it interesting and appealing. Soups, historically, were "dressed" when brought to the table. We're not so inclined these days, but you can't deny how tempting a little dollop of sour cream looks on a bowl of steaming hot tomato soup. Oh yes, don't forget to set out the soup spoons.

6	ears fresh corn	3	medium tomatoes, peeled, seeded and chopped
6	strips bacon	1	teaspoon salt
1	small onion, chopped	½	teaspoon allspice
1	jalapeño pepper, seeded and chopped		Pinch of sugar
1	small stalk celery, finely chopped	1	bay leaf
1	red bell pepper, seeded and cut into thin strips	2	cups light cream, room temperature
2	medium potatoes, peeled and diced	1	cup milk
			Black pepper to taste
			Chopped fresh parsley to garnish

Cut corn from cob, scrape corn milk and reserve. Cook bacon in a pot. Remove bacon and crumble, reserving drippings in pot. Add onions and sauté. Add jalapeño peppers, celery and bell peppers. Cook 2 minutes or until slightly softened. Add potatoes, tomatoes, salt, allspice, sugar and bay leaf. Stir in corn and corn milk. Cook over medium heat until mixture begins to sizzle. Reduce heat, cover and cook 35 to 45 minutes or until potatoes are tender. Stir in cream and milk and heat until it just comes to a boil. Season with black pepper. Sprinkle individual servings with crumbled bacon and parsley.

Yield: 10 to 12 servings

Chowder: A milk or tomato based soup containing seafood or a vegetable.

Baked Potato Soup

Real comfort food

Preheat oven to 400°.

4	large baking potatoes, washed	4	green onions, chopped, divided
⅔	cup butter or margarine	12	slices bacon, cooked and crumbled, divided
⅔	cup all-purpose flour	1¼	cups grated cheddar cheese, divided
6	cups milk		
¾	teaspoon salt	1	(8-ounce) container sour cream
½	teaspoon black pepper		

Pierce potatoes several times with a fork. Bake for 60 minutes or until tender. Cool and cut in half lengthwise. Scoop out pulp. Melt butter in a heavy soup pot over low heat. Add flour and stir until smooth. Cook 1 minute, stirring constantly. Gradually add milk. Cook, stirring constantly, until mixture is thickened and bubbly. Add potato pulp, salt, pepper, 2 tablespoons green onions, ½ cup crumbled bacon and 1 cup cheese. Cook until thoroughly heated. Stir in sour cream. Top individual servings with remaining green onions, bacon and cheese.

Yield: 6 servings

An Athens Tailgate

Fall in Athens means tailgates before the Spartans' game on Friday night, tailgates before the Bulldogs play on Saturday, and sometimes, tailgates before the Falcons' big game on Sunday.

~

Menu

Hoedown Ribs and Chicken

Poss's Famous Hash

Tailgate Baked Beans

Sweet Pickle Cole Slaw

No Bake Granola Bars

Chocolate Chip Toffee Cookies

Beer, Wine, and Cold Drinks

Roasted Red Pepper Soup

Deliciously spicy

3	large cloves garlic, minced	1	(14.5-ounce) can Italian tomatoes
1	tablespoon olive oil		Salt to taste
1	medium yellow onion, chopped		Crushed red pepper flakes to taste
3	red bell peppers, chopped, or 1 (12-ounce) can roasted peppers	10	basil leaves
		1	pint heavy cream

Brown garlic in oil. Add onions, bell peppers, tomatoes, salt and pepper flakes. Simmer 10 minutes. Remove from heat and cool. Combine tomato mixture and basil leaves in a blender and process. Return to heat and add cream. Serve hot or chilled.

Yield: 4 to 6 servings

Note: For a lighter soup, substitute tomato juice for the cream.

Cuban Soup

Wonderful with Francine's Sour Cream Cornbread

2	smoked ham hocks, split	3-4	large potatoes, cut into large cubes
1	large or 2 medium onions, chopped	2	(16-ounce) cans chickpeas, drained
3-5	cloves garlic, minced	2	teaspoons paprika
1	pound polish kielbasa sausage, sliced		Salt to taste

Cook ham hocks in 1 to 2 quarts of water or enough to cover. Cook until almost done. Add onions, garlic and sausage and cook 15 minutes longer. Add potatoes and cook 10 minutes. Stir in chickpeas and simmer 15 minutes. Add paprika and salt. Remove ham hocks and serve hot.

Yield: 4 to 6 servings

Chickpeas: A round, buff colored legume that has a mild nut-like taste. Also known as garbanzo beans, these beans are commonly used in soups, stews and salads.

Roasted red bell peppers may be purchased already prepared or you can make your own using peppers right from your garden. First, cut each pepper in half lengthwise. Take out the stem, seeds and white membrane. Flatten each half with the palm of your hand. Place pepper halves, skin side up, on a baking sheet. Broil 15 to 20 minutes or until charred and blistered. Using tongs or a fork, place peppers in a bowl of ice water until cool enough to handle. Peel off the blistered skin with a knife.

~

A ham hock is the knuckle above the pig's foot that has meat, fat and bone. It is cured and smoked and used to flavor foods such as dried beans, soups, stews and vegetables.

Spinach Tortelloni Soup

A meal in itself

1 tablespoon margarine or butter	1 (10-ounce) package frozen chopped spinach, unthawed
2 cloves garlic, minced	1 teaspoon dried basil
4 (14½-ounce) cans chicken broth	2 (28-ounce) cans Italian tomatoes
1 (9-ounce) package refrigerated cheese tortelloni	Parmesan cheese

Melt margarine in a pot. Add garlic and sauté until tender. Add broth and tortelloni. Bring to a boil. Stir in spinach, basil and tomatoes. Simmer at least 30 minutes. Top individual servings with Parmesan cheese.

Yield: 8 to 10 servings

Tortellini: small rolls of filled pasta formed into a ring or hat shape. Tortelloni are simply a larger version of tortellini.

Calabacitas Cheese Soup

A hearty alternative to chili

1 tablespoon olive oil	2 medium yellow squash, sliced ¼-inch thick
1 cup diced onions	1 (8¾-ounce) can corn, drained
2 cloves garlic, minced	1 (4-ounce) can diced green chiles, drained
½ teaspoon dried oregano	12 ounces processed cheese loaf, cut into ½-inch cubes
2 (14½-ounce) cans chicken broth	½ teaspoon black pepper
1 (14½-ounce) can stewed tomatoes	¼ cup chopped fresh cilantro
2 medium zucchini, sliced ¼-inch thick	

Heat oil in a 4- or 5-quart pot over medium heat. Add onions and garlic and sauté until tender. Add oregano; cook and stir 1 minute. Stir in broth and tomatoes. Cover and bring to a boil. Stir in zucchini, yellow squash, corn and chiles. Bring to a boil. Reduce heat and cover. Simmer 7 to 9 minutes or until squash is tender. Stir in cheese loaf and black pepper. Cook and stir until cheese melts. Mix in cilantro and serve.

Yield: 6 servings

What better way to beef up a pot of soup than to throw in a handful of pasta? Some types make a soup almost a stew, while other more delicate varieties can make an elegant offering out of clear consommé.

~

Impress the guests at your next casual get-together by serving a thick, hearty soup out of individual bread bowls. All you need are as many loaves of round, coarse-grain crusty bread as you have guests. Cut the top fourth off each loaf to make a lid, then hollow out the inside, being careful not to break through to the bottom. Save the "innards" to make croutons or breadcrumbs. Brush around the inside with olive oil and toast the "bowls" and "lids" at 350° for 10 minutes or until crusty. Ladle soup into bowls, replace lids and serve immediately.

Cyrilla's Texas Style Bean Soup

Nice change from traditional winter soups

2	cups dried pinto beans	1	teaspoon black pepper
1	cup cubed ham	1	teaspoon crushed bay leaves
1	quart water	1	teaspoon oregano
1	(22-ounce) can tomato juice	½	teaspoon ground cumin
4	cups chicken broth	½	teaspoon crushed rosemary
3	onions, chopped	½	teaspoon celery seed
3	cloves garlic, minced	½	teaspoon ground thyme
3	tablespoons chopped parsley	½	teaspoon marjoram
¼	cup chopped bell peppers	½	teaspoon sweet basil
¼	cup brown sugar	¼	teaspoon curry powder
1	tablespoon chili powder	4	cloves
1	teaspoon salt	¾	cup sherry

Soak pinto beans overnight in enough water to cover. Drain and place beans in a pot with all remaining ingredients except sherry. Bring to a boil. Cook slowly for 2 to 3 hours or until beans are tender. Add sherry and serve.

Yield: 8 to 12 servings

Rosemary: An aromatic herb whose flavor hints of both lemon and pine. Used to season a variety of dishes including soups, salads, vegetables, meats, eggs, stuffings and dressings.

Get a jump on soup making by soaking more dried beans than needed and freezing the extra. The next time you need dried beans, take them out of the freezer and thaw. Soaked and cooked beans can be frozen for up to 1 month. Then all that's left to do when you're ready to make soup is to heat them along with the other ingredients.

Mex Tex Soup

Hot and spicy

1	cup chopped onions	¼	teaspoon salt
1	cup chopped bell peppers	¼	teaspoon black pepper
1	cup chopped tomatoes	1	bay leaf
½	cup chopped fresh parsley	1	cup cooked and shredded
2	(10½-ounce) cans chicken		chicken breast
	broth, or 3 cups	2	tablespoons grated sharp
1	teaspoon dried oregano		cheddar cheese
1	teaspoon chili powder		Coarsely crushed tortilla
¾	teaspoon ground cumin		chips

Combine onions, bell peppers, tomatoes, parsley, broth, oregano, chili powder, cumin, salt, black pepper and bay leaf in a Dutch oven. Bring to a boil. Cover, reduce heat and simmer 30 minutes. Remove bay leaf and stir in chicken. Cook until thoroughly heated. Top individual servings with cheese and tortilla chips.

Yield: 4 servings

Curried Carrot Soup

Won't your family be surprised to find out it's carrots!

2	medium onions, chopped	½	teaspoon curry powder or to
½	stick butter		taste
2	pounds carrots, chopped		Salt and pepper to taste
3	bay leaves	4	cups chicken broth
		1	cup cooked rice (optional)

Sauté onions in butter until brown. Stir in carrots, bay leaves, curry powder, salt and pepper. Stir in broth, cover and simmer 1 to 2 hours. Remove bay leaves. Add rice, if using, and purée in a blender. Serve hot or cold.

Yield: 8 servings

Sauté: To cook food quickly over direct heat in a small amount of oil.

Homemade Chicken Stock

4 cups cold water
1 medium onion
1 clove garlic, quartered
1 stalk celery, cut into large pieces
1 carrot, cut into large pieces
1 bay leaf
1½ pounds chicken backs, necks or other bones

Combine all ingredients in a stockpot or saucepan. Bring to a boil over high heat. Reduce heat and simmer, partially covered, at least 4 hours. Add extra water as needed to maintain 1 quart liquid. After cooking, strain, cool and refrigerate or freeze stock until ready to use. If you find you don't have 4 hours of simmering time available, just remember: a 30-minute stock is at least half an hour better than plain water.

~

Freeze leftover soup in 1-pint containers. They take up less space and are easier to store. They will be greatly appreciated by a hungry teenager who gets home too late for dinner.

Lewis and Clark's White Chili

A new version of an old favorite

2	pounds boneless, skinless chicken breast	¼	teaspoon ground cloves
1	tablespoon olive oil	3	pounds canned or jarred great Northern beans, drained
2	medium onions, chopped		
4	cloves garlic, minced	4	cups chicken broth
2	teaspoons ground cumin	5	cups Monterey Jack cheese, divided
¼	teaspoon cayenne pepper		
1	teaspoon ground oregano		Sour cream
2	(4-ounce) cans chopped mild or hot green chiles		Canned jalapeño peppers, chopped

Simmer chicken in a large saucepan in enough water to cover. Cook 15 to 20 minutes or until tender. Drain chicken, discarding liquid, and dice into ½-inch cubes. Using the same saucepan, heat oil over medium heat. Add onions, and cook until translucent. Stir in garlic, cumin, cayenne pepper, oregano, chiles and ground cloves. Sauté 2 to 3 minutes. Add chicken, beans, broth and 3 cups of cheese. Simmer 15 minutes. Ladle into large individual bowls. Top each serving with 1 ounce of cheese. Serve with sour cream and jalapeño peppers on the side.

Yield: 8 to 10 servings

Poss' Famous Hash

"We make this hash to eat, not to sell!" Robert E. Poss, Sr.

3	chicken fryers, cut up, or 6 pounds chicken breast	2	large onions
3	pounds beef chuck roast	5	(14½-ounce) cans tomatoes, puréed
3	pounds Boston butt pork roast	⅔	cup brown sugar
3	baking potatoes, peeled	⅔	cup cider vinegar
		½	cup ketchup

Combine chicken, beef and pork in a large pot. Cover with water and cook until meat is almost done. About 30 minutes before meat is done, add potatoes and onions and cook until meat is done and vegetables are tender. Drain, reserving stock. Remove meat from bones. Place meat, potatoes and onions in a food processor and blend. Return mixture to pot. Add puréed tomatoes, brown sugar, vinegar and ketchup. Bring to a simmer. Use reserved stock to thin as needed.

Yield: 7 to 8 quarts

Seafarer's Bisque

Rich, creamy and wonderful

½	stick butter	1	pound unpeeled medium shrimp, peeled and deveined
1	cup sliced mushrooms		
¼	cup chopped green onions		
1	clove garlic, minced	½	cup dry white wine
3	tablespoons all-purpose flour	½	cup heavy cream
1	(10½-ounce) can chicken broth	1	tablespoon chopped fresh parsley

Melt butter in a saucepan. Add mushrooms, onions and garlic. Sauté 5 minutes or until tender. Add flour and stir until smooth. Cook over medium heat, stirring constantly, for 1 minute. Gradually add broth and cook and stir until mixture is thickened and bubbly. Add shrimp, reduce heat, and simmer 3 minutes, stirring often. Add wine, cream and parsley. Cook until thoroughly heated.

Yield: 4 servings

Bisque: (bihsk) A creamy, thick soup usually consisting of puréed seafood (sometimes poultry or vegetables) and cream.

A famous landmark for years in Athens, Poss' Restaurant was a slab-sided building on the Atlanta highway where many a student enjoyed a crown steak dinner for less than five dollars. A quote reprinted from the restaurant's menu says "Made in the Country by Country People…Famous Poss' old fashioned Brunswick stew, Southern hash and barbecue sauce are made from carefully guarded country recipes famous in Dixie since ante-bellum days. These famous recipes have been enjoyed by Southerners and visitors to the South for many, many years".

Former University of Georgia football players Bob Poss and his son Bobby also operated Poss' Lakeview, the scene of many local parties, and provided concessions for UGA sporting events.

Juan's Colombian Stew

From someone who knows

Herbed Croutons

1 stick butter, melted
1 tablespoon Parmesan cheese
1 tablespoon dried parsley
1 teaspoon garlic salt
1 teaspoon dried oregano
½ teaspoon paprika
2 cups cubed day old bread

Combine butter, cheese, parsley, garlic salt, oregano and paprika. Pour mixture over bread cubes and toss. Bake in preheated 200° oven for 60 minutes, turning frequently while baking.

6-8 cups water
½ cup chopped onions
¾ cup chopped celery
4-6 boneless, skinless chicken breasts
6-8 white potatoes, peeled and chopped
1 (16-ounce) can yellow or shoe peg corn, drained

½-1 cup milk or half-and-half
1 stick butter
2 tablespoons chopped cilantro
Dash of cayenne pepper
Salt and white pepper to taste
Salsa
Sour cream, 1 tablespoon per serving
Chopped ripe avocado

Bring 6 to 8 cups of water to a boil in a large pot. Add onions and celery and boil 3 to 5 minutes. Add chicken and cook 10 to 15 minutes or until done. Remove chicken, cool and chop, leaving remaining contents in pot. Add potatoes to pot and cook over medium heat for 30 to 45 minutes or until potatoes are very soft. Add chicken, corn, milk, butter, cilantro, cayenne pepper, salt and white pepper. Simmer on low for 30 minutes. Top individual servings with salsa, sour cream and avocado.

Yield: 4 to 6 servings

Cilantro: An herb commonly used in Latin American, Caribbean, Indian and Asian dishes. It is also known as coriander and Chinese parsley. Cilantro has a lively, pungent fragrance that some describe as "soapy", and its distinctive flavor lends itself to highly spiced foods. Both the leaves and stem can be used in fresh or cooked foods.

Athens Country Club's Gazpacho

A club favorite from Executive Chef Christopher McCook

2½ pounds vine-ripened tomatoes, peeled, seeded and finely chopped	¼ cup extra virgin olive oil
	¼ cup red wine vinegar
	1 cup tomato juice
½ pound seedless cucumber, cut into ½-inch cubes	1 cup beef broth
1 cup minced onions	1 tablespoon tomato paste
1 red bell pepper, finely chopped	1 teaspoon ground cumin
	1 teaspoon salt
1 yellow bell pepper, finely chopped	Black pepper to taste
	1 tablespoon Worcestershire sauce
1 jalapeño pepper, seeded and minced	½ cup ice cubes
¾ teaspoon minced garlic	Thin cucumber slices and julienne strips of red and yellow bell pepper for garnish

Combine all ingredients except ice cubes and garnishes in a non-reactive bowl. Mix well. Stir in ice cubes. Chill in refrigerator 4 hours or overnight. Garnish individual servings with cucumber slices and bell pepper strips.

Yield: about 8 cups, 6 servings

Gazpacho is a cool, summertime soup that can be used as a first course, or with the addition of extra fresh vegetables, can be a meal in itself. Make ahead and serve cold in chilled bowls or mugs. Garnish with croutons, a dab of sour cream or slices of hard cooked egg.

Tom's Fish Chowder

A Dyer family favorite

1 small onion, chopped	1 large or 2 small potatoes, cubed
2 tablespoons butter	Salt and pepper to taste
2-3 cloves garlic, minced	2 tablespoons butter, softened
2 (8-ounce) bottles clam juice	2 tablespoons all-purpose flour
1 (14½-ounce) can chicken broth	
1 chicken broth can filled with water	2½ cups half-and-half
	2 pounds cod or orange roughy

Brown onions in butter in a saucepan. Add garlic, clam juice, broth, water, potatoes, salt and pepper. Simmer 20 minutes. In a small bowl, mix together butter and flour until smooth. Add a small amount of liquid from saucepan to butter mixture and stir until smooth. Add mixture slowly back into saucepan. Cook and stir 2 minutes. Add half-and-half and bring to a simmer. Add fish and cook 5 to 10 minutes longer.

Yield: 4 to 6 servings

Chilled Strawberry Soup

Serve in a glass punch bowl for an elegant presentation.

1 pint fresh strawberries, hulled	¼ cup sugar
1 cup sour cream	1 teaspoon vanilla
½ cup milk	1 tablespoon lemon juice

Combine all ingredients in a blender. Process until smooth. Refrigerate at least 60 minutes. Serve in chilled bowls with a strawberry slice for garnish.

Yield: 4 to 6 servings

Note: When buying strawberries, look for fresh green caps. Brown, wilted caps indicate they are past their prime. A large amount of white flesh around the top of the berry means it was picked before ripening.

How do you know when summer arrives in the South? The days get longer, the nights get hotter, the mosquitoes get nastier and the "U Pick" signs pop up everywhere. Fresh fruits and vegetables of all kinds — can you imagine anything better? Try this refreshing soup when strawberries are plentiful and at their best.

~

Tangy Salad Dressing

1 teaspoon dry mustard
1 teaspoon salt
Black pepper to taste
½ teaspoon Worcestershire sauce
½ cup vegetable oil
¼ cup or less sugar
¼ cup tarragon vinegar
2 tablespoons minced fresh parsley
1 tablespoon minced red onion

Combine all ingredients. Refrigerate at least 2 hours.

Tossed Fruit and Nut Salad

Made with a few of our favorite things

2 heads romaine lettuce, or lettuce of choice	1 (11-ounce) can mandarin oranges, drained
1 ripe avocado, cut into bite-size pieces	1 cup walnuts, pecans or cashews
¼ cup lemon juice	1 cup feta or bleu cheese, finely crumbled

Wash, dry and tear lettuce into bite-size pieces. Place lettuce in a serving bowl. Soak avocado briefly in lemon juice and drain. Place avocado, oranges, walnuts and cheese on lettuce in a decorative fashion on top. Serve with your favorite oil and vinegar Italian dressing or try the dressing we've included (see side bar).

Yield: 6 to 8 servings

Variation: Apples may be substituted for the avocado. Pineapple cubes may be substituted for the oranges, or use a combination of the two.

California Fruit Plate

Not your average fruit plate

Fruit Plate

Romaine lettuce leaves	1 cup raisins or chopped dates
4 cups torn mixed salad greens	½ cup slivered almonds
1 medium apple, cubed	½ cup grated carrot
¼ cup flaked coconut	

Dressing

½ cup mayonnaise	¼ cup orange marmalade
½ cup sour cream	1 tablespoon milk

Line a large shallow salad bowl with lettuce leaves. Place mixed greens in center of bowl. Arrange apples around the outer edge of the greens. Sprinkle with coconut. Arrange raisins, almonds and carrots in a circular design on top of greens in center of bowl. Cover and chill.

To make dressing, combine all ingredients. Cover and chill. When ready to serve, spoon dressing over salad and toss to coat.

Yield: 6 to 8 servings

Romaine Lettuce: (roh MAYN) A type of lettuce having an elongated head, dark green outer leaves and lighter leaves in the center. Its crisp and slightly bitter leaves are used to add texture and flavor to mixed green salads.

Peach Apricot Freeze

Delicious and different

2 (8-ounce) cartons peach flavored yogurt	½ cup sugar
	⅓ cup coarsely chopped pecans
1 (17-ounce) can apricot halves, drained and chopped	

Stir yogurt in carton to blend. Combine yogurt, apricot, sugar and pecans. Mix well. Spoon mixture into 12 paper- or foil-lined muffin tins. Freeze until firm. Remove liners and let stand at room temperature a few minutes before serving.

Yield: 12 servings

Variation: If desired, spoon mixture into a pan and cut into squares to serve.

For a quick and easy main dish salad, pick up a barbecued chicken from the deli and try this recipe.

Continental Waldorf Salad

3 red apples, chopped
4 ounces walnuts, chopped and toasted
2 stalks celery, chopped
¾ cup grapes
1 barbecued chicken, skinned, deboned and shredded
1 cup mayonnaise
¼ cup plain yogurt
1 teaspoon curry powder

Combine apples, walnuts, celery, grapes and chicken. Stir together mayonnaise, yogurt and curry for a dressing. Just before serving, fold dressing into apple mixture. Serve on a bed of lettuce.

Yield: 4 servings

Rainbow Fruit Salad
with Poppy Seed Dressing
Beautiful served in a clear salad bowl or even a trifle bowl

Poppy Seed Dressing

1½ cups sugar
⅔ cup balsamic vinegar
3 tablespoons lemon juice
1 teaspoon salt
2 cups vegetable oil
2 tablespoons poppy seeds

Combine sugar, vinegar, juice and salt in a blender. Blend well. Add oil slowly while blender is running. Continue to blend until mixture is thick. Stir in poppy seeds. Cover and refrigerate until chilled. Stir before serving.

Yield: 3½ cups

1 large ripe mango, seeded and chopped (about 2 cups)	2 cups halved strawberries
2 cups fresh blueberries	2 nectarines, sliced
2 bananas, sliced	1 kiwi fruit, peeled and sliced
2 cups seedless green grapes	Poppy Seed Dressing (see side bar)

In a clear, straight-sided serving bowl, arrange a layer of mango slices. Continue to layer fresh fruits in the order listed. Serve with Poppy Seed Dressing.

Yield: 8 to 10 servings

Strawberry Pretzel Salad
Unique combination of flavors

Preheat oven to 350°.

1½ sticks margarine, melted	2 cups boiling water
3 tablespoons plus ¾ cup brown sugar, divided	3 cups strawberries, chilled
2½ cups crushed pretzels	1 (8-ounce) package cream cheese
1 (6-ounce) package strawberry gelatin	1 (12-ounce) container frozen whipped topping

Combine margarine, 3 tablespoons brown sugar and pretzels and press into a 9x13-inch baking dish. Bake for 10 minutes. Cool and set aside. Dissolve gelatin in boiling water. Cool slightly and stir in strawberries. Chill until mixture just starts to set. Blend cream cheese and remaining ¾ cup brown sugar. Fold in whipped topping. Spread on crust. Pour strawberry mixture over top. Chill until set.

Yield: 8 to 10 servings

Cranberry Orange Mold

A must for holiday meals

1½ cups boiling water
2 (3-ounce) packages cranberry
  gelatin
1 (16-ounce) can whole berry
  cranberry sauce

1 cup cold water
1 orange, sectioned and diced
½ cup chopped walnuts
½ cup chopped celery

Mix boiling water and gelatin in a large bowl. Stir 2 minutes or until completely dissolved. Stir in cranberry sauce until melted. Stir in cold water and refrigerate 2 hours or until thickened. Add orange sections, walnuts and celery. Spoon into a 5-cup mold. Refrigerate 4 hours or until firm. Unmold and garnish as desired. Refrigerate leftovers.

Yield: 10 servings

Congealed Broccoli Salad

Even broccoli haters like this

1 envelope unflavored gelatin
2 tablespoons cold water
1 (10½-ounce) can consommé
  Dash of Worcestershire sauce
  Hot pepper sauce to taste

1 (10-ounce) package frozen
  chopped broccoli, cooked
  and drained
¾ cup mayonnaise
¾ cup cottage cheese
2 eggs, hard-cooked and chopped

Soak gelatin in cold water until softened. Heat consommé. Add gelatin and stir until dissolved. Add Worcestershire sauce and hot pepper sauce. Stir in broccoli, mayonnaise, cottage cheese and eggs. Mix thoroughly. Spoon into individual salad molds or a 9-inch square pan. Refrigerate until set. Unmold when ready to serve.

Yield: 8 servings

Consommé: (KON suh may) A clarified meat or fish broth.

Southern holiday dinners without cranberry sauce would be unthinkable! It's like serving turkey without dressing. Whether from a can or from the creative hands of a good cook, cranberries offer that little bit of tartness that helps balance the flavors on the holiday table. After the holidays, leftover cranberry sauce can be substituted for fruit jellies when making peanut butter and jelly sandwiches.

~

To make unmolding easier, spray salad molds with vegetable spray before filling.

~

Fold fruits or vegetables into congealed salads when the mixture is the consistency of egg whites.

Cucumber and Onion Gelatin Salad

A welcome change from sweet refrigerated salads

1	(3-ounce) package lime gelatin	¼	cup minced green onions
1	cup cottage cheese, or 3 ounces cream cheese, softened	2	tablespoons lemon juice
1	cup mayonnaise	1	teaspoon prepared horseradish
¾	cup grated and drained cucumbers	¼	teaspoon salt
		½	cup chopped pecans

Prepare gelatin according to package directions. When gelatin starts to set, add cottage cheese or beat in cream cheese. Add mayonnaise, cucumbers, onions, juice, horseradish, salt and pecans. Stir until creamy. Transfer to a mold and refrigerate until set. Serve on romaine lettuce leaves.

Yield: 6 to 8 servings

Crunchy Broccoli Toss

A delicious way to add color and texture to your meal

1	bunch broccoli, separated into florets and chopped	½	cup golden raisins
6	slices bacon, cooked and crumbled	½	cup chopped walnuts
		1	cup mayonnaise
¼	cup chopped onions	⅓	cup sugar
		2	tablespoons cider vinegar

Combine broccoli, bacon, onions, raisins and walnuts. Make a dressing by mixing together mayonnaise, sugar and vinegar. Pour dressing over broccoli mixture and toss. Chill before serving.

Yield: 4 to 6 servings

Variation: Omit raisins and walnuts and add 1 cup grated Monterey Jack cheese. For added flavor and texture, chop broccoli stems and add to mixture.

Because the South is warm for most of the year, gelatin salads have long been a mainstay in most Southern kitchens. Unfortunately, many cooks only think of sweet salads when planning their menus. While sweet salads are truly delicious, vegetable congealed salads have so much more to offer; an interesting taste and texture, beautiful color combinations and exciting variety. If you've never tried one before, this recipe for Cucumber and Onion Gelatin Salad would be a good place to start. It's easy, delicious and goes well with any meat.

Asparagus Mousse
with Aioli (Garlic Mayonnaise)
They'll think you worked for hours!

¼ cup unflavored gelatin	½ cup heavy cream, whipped
1 (16-ounce) can asparagus, cut into short lengths, liquid reserved	1 teaspoon salt
	Juice of 2 lemons
	Shelled, blanched almonds
½ cup mayonnaise	Aioli (see side bar)

Dissolve gelatin in cold water. Heat asparagus liquid and add to gelatin. Cool. Fold in mayonnaise, cream, salt, lemon juice and almonds. Add asparagus. Pour into individual molds or a large ring mold. Refrigerate until set. Unmold onto lettuce cups or a lettuce-lined platter. Top with Aioli.

Yield: 12 servings

Note: Aioli, or garlic mayonnaise, is a wonderfully different accompaniment that can be used with most vegetables and is especially good with fish.

Green Bean, Walnut and Feta Salad
Interesting combination of ingredients

1½ pounds fresh green beans, strings removed and halved crosswise	1 clove garlic, minced
	¾ teaspoon salt
	¼ teaspoon black pepper
¾ cup olive oil	1 cup chopped walnuts, toasted
½ cup loosely packed fresh mint leaves	½ cup chopped red onions
¼ cup white wine vinegar	1 cup crumbled feta cheese

Cook beans in a small amount of boiling water for 5 minutes or until tender. Drain and plunge into ice water. Drain again and pat dry. Cover and chill. To make a dressing, combine oil, mint, vinegar, garlic, salt and pepper in a food processor or blender. Process about 20 seconds or until well blended. Refrigerate until needed. Transfer beans to a serving bowl. Top with walnuts, onions and cheese. Just before serving, pour dressing over salad and toss.

Yield: 6 servings

Aioli (Garlic Mayonnaise)

8 cloves garlic, pressed
¼ teaspoon salt
¼ cup egg substitute
1 teaspoon lemon juice
1 cup olive oil

Combine garlic and salt and mix well. Place mixture in a food processor. Add egg substitute and lemon juice and process for 3 to 5 seconds. With motor running, drizzle in oil until thickened to a mayonnaise consistency. Refrigerate until ready to use.

~

Cold Asparagus Salad

Cook a 10-ounce package of frozen asparagus according to package directions. Chill. Arrange on a serving platter. Top with shavings of Parmesan cheese. Drizzle with balsamic vinegar and extra virgin olive oil. Sprinkle generously with cracked black pepper.

Roasted Corn Salad

Can be used as a salad or relish

½ cup olive oil	1 medium cucumber, peeled, seeded and chopped
⅓ cup lemon juice	
1 tablespoon red wine vinegar	2 large tomatoes, seeded and chopped
2 cloves garlic, pressed	
½ teaspoon salt	2 avocados, peeled and chopped
1 tablespoon vegetable oil	
1 (16-ounce) package frozen yellow corn, thawed	4 slices bacon, cooked and crumbled

Combine olive oil, juice, vinegar, garlic and salt in a jar. Cover and shake to mix well. Set aside. Drizzle vegetable oil over corn and place in a 9x13-inch baking pan. Broil 5 inches from the heat source, stirring occasionally, for 10 minutes or until edges of corn are brown. Cool. Combine olive oil mixture, corn, cucumbers and tomatoes. Cover and chill 2 hours or more. Mix in avocados. Sprinkle with bacon and toss gently.

Yield: 4 servings

Chunky Sweet Potato Salad

You won't believe how good this is!

4 medium sweet potatoes, peeled and cubed	½ cup chopped pecans
	½ cup sour cream
1 medium Granny Smith apple, unpeeled and chopped	½ cup mayonnaise
	1 teaspoon lemon zest
	2 tablespoons lemon juice
½ cup chopped celery	2 tablespoons honey
½ cup raisins	Salt and pepper to taste

Cook potatoes in boiling water until tender; do not overcook. Drain and cool. Combine potatoes, apples, celery, raisins and pecans in a large bowl. Mix well. Combine sour cream, mayonnaise, zest, juice, honey, salt and pepper in a separate bowl. Mix well and pour over potato mixture. Toss gently so as not to mash potatoes. Cover and chill.

Yield: 6 to 8 servings

Avocados are known for their rich, buttery texture and mild, slightly nutlike flavor. Like many fruits, avocados actually ripen best off the tree. Ripe avocados will yield to gentle pressure. Most avocados found in grocery stores are firm and unripe. It's a good idea to buy avocados several days before you need them. You can hasten the ripening process by placing them in a brown paper bag and leaving for 2 to 4 days. Once cut and exposed to air, avocados discolor rapidly. For this reason, it's a good idea to add cubed or sliced avocado to a dish at the last minute. If a dish contains mashed avocado, adding a little lemon or lime juice will help prevent discoloration, and no, it's not true that burying the avocado pit in guacamole will help maintain its color.

Tart and Tangy Vegetable Pasta Salad

Good for dinner under the stars

8	ounces dry farfalle (bow tie) pasta	2	tablespoons sour cream
⅓	cup olive oil, divided	1	tablespoon lemon juice
8	ounces broccoli florets	2	teaspoons lemon zest
4	ounces snow peas		Salt and pepper to taste
4	small yellow squash, quartered	1	stalk celery, finely sliced
		1	tablespoon chopped chervil

Cook pasta in boiling water until al dente. Drain and toss with 1 tablespoon olive oil. Set aside to cool. Combine broccoli, peas and squash and steam 5 minutes. Plunge into cold water, drain and let dry. For dressing, mix together sour cream, lemon juice, zest and remaining olive oil. Season with salt and pepper and set aside. Fold together pasta, steamed vegetables and celery. Sprinkle with chervil and drizzle dressing over the top. Toss to combine. Garnish with chervil sprigs. Serve at room temperature.

Yield: 4 servings

Chervil: (CHER vehl) A mild flavored member of the parsley family with curly, dark green leaves and an elusive anise flavor.

Wilted Lettuce Salad

It's Southern, after all!

Salad

1	bunch leaf lettuce, torn into pieces	6-8 radishes, thinly sliced (optional)
		4-6 green onions with tops, thinly sliced

Dressing

4	slices bacon	1	teaspoon sugar
2	tablespoons red wine vinegar	½	teaspoon black pepper
1	tablespoon lemon juice		

Toss lettuce, radishes and onions in a large salad bowl. Set aside. To make dressing, cook bacon in a skillet until crisp. Remove bacon and drain on paper towels, reserving drippings in skillet. Add vinegar, lemon juice, sugar and pepper to drippings. Stir well. Pour dressing over salad greens and toss gently. Crumble bacon over top.

Yield: 6 to 8 servings

Cornbread Salad

8 corn muffins

1 (8-ounce) can green peas, drained

1 (11-ounce) can Mexi-corn, drained

2 eggs, hard-cooked and chopped

½-1 bell pepper, chopped

½-1 onion, chopped

½-1 cup mayonnaise

Salt and pepper to taste

Crumble muffins into a salad bowl. Combine peas, corn, eggs, bell peppers, onions, mayonnaise, salt and pepper, and spoon over muffin crumbs. Toss lightly.

Strawberry Spinach Salad

Good way to get kids to eat their greens

How do you describe the elusive flavor of kiwi? Some say it's strawberry, some say pineapple. But all agree that its sweet but tart flavor is unlike any other. Kiwi fruit are available pretty much all year. Ripe kiwi fruit will give slightly when squeezed. They can be cut in half and the flesh scooped out like a melon or peeled, sliced and used in salads, desserts or as a garnish. And there's an added advantage to kiwis — they're a good source of Vitamin C.

8 cups torn spinach	2 tablespoons strawberry jam
3 kiwi fruit, peeled and sliced	2 tablespoons balsamic,
1 cup fresh strawberries, thickly sliced	strawberry or cider vinegar
¾ cup chopped pecans or macadamia nuts	⅓ cup vegetable oil

Combine spinach, kiwi fruit, strawberries and pecans in a large bowl, reserving a few kiwi and strawberry slices for garnish. Combine jam and vinegar in a blender and process until smooth. With blender running, add oil in a steady stream until blended. Pour dressing over spinach mixture and toss gently. Top with reserved fruit slices or arrange salad on individual salad plates and garnish each serving.

Yield: 6 to 8 servings

Orange Kiwi Avocado Salad

Three great tastes in one

2-3 oranges	2 tablespoons safflower or almond oil
½ cup lime juice	
¼ teaspoon salt	2 large avocados, peeled and sliced
1 teaspoon honey	
2 tablespoons walnut oil	4 kiwi fruit, peeled and sliced

Working over a bowl to reserve the juice, peel and section oranges. Set orange sections aside. Add lime juice, salt, honey and oils to orange juice in bowl for a dressing. Arrange orange sections, avocado slices and kiwi slices in a circular fashion on a large platter. Drizzle half of the dressing over the top. Cover and chill 30 to 60 minutes. (Browning of the avocado will occur after 60 minutes.) Serve remaining dressing on the side.

Yield: 6 to 8 servings

Winter Greens with Pears

A deliciously different kind of green salad

1	small head romaine lettuce, torn into pieces	½	teaspoon dried rosemary
1	large head endive, torn into pieces	½	teaspoon dried thyme
1	head radicchio, torn into pieces	½	teaspoon dry mustard
4	ounces bacon	½	cup balsamic vinegar
1	medium sweet onion, chopped	½	cup cider vinegar
¼	teaspoon black pepper	½	cup brown sugar
½	teaspoon celery seed	½	cup salad or olive oil
		3	medium green pears, thinly sliced and dipped in lemon juice
		1	cup pecan halves, toasted

Combine romaine, endive and radicchio in a bowl and chill. Cook bacon, crumble and set aside, reserving drippings in pan. Add onions to drippings and sauté until tender. Stir in pepper, celery seed, rosemary, thyme and mustard. Cook until onions are very soft. Place mixture in a food processor and process a few seconds. Combine vinegars, sugar and oil. Stir in onion mixture to make a dressing. If dressing is made ahead and refrigerated, allow it to reach room temperature before using. Add pears and bacon to bowl of greens. Add dressing and toss. Sprinkle with pecans.

Yield: 6 servings

Radicchio: (rah DEE kee oh) A red-leafed Italian lettuce with a slightly bitter taste that is often used as a salad green.

Balsamic vinegar is made from the newly pressed juice of selected white grapes. The juice is boiled until reduced to a third of its original volume. The syrup is then aged over a period of years in a series of wooden barrels until it becomes very dark and concentrated, mellow and aromatic. It is best used sparingly, not as a regular vinegar, but more as a condiment.

Crunchy Romaine Toss

Interesting blend of textures

Sweet and Sour Dressing

1	cup vegetable oil	½	cup wine vinegar
1	cup sugar	1	tablespoon soy sauce
			Salt and pepper to taste

Salad

1 cup chopped walnuts
1 (3-ounce) package ramen noodles, uncooked and broken, discard flavor packet
4 tablespoons unsalted butter

1 bunch broccoli, coarsely chopped
1 head romaine lettuce, torn into pieces
4 green onions, chopped
1 cup Sweet and Sour Dressing

To make dressing, combine all ingredients and mix. To prepare salad, brown walnuts and noodles in butter. Cool on paper towels. Combine walnuts and noodles in a bowl with broccoli, lettuce and onions. Pour 1 cup dressing over the top and toss to coat well.

Yield: 2½ cups dressing, 6 to 8 salad servings

Ramen Noodles: Small, Asian deep-fried noodles that are packaged dry, often with dehydrated vegetables and broth mix. When added to water, they rehydrate to make a quick and easy soup.

When making a large tossed salad, place the dressing in the bottom of the bowl. Then add the ingredients that taste best marinated, like cucumbers, artichokes, green onions and mushrooms. Top with salad greens. Cover and refrigerate. Toss before serving.

Sweet Pickle Coleslaw

It's Southern, after all!

1 medium head cabbage, grated (about 8 cups)
1 small onion, finely chopped
½ cup chopped sweet pickles
½ cup mayonnaise
2 tablespoons sugar

2 tablespoons white vinegar
1 teaspoon dill seeds
1 teaspoon celery seeds
¾ teaspoon salt
¼ teaspoon black pepper
Leaf lettuce

Combine cabbage, onions and pickles. Set aside. Combine mayonnaise, sugar, vinegar, dill seeds, celery seeds, salt and pepper. Spoon over cabbage mixture and toss well. Cover and chill at least 2 hours. Serve in a lettuce lined bowl.

Yield: 8 to 10 servings

Summer Potato Salad in Sherry Vinaigrette

It gets better every day.

6 tablespoons extra virgin olive oil	2 medium tomatoes, cut into wedges
2 tablespoons sherry vinegar Salt and pepper to taste	3 eggs, hard-cooked and cut into wedges
1½ pounds new or red potatoes	1¼ cups finely diced cucumber
¼ cup freshly squeezed lemon juice	2 green onions, finely diced
	1¼ cups finely diced bell pepper
	12 black olives

Whisk together oil, vinegar, salt and pepper in a small bowl. Boil potatoes in salted water with lemon juice until tender. Drain, cool and cut into ¼-inch slices. Layer potato slices in a serving bowl. Drizzle each layer with a small amount of vinaigrette and season lightly with salt and pepper. Arrange tomato and egg wedges on potatoes. Scatter cucumbers, green onions, bell peppers and olives over the top. Pour remaining vinaigrette over salad. Serve chilled or at room temperature.

Yield: 6 servings

Tomato Basil Tortellini Salad

A great main dish salad

1 pound cheese tortellini	3 tablespoons olive oil
2 cups frozen yellow corn, thawed	1 tablespoon red wine vinegar
1½ pounds fresh tomatoes, seeded and diced	1 clove garlic, crushed
¼ cup chopped fresh basil	½ teaspoon salt
2 tablespoons chopped fresh parsley	½ teaspoon black pepper
	2 tablespoons Parmesan cheese

Cook tortellini according to package directions. Drain and cool. In a large bowl, combine corn, tomatoes, basil and parsley. Whisk together oil, vinegar, garlic, salt and pepper. Pour over vegetable mixture and stir. Add tortellini and toss gently. Sprinkle cheese on top.

Yield: 6 to 8 servings

Southern families have waged war over whose potato salad or coleslaw is the best. Some people like them sweet, others prefer tart. Some only like mayonnaise dressings while others prefer the taste of vinegar. Basically, it boils down to what you're used to, which usually means "the way mama always made it". Why not try some different ingredients and combinations such as potato salad made with sweet potatoes or coleslaw with fruit added to it. You might be surprised at what you end up liking!

~

To cut large amounts of basil, stack up 8 to 10 leaves, roll loosely and slice diagonally with a sharp knife or kitchen scissors.

Pine Nut Wild Rice Salad

Well worth the trouble

Pine nuts, also called pinon or pignoli, are derived from the pinecones of several varieties of pine trees. The process of retrieving these nuts is very labor intensive, which accounts for their expense. Because they are high in fat, pine nuts turn rancid quickly. They should be stored in an airtight container in the refrigerator for up to 3 months or frozen for up to 9 months.

~

To toast pine nuts, cook in a dry frying pan over medium heat for 1 to 2 minutes or until lightly golden.

~

If pine nuts are not available, other nuts, such as slivered almonds, could be substituted in a recipe.

1	(7-ounce) package long-grain wild rice, cooked and cooled	⅔	cup chopped green or Vidalia onions
1	(7- to 9-ounce) package yellow saffron rice, cooked and cooled	1	cup pine nuts, toasted
		1	(2-ounce) jar diced pimentos, drained
6-10	ounces crumbled feta cheese	1	(6- to 10-ounce) bottle vinaigrette salad dressing
1	cup chopped bell peppers, any color		

Combine long-grain and saffron rice, cheese, bell peppers, onions, pine nuts and pimentos in a large bowl. Mix well. Pour vinaigrette over salad and toss, using enough dressing to coat but so as to not have dressing standing in bottom of bowl.

Yield: 10 to 12 servings

Variation: Add cooked chicken or ham for a main dish salad.

Saffron: Better known as the world's most expensive spice. It has a bright yellow color, a bittersweet flavor and an exotic aroma.

Tuscan Warm Pasta Salad

Fabulous one dish meal

1 (1-pound) box rigatoni	½ cup sun-dried tomatoes in oil, drained and thinly sliced
⅓ cup olive oil	
1 clove garlic, crushed	¼ cup shredded fresh basil leaves
1 tablespoon balsamic vinegar	
1 (14-ounce) can artichoke hearts, drained and quartered	2 cups spinach leaves
	¼ cup pine nuts, toasted
	¼ cup small black olives
8 thin slices prosciutto, chopped	Salt and pepper to taste

Cook rigatoni until al dente. Drain and place hot pasta in a large serving dish. Whisk together oil, garlic and vinegar and pour over hot pasta. Toss and cool slightly. Add artichoke hearts, prosciutto, tomatoes, basil, spinach, pine nuts and olives. Toss. Season with salt and pepper.

Yield: 6 servings

A salad where all or some of the ingredients are warm makes an appetizing first course or entrée. Combined soon after cooking, the warm ingredients are still bright and flavorful while the more traditional salad ingredients add crispness and freshness.

~

Chicken Club Salad

Just like a BLT

1 head iceberg lettuce, shredded, divided	1 pint cherry tomatoes, halved
Salt and pepper to taste	1 pound bacon, cooked crisp and crumbled
3 eggs, hard-cooked and sliced	Mayonnaise
3 large skinless chicken breasts, cooked and chopped	¼ cup Parmesan cheese
	1 cup grated Swiss or Monterey Jack cheese
2 tablespoons chopped green onions	Crispy Golden Croutons

In a large glass salad bowl, layer ingredients as follows: half the lettuce, sprinkle with salt and pepper, egg slices, chicken, green onions, tomatoes, bacon and remaining lettuce. Spread mayonnaise over top, using enough to cover lettuce completely. Sprinkle with cheeses. Cover loosely and refrigerate. Just before serving, sprinkle with croutons.

Yield: 6 servings

Crispy Golden Croutons

6-8 slices French or Italian bread
4 tablespoons butter
¼ cup vegetable oil
Garlic salt
Parmesan cheese

Trim crusts and cut bread into ½-inch cubes. Sauté bread in butter and oil over low heat until golden brown. Sprinkle lightly with garlic salt and cheese. Store in an airtight container in the refrigerator.

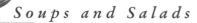

Tabbouleh
A Middle Eastern treat

Seasoned Salt

2 tablespoons
celery salt
2 tablespoons
garlic salt
2 tablespoons onion salt
1½ teaspoons paprika
1¼ teaspoons chili
powder
½ teaspoon black pepper
⅛ teaspoon cayenne
pepper

Combine all ingredients and sift together 3 to 4 times. Store in an airtight container, preferably one with a shaker top lid.

½ cup fine (#1 grade) bulgar
5 ripe tomatoes, minced
6 green onions, minced
4 bunches fresh parsley,
     minced
½ bunch fresh mint, minced

1 cup olive oil
1 cup freshly squeezed lemon
     juice
   Salt to taste
   Cayenne pepper to taste
   Romaine lettuce leaves for
     garnish

Combine bulgar and tomatoes. Allow to sit 15 minutes. Add onions, parsley and mint and mix gently. In a separate bowl, combine oil, juice, salt and cayenne pepper. Pour dressing over bulgar mixture. Mix and chill. Surround with romaine lettuce for garnish.

Yield: 6 to 8 servings

Tabbouleh: (tuh BOO luh) a Middle Eastern dish of bulghur wheat mixed with chopped tomatoes, onions, parsley and mint plus olive oil and lemon juice. Served cold, usually with a crisp bread like lavosh or the more readily available pita.

Bulgar: (BUHL guhr) Wheat kernels that have been steamed, dried and crushed. Bulgar has a tender, chewy texture and is used in salads, meat and vegetable dishes.

Chicken Salad Amandine
with Frozen Fruit Salad

"No bride in the 1950's would have had a luncheon without it."
Helen Gregory

Frozen Fruit Salad

1	(8-ounce) package cream cheese, softened
½	cup powdered sugar
⅓	cup mayonnaise
2	teaspoons vanilla
1	(8¾-ounce) can sliced peaches, well drained

½	cup halved maraschino cherries, well drained
2	cups miniature marshmallows
½	cup heavy cream, whipped
	Food coloring (optional)

Chicken Salad

3½	pounds chicken breasts
6	stalks celery, diced
½	cup pickle relish

1½	teaspoons white pepper
2	cups mayonnaise
½	cup almond slices, toasted

Blend cream cheese and sugar in a mixing bowl. Blend in mayonnaise. Add vanilla. Fold in peaches, cherries and marshmallows. Gently fold in whipped cream. Add a few drops of food coloring, if desired. Spoon into large paper soufflé cups or muffin tin liners. Freeze immediately. Thaw 15 minutes and remove soufflé cups before serving. Do not allow to soften.

To make chicken salad, boil chicken in salted water until meat is tender. Cool, skin, debone, and cut chicken into medium size strips. Fold together celery, relish, pepper and mayonnaise. Fold in chicken. Cover with plastic wrap and refrigerate until ready to serve. Garnish with almond slices.

Yield: 6 to 8 servings

When planning where people will sit at a dinner party, keep in mind the old Spanish proverb: "Two great talkers will not travel far together".

Turkey, Black Bean and Orzo Salad

Will serve a crowd

Black beans, also called turtle beans or frijoles negros, have a black skin, a cream-colored flesh and a sweet flavor. Four ounces dry black beans will yield 1½ cups packed cooked beans.

Dressing

3 tablespoons fresh lime juice	Tabasco to taste
1½ tablespoons white wine vinegar	1½ teaspoons ground cumin
	Salt and pepper to taste
2 large cloves garlic, minced	⅔ cup olive oil

Salad

8 ounces orzo pasta	2 (15-ounce) cans black beans, drained and rinsed
1 turkey breast, cooked and chopped	⅓ cup finely chopped fresh cilantro
1 red bell pepper, chopped	
1 yellow bell pepper, chopped	Shredded romaine lettuce
1½ cups thinly sliced red onions	2 avocados, peeled and sliced

In a blender or food processor, blend lime juice, vinegar, garlic, Tabasco, cumin, salt and pepper until smooth. With blender running, add oil in a steady stream until smooth and thickened.

To make the salad, cook orzo in salted boiling water until al dente. Drain and rinse with cold water. Place cooled orzo in a large bowl. Add turkey, bell peppers, onions, beans and cilantro. Pour dressing over top and toss. Spread lettuce on a large serving platter. Spoon turkey salad over lettuce. Arrange avocado slices on top.

Yield: 6 to 8 large servings

Variation: The meat in this dish may be omitted for an equally good salad. If desired, grilled chicken breasts may be substituted for turkey.

Orzo: A tiny rice-shaped pasta that may be substituted for rice.

Tailgate Taco Salad

A favorite for Friday night football tailgating

1 head iceberg lettuce	1 (8-ounce) bottle Green
2 tomatoes, chopped	Goddess salad dressing
1 (15-ounce) can chili beans, rinsed	1 (9-ounce) bag nacho flavored tortilla chips, crushed
1 cup finely grated cheddar cheese	

Tear lettuce into bite-size pieces and place in a large salad bowl. Add layers of tomatoes, beans and cheese. When ready to serve, pour dressing on top and add chips. Toss.

Yield: 10 servings

Variation: Brown ½ pound ground beef in a skillet. Add ½ cup chopped onions and cook until tender. Stir in 1 teaspoon chili powder and ¼ teaspoon salt. Add meat mixture with dressing and toss just before serving.

Susan's Hot Seafood Salad

Good hot or cold - a favorite for buffets

Preheat oven to 350°.

2 cups sliced celery	2 pounds small, shelled and cooked shrimp
½ cup chopped onions	¾ cup sliced mushrooms
1 medium bell pepper, finely chopped	1 cup mayonnaise
1 (8-ounce) can sliced water chestnuts	4 eggs, hard-cooked and chopped
1 (6-ounce) can crabmeat, flaked	½ teaspoon salt
	½ teaspoon paprika
	½ cup buttered breadcrumbs

Combine all ingredients except breadcrumbs and place in a 2-quart casserole dish. Sprinkle breadcrumbs on top. Bake for 30 minutes.

Yield: 6 servings

Water Chestnuts: The edible tuber of a water plant indigenous to Southeast Asia. Its skin resembles that of a true chestnut, but the flesh is white, crunchy and juicy, the flavor bland with a hint of sweetness. Popular in Asian cooking.

If you have trouble finding commercially prepared Green Goddess dressing, make your own.

Green Goddess Dressing

1 cup mayonnaise
½ cup sour cream
⅓ cup chopped fresh parsley
3 tablespoons minced chives
2 tablespoons anchovy paste
3 tablespoons tarragon vinegar
1 teaspoon Worcestershire sauce
Dash dry mustard
¼ teaspoon black pepper
1 clove garlic, minced

Combine all ingredients until thoroughly blended.

Yield: 2 cups

~

Enhance the taste of any recipe by making fresh breadcrumbs. In a food processor, place day old bread that has the crusts removed. Process until crumbled. If the bread is more than two days old, the flavor can deteriorate and cause a stale taste.

Aloha Crab Salad

Perfect for a bride's luncheon

1	(6-ounce) package frozen king or snow crab meat	⅓	cup sliced water chestnuts
1	fresh pineapple	1	green onion, finely chopped
1	ripe avocado	1	cup mayonnaise
1	tablespoon lemon juice	¼	teaspoon curry powder

Thaw crab meat, drain and separate into chunks. Halve pineapple lengthwise and remove core. Scoop out fruit and cut into chunks, reserving pineapple shells. Peel avocado, coarsely dice, and sprinkle with lemon juice. Toss together crabmeat, pineapple chunks, avocado, water chestnuts and onions. Spoon into pineapple shells. Combine mayonnaise and curry powder. Garnish salad with mayonnaise mixture.

Yield: 4 or 5 servings

Cutting a pineapple is easier than it looks. To remove the crown, grasp the leafy top with one hand, the pineapple with the other and twist. Cut the pineapple in half lengthwise. If the shell is to be used for serving, cut all around the pineapple to within ½ inch of the shell and lift out pulp. If only the fruit is to be used, cut each pineapple half into quarters. Hold each quarter securely and slice fruit from rind. Cut off the pineapple core and remove any "eyes". Cut into desired size pieces.

Cilantro Jalapeño Dressing

Good over romaine lettuce and red bell pepper strips

1	cup mayonnaise	1	large clove garlic
¼	cup buttermilk	½-2	fresh jalapeño peppers with seeds, divided
½	cup chopped fresh parsley		
1	bunch fresh cilantro, chopped	2	tablespoons Worcestershire sauce
3	tablespoons apple cider vinegar	1	teaspoon paprika
		¾	teaspoon salt
3	green onions, chopped	½	teaspoon black pepper

Combine mayonnaise, buttermilk, parsley, cilantro, vinegar, onions, garlic, ½ of a jalapeño pepper, Worcestershire sauce, paprika, salt and pepper in a food processor. Process until smooth. Adjust seasonings, adding more jalapeño pepper if desired. If mixture is too thick, thin with extra buttermilk. Cover and refrigerate.

Yield: 1 cup

Judith's Company Dressing

Makes a simple salad unforgettable

2-4 cloves garlic, crushed	Black pepper to taste
1 teaspoon dry mint, crushed	Juice of 1 or 2 lemons
1 teaspoon dry oregano, crushed	1 cup virgin cold-pressed olive
½-1 teaspoon salt	oil

Combine garlic, mint, oregano, salt and pepper in a bowl. Mash together with a fork. Mix in juice of 1 lemon. Whisk in oil. Taste and add juice of second lemon if a tarter flavor is desired. Adjust salt and pepper to taste.

Yield: 1¼ cups

Note: Try this as a marinade as well — it's delicious.

Raspberry Vinegar Poppy Seed Dressing

Try over your favorite fruit salad

¼ cup sugar	2 tablespoons minced onions
½ cup raspberry vinegar	1¾ cup peanut oil
1½ teaspoons dry mustard	2 tablespoons poppy seeds
¾ teaspoon salt	

In a food processor or blender, blend sugar, vinegar, mustard, salt and onions until smooth. With motor running, add oil in a slow, steady stream until thoroughly combined. Add poppy seeds and blend just until seeds are well distributed.

Yield: 2½ cups

Roquefort Dressing

So tasty

¼ cup garlic red wine vinegar	1 teaspoon salt
¼ cup lemon juice	½ cup sugar
1 teaspoon paprika	1 cup olive oil
1 teaspoon dry mustard	4-5 ounces Roquefort cheese

Stir together vinegar, lemon juice, paprika, mustard, salt and sugar until partially dissolved. Add oil and cheese. Shake well and refrigerate for up to 1 month. Remove from refrigerator 2 to 3 hours before serving.

Yield: 1 quart

Ever wonder what makes blue cheese blue? It has been injected with or exposed to a mold that gives it the characteristic blue veining and then aged for 3 to 6 months. You may find it labeled as Roquefort, Stilton or Gorgonzola, but they are all blue cheese. Some of these cheeses are mild in flavor while others are quite potent. Your nose can tell the difference.

Sweet and Sour Salad Dressing

Very versatile

1	teaspoon paprika	1	teaspoon grated onion
1	teaspoon celery seed	½	cup sugar
1	teaspoon dry mustard	1	cup vegetable oil
1	teaspoon salt	½	cup white vinegar

Combine all ingredients in a small covered container. Shake vigorously to mix. Chill several hours before serving. Serve over mixed greens.

Yield: 1½ cups

Variation: For a change, add pistachios and crumbled bleu cheese to the dressing.

Crispy Topping

Sprinkle over your favorite salad.

1	(3-ounce) can Chinese noodles	1	teaspoon curry powder
3	tablespoons butter, melted	½	teaspoon seasoned salt
2	teaspoons Worcestershire sauce		

Combine all ingredients and place in a jelly-roll pan. Bake in a preheated 225° oven for 60 minutes or until crispy and toasted, stirring frequently.

"There was no finer place to grow up than in Athens. One hour from Atlanta, one hour from the mountains, four from the beach, UGA in our backyard and 10 minutes from the country."

Doc Eldridge, Mayor, Athens/Clarke County Unified Government

ENTRÉES

University of Georgia

DePALMA'S
ITALIAN CAFE

Chicken Scaloppine

2   pounds boneless, skinless chicken breast
2-4 cups all-purpose flour
    Salt and pepper to taste
2   sticks butter
2   cups chicken broth
    Lemon Juice
5   cloves garlic, minced

2   (10-ounce) cans artichokes in water,
    quartered
1   (3½-ounce) jar capers
    Chardonnay white wine
2-3 pounds fresh spinach, washed and
    stemmed

Pound chicken with a meat hammer to thin it out a bit, being careful not to tear or shred the meat. In a mixing bowl, combine flour with a palm's worth of salt and pepper. Dredge chicken in flour mixture and set on wax paper until ready to cook. To clarify butter, heat butter in a small saucepan until liquid. Let sit until butter solids separate from the oil or clarified butter. Pour off clarified butter into a separate bowl. Heat a saucepan over medium-high heat. Coat generously with some of the clarified butter. When hot, add half of the chicken pieces, or as many as will fit in the bottom of the pan and still leave some room for other ingredients to be added. Brown on one side for about 1 minute, 30 seconds. Turn and add enough broth to cover the bottom of the pan. Add a splash of lemon juice and a couple pinches of garlic. Cook until juices thicken to a glaze. Add 12 pieces of quartered artichokes, a small palmful of capers and a splash of wine. Cook another 20 to 30 seconds. Cover chicken with a generous amount of spinach. Cook briefly until spinach is wilted and soft but still leafy and bright green. Remove from heat and serve. Repeat cooking steps with remaining chicken. Serve with a dry Chardonnay.

Yield: 4 servings

DePalma's

A popular Italian eatery whose location in downtown Athens offers a picturesque view of the old campus of the University of Georgia.

Southern Fried Chicken

It's Southern, after all!

1	(2½- to 3-pound) chicken, cut into pieces, or 2 pounds boneless chicken breast with skin
1	quart buttermilk
1	teaspoon salt, plus extra to taste, divided

1	teaspoon black pepper, plus extra to taste, divided
2	cups all-purpose flour
½	teaspoon cayenne pepper or to taste (optional)
	Vegetable shortening, melted, or peanut oil for frying
3	tablespoons bacon drippings

Soak chicken in buttermilk in the refrigerator for 8 to 10 hours or overnight. Drain and lightly pat dry. Sprinkle with 1 teaspoon salt and 1 teaspoon pepper. Combine flour, cayenne pepper, salt and black pepper to taste in a large plastic zip-top bag. Add chicken, 2 to 3 pieces at a time, seal bag and shake to coat. Combine shortening and bacon drippings in a large heavy skillet, preferable cast iron, to a height of about 1 inch. Heat oil to 300° to 325°. Add chicken to skillet one piece at a time so temperature does not drop. Cook 10 to 12 minutes per side or until juices run clear when pierced in the thickest part of the meat. Thicker pieces may take longer to cook. Transfer cooked pieces to paper towels to drain. Place in a non-recycled paper bag in a warm oven until ready to serve.

Yield: 4 to 6 servings

Fried Chicken Gravy

A must with fried chicken

4-5 tablespoons pan drippings
4-5 tablespoons all-purpose flour

3 cups hot milk or water
Salt and pepper to taste

After frying chicken, pour oil into another container, leaving 4 to 5 tablespoons of drippings and oil in the skillet. Stir in flour until smooth over medium heat. Gradually add milk, cook and stir until thickened. Season with salt and pepper.

Yield: 2½ to 3 cups

Note: This same method can be used to make gravy from other fried meats. (See gravy variations, page 106.)

Sunday Dinner Chicken and Dressing Casserole

Same great taste in half the time

Preheat oven to 350°.

Gravy Variations

Use cooking water from vegetables, consommé or tomato juice as part of gravy liquid.

~

For cream gravy: substitute milk for part of the liquid.

~

For mushroom gravy: Before adding flour, cook and stir 1 cup sliced fresh mushrooms in pan drippings until brown. Add ½ teaspoon Worcestershire sauce to gravy. If using canned mushrooms, use some of liquid from can as part of the gravy liquid.

~

For sausage gravy: Add cooked and crumbled sausage to cream gravy.

~

Buy mushrooms before they "open". When stems and caps are attached snugly, mushrooms are truly fresh.

¾ cup chopped celery	1 teaspoon salt
½ cup chopped onions	Dash of black pepper
2 tablespoons snipped parsley	½ teaspoon poultry seasoning
1 stick plus 2 tablespoons butter, divided	3 cups chicken broth
	4 cups diced cooked chicken
6 cups day old bread cubes	1 cup fine dry breadcrumbs

Sauté celery, onions and parsley in 1 stick butter for 5 minutes. Add bread cubes, salt, black pepper and poultry seasoning. Toss lightly. Stir in broth and chicken. Mix well. Turn into a greased, shallow 3-quart casserole dish. Brown breadcrumbs in remaining 2 tablespoons butter and sprinkle over casserole. Bake for 20 to 25 minutes.

Yield: 6 to 8 servings

Note: Divide mixture between two 1½-quart casserole dishes. Bake one dish now and freeze the other for later.

Stir-fry Chicken and Snow Peas

Good last minute dish

1 teaspoon ginger	1½ pounds boneless, skinless chicken breast, cut into ½-inch cubes
2 teaspoons sugar	
1 tablespoon cornstarch	
6 tablespoons soy sauce	2 (6-ounce) packages frozen snow peas, thawed
⅓ cup sherry	
¼ cup vegetable oil	8 ounces fresh mushrooms, sliced
¾ cup whole blanched almonds	

Combine ginger, sugar, cornstarch, soy sauce and sherry. Set aside. Heat oil in a wok or heavy skillet over medium heat. Add almonds. Cook and stir about 3 minutes. Add chicken and cook just until meat turns white; do not overcook. Drain oil. Add sherry mixture and cook until sauce thickens. Add pea pods and mushrooms. Cook and stir until hot and glazed. Serve over rice.

Yield: 4 servings

Snow Pea: An almost translucent, bright green legume with tiny seeds that are tender and sweet. The snow pea is entirely edible.

Chicken Breast Sauté with Wild Rice

As good for family dinner as for guests

Preheat oven to 325°.

White and Wild Rice Bake

1	stick margarine	1	cup chopped celery
1	cup chopped green onions	½	cup slivered almonds
1	bell pepper, chopped	3	cups cooked long grain and
2	cloves garlic, minced		wild rice mix
1	(5-ounce) can water	2	cups chicken broth
	chestnuts, sliced	1½	cups port wine
1	cup sliced mushrooms		

Chicken

1	stick butter	Salt to taste
10	chicken breasts	Toasted almonds

To make rice, melt margarine in a large saucepan. Add onions, bell peppers, garlic, water chestnuts, mushrooms, celery and slivered almonds. Sauté until vegetables are tender. Add rice, broth and wine. Transfer to a large baking dish and cover. Bake for 20 to 25 minutes or until liquid is absorbed.

To prepare chicken, melt butter in a saucepan. Add chicken and sauté until brown. Season with salt and transfer to a baking dish. Cover and bake for 30 minutes or until tender. Serve chicken over Rice Bake. Sprinkle toasted almonds on top.

Yield: 10 servings

Note: Packaged mixtures of long grain and wild rice are available commercially. The wild rice has been partially cooked which makes it possible for both rices to cook in the same amount of time.

Port Wine: A sweet wine most often served after a meal.

**Come For
Dinner At 8**

You can go out to eat anytime, but to be invited to someone's home for dinner — well, it's quite simply the sincerest form of flattery.

~

Menu

*Poached Salmon
à la Elegant*

Mini Beef Wellingtons

Mrs. Cobb's Casserole

Zesty Carrots

*Creamed Mushrooms
in Wild Rice Ring*

Cheese Stuffed Tomatoes

*Mama's Refrigerator
Yeast Rolls*

Tiramisu

Iced Tea

Coffee

Raspberry Kiss

Entrées

Easy Oven Crisp Chicken

So tender you won't even need a knife

Preheat oven to 350°.

1 cup dairy sour cream	⅛ teaspoon black pepper
¼ cup lemon juice	2 teaspoons celery salt
4 teaspoons Worcestershire sauce	8 skinless chicken breast halves
2 teaspoons paprika	1 (8-ounce) package herb-seasoned stuffing mix
1 teaspoon garlic salt	4 tablespoons butter, melted
1 teaspoon salt	

Combine sour cream, lemon juice, Worcestershire sauce, paprika, garlic salt, salt, black pepper and celery salt. Mix well. Add chicken and marinate in refrigerator overnight. Remove chicken from marinade and roll in stuffing mix. Place chicken in a shallow baking dish. Drizzle with butter. Bake for 60 minutes or until meat is tender and coating is browned.

Yield: 8 servings

Rice Stuffed Chicken Breasts

Chicken and rice — a natural fit

Preheat oven to 350°.

4 tablespoons butter or margarine	1½ teaspoons salt
1½ cups sliced mushrooms	½ teaspoon dried oregano
1⅓ cups instant rice, uncooked	½ teaspoon rubbed sage
¼ cup chopped onions	½ teaspoon dried thyme
¼ cup chopped celery leaves	¼ teaspoon black pepper
1½ cups water	⅓ cup chopped pecans, toasted
	6 bone-in chicken breast halves

In a large skillet, melt butter over medium heat. Add mushrooms, rice, onions and celery leaves, and sauté until onions are tender. Add water, salt, oregano, sage, thyme and black pepper. Bring to a boil. Reduce heat, cover and simmer 5 to 7 minutes or until rice is tender and liquid is absorbed. Stir in pecans. Stuff ½ cup of mixture under the skin of each chicken breast. Place breasts in a greased 9x13-inch baking dish. Bake, uncovered, for 1 hour, 30 minutes or until juices run clear.

Yield: 6 servings

This is an easy recipe to put together. Marinating the chicken overnight in the delicious marinade will assure a tender entrée the next day.

~

"When we moved to Athens during the Depression, my mother would serve our friends Chicken a la King because she could stretch this dish further than any other. There was no written recipe, but a small spoonful of mustard was the ingredient that made it so good. Mother's specialty was the forerunner of Mrs. Cobb's famous Chicken Boudini."

Betsy Powell, former Red Cross Prisoner of War Communications Correspondent, recipient of a Presidential Citation and Associate Director for Off-Campus Credit Programs at the UGA Center for Continuing Education.

"Old Timey" Chicken and Dumplings

It's Southern, after all!

Rolled Dumplings
½ cup vegetable shortening
4 cups self-rising flour, divided
1 cup buttermilk

Chicken
1 (2- to 3-pound) chicken fryer, cut into pieces
3 quarts water
1 carrot, cut into chunks
1 medium onion, coarsely chopped
1 tablespoon salt
½ teaspoon black pepper
4 tablespoons butter or margarine
1-2 cups milk

To make dumplings, cut shortening into 3 cups flour until crumbly. Stir in buttermilk to form a stiff dough. Gradually add remaining flour as needed. Turn dough onto a floured surface and knead until smooth. Roll dough until very thin. Let rest 15 to 20 minutes. Cut into 1x3-inch strips. Drop into broth as directed below.

To prepare chicken, combine chicken, water, carrots, onions, salt and pepper in a large pot. Cover and boil 50 minutes or until tender. Remove chicken; strain broth and return to pot. Debone chicken and cut meat into bite-size pieces. Bring broth to a boil. Add butter. Adjust seasonings as desired. Drop dumplings, a few at a time, into broth. Cover and simmer 15 minutes. Stir in milk and chicken. Turn off heat, cover, and let stand 5 minutes before serving.

Yield: 4 to 6 servings

This dish is great on cold winter nights or when someone in the family is "under the weather". It makes a wonderful dish to take to neighbors, and children love it.

~

Some people prefer dropped to rolled dumplings. They are just as good — really just a personal preference.

Dropped Dumplings

½ cup shortening
3 cups self-rising flour
1⅓ cups ice water

Cut shortening into flour until crumbly. Stir in just enough water to make a soft dough. Drop by rounded teaspoonfuls into boiling broth, spacing to prevent sticking.

Chicken Alouette

It takes time to prepare, but you'll be glad you did.

1 pound boneless chicken = 2 cups chopped, cooked chicken

Preheat oven to 400°.

1 (17-ounce) package puff pastry sheets, thawed
1 (4-ounce) container garlic and herb Alouette cheese
6 boneless, skinless chicken breast halves

½ teaspoon salt
¼ teaspoon black pepper
1 egg, beaten
1 tablespoon water

Unfold pastry onto a lightly floured surface. Roll each sheet into a 12x14-inch rectangle. Cut one sheet into four 7x6-inch rectangles. Cut second sheet into two 7x6-inch rectangles and one 12x7-inch rectangle. Set large rectangle aside. Shape each of the 6 small rectangles into ovals by trimming off corners. Spread cheese evenly over the oval pastries. Sprinkle chicken breasts with salt and pepper. Place a chicken breast in the center of each oval. If chicken breasts are too large, trim them to fit. Lightly moisten the pastry edges and fold ends and sides over the chicken as if wrapping a package. Press edges to seal. Place chicken packages, seam-side down, on a greased baking sheet. Using cookie cutters, cut pastry shapes out of the large rectangle. Moisten and place on top of each package. Combine egg and water and brush mixture over packages. Bake for 25 minutes or until golden brown. If pastry starts to brown too quickly, cover loosely with foil.

Yield: 6 servings

Note: This recipe may be made the day before. Cover chicken packages tightly with plastic wrap and refrigerate. When ready to serve, brush with egg mixture and bake as directed above.

Chicken and Sausage Cassoulet
A meal in itself

3   medium carrots, cut into
    ½-inch pieces
1   medium onion, chopped
⅓   cup water
1   (6-ounce) can tomato paste
½   cup dry red wine
1   teaspoon garlic powder
½   teaspoon dried thyme,
    crushed

⅛   teaspoon ground cloves
2   bay leaves
2   (15-ounce) cans navy beans,
    drained
4   boneless, skinless chicken
    breast halves, frozen
½   pound fully cooked Polish
    sausage, cut into ¼-inch
    slices

In a small saucepan, combine carrots, onions and water. Bring to a boil. Reduce heat, cover and simmer 5 minutes. Transfer to a 3½- to 4-quart crock pot. Stir in tomato paste, wine, garlic powder, thyme, cloves and bay leaves. Add beans. Place frozen chicken on top of beans. Place sausage on chicken. Cover. Cook on low for 9 to 10 hours or on high for 5 hours, 30 minutes to 6 hours. Remove bay leaves before serving.

Yield: 4 servings

Note: Use frozen chicken rather than thawed so that chicken cooks tender without being overdone.

Cassoulet: (ka soo LAY) A classic French dish of white beans and meat, traditionally cooked very slowly.

Spray sheets of foil with nonstick cooking spray before wrapping meat for the freezer. When unwrapped, the foil comes right off without sticking or tearing.

Chicken skin contains a lot of fat. Remove skin either before or after cooking. If the chicken is cooking in a broth mixture, remove the skin before cooking. If you're baking or broiling the chicken, remove the skin after cooking. This keeps the meat moist and retains the flavor, while only a small amount of the fat from the skin is absorbed by the meat.

Greek Chicken Breasts

A different way to prepare chicken

Preheat oven to 350°.

4	bone-in chicken breast halves	2	teaspoons dried oregano
8	cloves garlic, crushed	4	lemons, thinly sliced
2	tablespoons olive oil	16-20	kalamata olives, pitted
1	teaspoon salt	1	(4-ounce) container crumbled feta cheese
1	teaspoon black pepper		Fresh oregano sprigs and lemon slices for garnish

Lift skin gently from chicken breasts without detaching it. Place 2 garlic cloves under each skin and replace skin. Rub breasts with oil and sprinkle with salt, pepper and oregano. Cover the bottom of a 9x13-inch baking dish with lemon slices. Arrange chicken on top. Sprinkle olives around chicken pieces. Bake for 45 minutes or until done. Sprinkle with feta cheese. Garnish as desired.

Yield: 4 servings

Cold Lemon Chicken

Refreshing cold dish on a hot summer day

½	cup dry white wine	¼	cup mayonnaise
1	cup water	4	teaspoons peeled, seeded and finely chopped cucumber
½	cup plus 2 teaspoons lemon juice, divided	2	teaspoons lemon zest
6	boneless, skinless chicken breast halves	¼	teaspoon salt
		¼	teaspoon black pepper
		6	lemon slices

Combine wine, water and ½ cup lemon juice. Bring to a boil. Add chicken and cover. Cook over medium heat for 20 minutes. Drain and set chicken aside to cool. Mix mayonnaise, cucumber, lemon zest, remaining 2 teaspoons lemon juice, salt and pepper. Spread over cooled chicken. Place a lemon slice on each breast. Wrap chicken in foil and chill thoroughly before serving.

Yield: 6 servings

Chicken Italiano
"Our children's favorite dish"

Preheat oven to 350°.

3 cloves garlic, finely minced	¼ teaspoon thyme
1 onion, minced	1 cup Italian breadcrumbs
6 tablespoons olive oil, divided	¾ cup Parmesan cheese, divided
1 (28-ounce) can diced tomatoes	8 boneless, skinless chicken breast halves, lightly salted
1 teaspoon salt	1 egg, beaten
¼ teaspoon black pepper	8 ounces mozzarella cheese, sliced
1 (8-ounce) can tomato sauce	

Sauté garlic and onions in 3 tablespoons oil until golden. Add tomatoes, salt and pepper. Simmer, uncovered, for 10 minutes. Add tomato sauce and thyme and simmer, uncovered, 20 minutes longer. Combine breadcrumbs and ¼ cup Parmesan cheese in a shallow dish. Dip chicken in egg, then roll in breadcrumb mixture. Sauté in remaining 3 tablespoons oil until golden brown, turning once. Transfer chicken to a 12x8x2-inch baking dish. Pour two-thirds of tomato mixture over chicken. Lay mozzarella slices over chicken and cover with remaining tomato mixture. Sprinkle with remaining ½ cup Parmesan cheese. Bake, uncovered, for 30 minutes.

Yield: 4 or 5 servings

Note: Sauce may be doubled and served with chicken over pasta or noodles.

"I have lived in Athens for 31 years. It is such an enjoyable place to live for so many reasons. Diverse seems an appropriate description of Athens—among the people, the institutions, and the climate and weather! Athens offers a friendly and warm atmosphere to everyone."

Jackie Anderson, faculty member at Athens Academy and teacher for more than 25 years.

DasGupta's Authentic Chicken Curry
It's the real thing!

Curry is a catch-all term that is used to refer to any number of hot, spicy, gravy based Indian and Asian foods.

Curry powder is a pulverized blend of up to 20 spices, herbs, and seeds.

2 tablespoons plain yogurt	¼ cup olive oil
2 tablespoons tomato sauce	1 medium onion, chopped
1 tablespoon vinegar	1 teaspoon garlic powder
Salt to taste	2 medium-size red potatoes,
½ teaspoon sugar	peeled and halved
1 teaspoon powdered turmeric	¼ teaspoon powdered cloves
1 tablespoon plus 1 teaspoon	¼ teaspoon cinnamon
powdered ginger, divided	¼ teaspoon cardamom
1 tablespoon instant onion flakes	4 ounces canned sweet green
Cayenne pepper to taste	peas, drained
8 chicken legs or breast pieces,	
or combination, skin	
removed	

Combine yogurt, tomato sauce, vinegar, salt, sugar, turmeric, 1 tablespoon ginger, onion flakes and cayenne pepper in a large bowl. Mix well. Coat chicken pieces with yogurt mixture. Place chicken and mixture in a large, shallow glass dish and marinate in refrigerator overnight. When ready to serve, heat oil in a large skillet over medium heat. Add onions, remaining 1 teaspoon ginger and garlic powder. Sauté 3 to 4 minutes. Add chicken, yogurt marinade and potatoes. Cook and stir 3 to 4 minutes. Cover and reduce heat to low. Cook 60 minutes or until chicken and potatoes are tender. Add cloves, cinnamon, cardamom and peas. Mix well and cook over low heat for 5 minutes. Serve hot with basmati rice.

Yield: 8 servings

Basmati Rice: (bahs MAH tee) Translated, basmati means "queen of fragrance". It is a long-grained rice with a fine texture and a nutlike flavor that results from the aging process used to decrease its moisture content.

Cardamom: An aromatic spice native to India. A member of the ginger family, it has a pungent aroma and a warm spicy sweet flavor. Widely used in Scandinavian and East Indian cooking.

Turmeric: Comes from the root of a tropical plant that is related to ginger. It has a bitter, pungent flavor and intense yellow-orange color and is used to add both flavor and color to recipes. It is a primary ingredient in mustard and is what gives it its bright yellow color.

Wilkins Paella

Mr. Wilkins' specialty

3	chicken breasts	½	teaspoon salt
	Salt and pepper to taste		Pinch of saffron
¼	cup olive oil	½	cup slices cooked sausage of
1	onion, chopped		choice
2	cloves garlic, minced	¼	cup chopped cooked ham
2	cups dry Arborio rice	12	shrimp, cooked, peeled and
4	cups mixture of chicken		deveined
	broth and clam juice	¼	cup green peas

Season chicken with salt and pepper. Brown on all sides in a skillet in oil. Remove chicken and set aside. Add onions and garlic to oil in skillet and sauté until softened. Add rice and sauté until translucent. Add broth/juice mixture, ½ teaspoon salt and saffron. Add chicken and cook over medium heat for 10 minutes. Add sausage and ham. Cover and simmer over low heat for 10 minutes or until chicken is done. Arrange shrimp on top. Sprinkle with peas. Add extra broth mixture if needed. Simmer 5 minutes.

Yield: 6 servings

Mary Donnan's Chicken Enchiladas

"This is a great meal!"

Preheat oven to 350°.

2	tablespoons olive oil	1	teaspoon ground cumin
½	cup chopped onions	10	flour tortillas
1	clove minced garlic	4-6	skinless chicken breasts,
2	teaspoons chili powder		cooked and chopped
2	(8-ounce) cans tomato sauce	8	ounces mozzarella cheese, grated
½	cup chicken broth		Shredded lettuce
	Salt and pepper to taste	8	ounces longhorn cheese

Heat oil in a saucepan. Add onions and garlic and sauté. Stir in chili powder, tomato sauce and broth. Season with salt, pepper and cumin. Using some of the tomato sauce, spread a thin layer over each tortilla. Fill center of tortillas with chicken, mozzarella cheese and lettuce. Roll tortillas and place, seam-side down, in a greased 9x13-inch pan. Pour remaining sauce over the top and sprinkle with longhorn cheese. Bake for 15 minutes or until thoroughly heated.

Yield: 8 to 10 servings

Sweet and Sour Chicken on the Grill

So, so good! Men love it.

1	(12-ounce) bottle chili sauce	2	teaspoons instant onion flakes
1	cup apple jelly or red plum jam	2	teaspoons Dijon mustard
3	chicken bouillon cubes	4	pounds chicken pieces

Combine chili sauce, jelly, bouillon cubes, onion flakes and mustard in a saucepan. Simmer sauce mixture over low heat for 20 minutes. Cook chicken on a grill for 20 minutes. Baste with sauce and turn. Continue to baste, turning every 10 minutes for 45 minutes or until chicken is done.

Yield: 6 servings

Grilled Whole Rosemary Lemon-Pepper Chicken

An elegant use of the grill

1	(3½- to 4-pound) chicken	1	tablespoon dried parsley
1	tablespoon olive oil	1	tablespoon sesame seeds
3	tablespoons dried rosemary	¼	teaspoon garlic powder
2	tablespoons lemon pepper	⅛	teaspoon ground thyme
		⅛	teaspoon paprika

Discard chicken giblets. Rinse chicken and pat dry. Rub oil over outside and inside cavity. Combine seasonings to make a rub. Coat chicken inside and out with rub and under the skin, if desired. Tie legs together with string and fold wings under the body. Prepare grill by lightly spraying with cooking spray. If using a charcoal grill, mound coals on one side. For a gas grill, light one side only and turn temperature to medium. Place chicken on one side of the grill, opposite the coals or heat source. Close the lid and cook slowly for 1 to 2 hours or until a meat thermometer reaches 180° and the juices run clear when pierced with a fork. Cooking time will vary depending on the intensity of the heat from the grill. Smokers may take up to 3 hours.

Yield: 4 servings

Variation: For added smoky flavor, add a few water-soaked hickory chips to the fire.

When grilling chicken breasts, place the bony sides down toward the heat first. The bones will act as insulation to keep the chicken from burning before it's done.

~

When a recipe has basting sauce that is served along side grilled chicken, the sauce must be boiled for 1 minute before serving to be safe for consumption.

~

Creamy Mustard Sauce

⅓ cup sour cream
⅓ cup mayonnaise
1 tablespoon dry mustard
1 tablespoon finely chopped green onions
1½ teaspoons wine vinegar
Salt and pepper to taste

Mix all ingredients well. Great with pork or chicken.

Honey Glazed Chicken Kebabs

A summer favorite

½ cup orange marmalade
¼ cup soy sauce
2 tablespoons honey
½ teaspoon ground ginger
½ teaspoon salt
1 clove garlic, minced

4 boneless, skinless chicken
     breast halves, cut into
     1-inch cubes
4 ounces mushrooms
3 green onions, cut into 2-inch
     pieces
8 ounces bacon, sliced

Combine marmalade, soy sauce, honey, ginger, salt and garlic in a bowl. Mix well. Add chicken, mushrooms and onions. Stir to coat well. Cook bacon just until limp. Drain and cut bacon slices in half. Wrap each chicken piece with a piece of bacon. Thread onto skewers in the following order: chicken, mushroom and onion. Repeat. Place skewers on a grill over medium coals and cook 15 minutes or until done. Baste occasionally with marinade. Pour remaining marinade into a saucepan and bring to a boil over high heat. Cook until reduced by half and slightly thickened.

Yield: 4 servings

When your recipe calls for the chicken breast to be sliced thinly before cooking, freeze for 1 hour or until firm. With a sharp knife, thinly slice across the grain of the meat.

~

Grilled Garlic Bread

1 stick butter, softened
1 clove garlic, pressed
1 teaspoon dried parsley
¼ teaspoon dried oregano
¼ teaspoon dried dill
1 loaf French bread

Combine butter, garlic, parsley, oregano and dill. Refrigerate several days to develop flavors. Remove from refrigerator 1 hour before using. Cut bread into ¾-inch slices without cutting through the bottom crust. Spread butter mixture generously between slices. Wrap in foil and grill 15 minutes.

Yield: 6 servings

Bill's Special Bar-B-Qued Chicken

The secret to this delicious chicken is turning and basting every few minutes.

½ cup vegetable oil
1 cup cider vinegar
1½ tablespoons salt
1½ teaspoons poultry seasoning

¼ teaspoon white pepper
6 chicken broiler halves or
bone-in chicken breasts
with skin

Combine oil, vinegar, salt, poultry seasoning and pepper to make a basting sauce. Brush chicken with basting sauce and place on heated grill, bone-side down. Turn chicken every 5 to 6 minutes, basting with sauce each time. Repeat process until tender.

Yield: 6 servings

Note: Basting sauce may be doubled as needed.

The mild flavor of chicken adapts well to different marinades, sauces and bastes. The secret is to baste often.

Mustard Honey Baste

Mix ½ cup honey, ¼ teaspoon prepared mustard, 2 tablespoons lemon juice and 1 teaspoon salt. Baste chicken during last 10 to 15 minutes of cooking time.

~

Herb Baste

Mix together ¼ cup melted butter, a dash of dried savory, a dash of dried rosemary and a dash of dried thyme. Brush chicken frequently with the baste while cooking.

~

Brown Sugar and Tarragon Vinegar Baste

Combine 1 cup brown sugar, ½ cup tarragon vinegar and 2 tablespoons butter in a saucepan. Bring to a boil to blend flavors. Baste chicken frequently while cooking.

Mexican Chicken Casserole

Easy to adjust to suit personal taste

Preheat oven to 350°.

12-16 boneless chicken breast
halves
1 cup all-purpose flour
¼ cup vegetable oil
½ cup chopped onions
1 (15-ounce) can tomato sauce
2 chicken bouillon cubes,
crushed

1 (4-ounce) can chopped green
chiles
1 (2½-ounce) can chopped
black olives
2 tablespoons white wine vinegar
¾ teaspoon ground cumin
¾ teaspoon garlic salt
2 cups grated Monterey Jack
cheese

Dredge chicken in flour. Cook chicken in oil until lightly browned. Place in a 9x13-inch casserole dish. Combine onions, tomato sauce, bouillon, chiles, olives, vinegar, cumin and garlic salt in a saucepan. Simmer 5 minutes or until mixed. Pour mixture over chicken and cover with foil. Bake for 45 to 50 minutes. Remove foil and sprinkle with cheese. Bake 10 to 12 minutes longer. Serve with white rice.

Yield: 8 to 10 servings

Chicken and Pesto

Makes a beautiful presentation

Pesto

⅓	cup chopped almonds	3	tablespoons reduced-sodium chicken broth
½	cup packed fresh basil leaves		
½	cup packed Italian parsley	3	tablespoons olive oil
2	large cloves garlic	2	tablespoons freshly squeezed lemon juice
3	tablespoons Parmesan cheese		

⅓ cup chopped almonds
½ cup packed fresh basil leaves
½ cup packed Italian parsley
2 large cloves garlic
3 tablespoons Parmesan cheese

3 tablespoons reduced-sodium chicken broth
3 tablespoons olive oil
2 tablespoons freshly squeezed lemon juice

Chicken

4 boneless, skinless chicken breast halves
¼ teaspoon black pepper
1 tablespoon plus 1 teaspoon hot pepper flavored oil, divided

½ cup reduced-sodium chicken broth
1 tablespoon unsalted butter
1 tablespoon drained capers
6 kalamata olives
1 teaspoon anchovy paste
Julienned lemon peel

To make pesto, place almonds, basil and parsley in a food processor and process until chopped. Add garlic, cheese, broth, oil and lemon juice. Process until blended; mixture will be gritty.

To prepare chicken, flatten breasts to ½-inch thick and sprinkle with pepper. Cook chicken in a skillet in 1 tablespoon pepper oil over high heat, cooking 3 minutes per side. Remove to a plate and keep warm. Add broth, butter, capers, olives and anchovy paste to skillet. Stir to loosen browned bits from skillet. Remove 2 tablespoons of mixture and add to pesto. To serve, spoon ¼ cup of pesto onto each of four individual heated plates. Top each with a chicken breast. Drizzle caper mixture over top. Garnish with remaining 1 teaspoon pepper oil and lemon peel.

Yield: 4 servings

Anchovy Paste: A combination of pounded anchovies, vinegar, spices and water that comes packaged in a tube.

Cutting fresh basil leaves with a knife or scissors will cause the cut edges to turn black. If it is to be used fresh in a salad, the basil will look nicer if torn by hand.

Lime-Buttered Turkey Tenderloin

4 tablespoons butter, divided
¼ cup lime juice
2 teaspoons dry mustard
2 teaspoons garlic salt
2 (12-ounce) turkey breast tenderloins

Combine first 4 ingredients. Divide in half and set aside. Grill turkey, covered, over medium-hot coals 4 to 5 minutes on each side, basting often with one half of butter mixture. Cook remaining half of mixture in a small saucepan until thoroughly heated. Serve mixture warm with sliced turkey.

Yield: 4 to 6 servings

~

For an easy way to prepare fresh turkey breast, rub softened butter or olive oil over the surface. Sprinkle liberally with a Cajun or Creole seasoning mixture. Bake at 350°, uncovered, until a meat thermometer reaches 170°. Spray lightly with butter-flavored or olive oil cooking spray 1 to 2 times while cooking to keep meat from drying out.

Turkey Pot Pie

Comfort food!

Filling

5¼ cups chicken broth
3 carrots, cut into 1-inch pieces
1 small onion, diced
4 ounces fresh mushrooms, sliced

⅔ cup frozen green peas, thawed
1½ sticks butter
⅔ cup all-purpose flour
Salt and pepper to taste
4 cups coarsely chopped cooked turkey

Crust

1 cup all-purpose flour
½ teaspoon salt
7 tablespoons shortening

3 tablespoons ice water
1 egg yolk
1 tablespoon light cream or milk

To make filling, bring chicken broth to a boil in a large saucepan. Add carrots and onions and cook until almost tender. Add mushrooms and peas and cook 5 minutes. Remove vegetables from broth and set aside. Strain broth, setting 4 cups aside and discarding the rest. Melt butter in saucepan. Stir in flour and cook 2 minutes, stirring constantly. Gradually add reserved 4 cups hot broth. Cook until sauce thickens. Season to taste with salt and pepper. Spoon sauce into a 2-quart baking dish to ¼-inch depth. Place about the same amount of sauce in a container and set aside. Mix turkey, vegetables and remaining sauce. Spoon turkey mixture into baking dish and cover with reserved sauce. Refrigerate until cool.

To make crust, combine flour and salt. Cut in shortening until coarse crumbs are formed. Add ice water, 1 tablespoon at a time and mix with a fork until pastry is moist enough to hold together. Turn out onto a lightly floured surface and knead until smooth. Wrap in wax paper and chill 1 hour. Preheat oven to 400°. Roll dough to about ¼-inch thickness. Cut dough to fit top of baking dish with a 1-inch overhang on all sides. Fit dough over filling and flute edges to seal. Cut a 1½-inch circle from center of dough to allow steam to escape. Combine egg yolk and cream and brush over top of pie. Bake 40 minutes or until crust is brown and filling is bubbly.

Yield: 6 servings

Note: A great way to use turkey leftovers. To save time, refrigerated pie crust may be substituted.

Bourbon Marinated Rib-Eye Steaks

A big hit with men

½ cup bourbon	1 teaspoon ground oregano
¼ cup olive oil	¼ teaspoon hot pepper sauce
1 tablespoon chili powder	4 (1-inch thick) beef rib-eye
2 medium cloves garlic, finely chopped	steaks

Make a marinade by combining all ingredients except steaks. Place steaks in a shallow dish or plastic zip-top bag. Pour marinade over the top. Marinate 30 minutes to 2 hours. Discard marinade and grill over medium coals for 9 to 12 minutes, turning once.

Yield: 4 servings

Rib-Eye Steak: A boneless steak cut from the eye of the rib section of beef. A very tender and flavorful cut that should be cooked quickly by grilling, broiling or frying.

Fillets with Brandy Mustard Cream Sauce

Elegant entrée for a special occasion meal

4 tablespoons butter	Freshly ground black pepper to taste
4 (1¼-inch thick) beef fillets	
¼ cup Dijon mustard	½ cup brandy
2 teaspoons Worcestershire sauce	1 cup heavy cream

Melt butter in a skillet over medium heat. Add fillets and cook 5 minutes per side for medium rare. Remove steaks and keep warm. Add mustard and Worcestershire sauce to skillet. Season with pepper and stir to combine. Remove skillet from heat. Add brandy and ignite with a match. When flames die, return skillet to heat. Add cream and cook 2 minutes or until mixture is reduced to a thin sauce. Spoon sauce over steaks and serve immediately.

Yield: 4 servings

Steaks are best cooked at a medium temperature. If your grill does not have a temperature gauge, this old fashioned test will work. Hold your palm over the grill at working height. If the heat forces you to pull away in 4 seconds, the coals are medium hot. Steaks will continue to cook for several minutes after removed from the heat, so you might expect meat slightly more cooked once you cut into it.

~

When buying meat to grill, allow three-fourths to one pound per serving for cuts with a bone and one-third to one-half pound per serving for boneless cuts.

Beef Steak En Roquefort En Champignons

Quite simply - luscious!

Don't throw mush-
room stems away —
chop them and
sauté in butter. Add
a clove of chopped
garlic, 3 or 4 chopped
green onions, a little
rosemary, a few sprigs
chopped parsley and
lime juice to taste.
Cook until tender and
serve on toasted bread
for a tasty Portobella
Bruschetta.

~

1 (6- to 8-ounce) can
of mushrooms equals
1 pound fresh
mushrooms

For 1 pint (10 to 12
medium mushroom
caps), substitute
1 (3- to 4-ounce) can
mushrooms

1	cup sour cream	½	teaspoon vinegar
1	tablespoon chopped chives	⅛	teaspoon celery salt
1	cup mayonnaise	⅛	teaspoon garlic salt
2	tablespoons red wine	⅛	teaspoon onion salt
⅓	cup buttermilk		Hot pepper sauce to taste
2	ounces Roquefort cheese, crumbled		Salt and pepper to taste
1½	teaspoons Worcestershire sauce	6	beef New York strip steaks or tenderloin fillets
1½	teaspoons lemon juice	4	tablespoons butter
		1	pound mushrooms, split lengthwise

Prepare a marinade by combining the following in order listed: sour cream, chives, mayonnaise, wine, buttermilk, cheese, Worcestershire sauce, lemon juice, vinegar, celery salt, garlic salt, onion salt, hot pepper sauce, salt and pepper. Place steaks in a shallow pan and pour marinade over the top. Cover and refrigerate 4 to 24 hours. Remove steaks from marinade, keeping as much of marinade clinging to the steaks as possible. Grill steaks to desired doneness. While steaks cook, melt butter in a skillet. Add mushrooms and sauté until just tender. Serve over steaks.

Yield: 6 servings

New York Strip Steak: A steak cut from the tenderest part of beef, the short rib. It's the boneless top loin muscle and equal to a porter-house steak minus the tenderloin and bone. May also be marketed as Delmonico, Kansas City Strip, shell steak or simply strip steak. May be broiled, grilled or sautéed.

Filet Mignon: (fih LAY mihn YON) An expensive, boneless cut of beef cut from the small end of the tenderloin. Extremely tender but lacks the flavor of beef with bones attached. Cook quickly by broiling, grilling or sautéing.

Teriyaki Glazed Flank Steak

Low in fat, high in flavor

1 cup prepared teriyaki marinade	1 tablespoon dark sesame oil
½ cup chopped onions	1 large clove garlic, crushed
⅓ cup honey	Freshly ground black pepper
⅓ cup orange juice	1 (1½- to 2-pound) flank steak
1 tablespoon chopped fresh rosemary	Orange slices and rosemary sprigs for garnish

Combine teriyaki marinade, onions, honey, orange juice, rosemary, sesame oil, garlic and pepper. Mix well. Remove ¾ cup of marinade mixture and set aside for basting. Lightly score both sides of steak in a crisscross pattern. Place in a dish and pour remaining marinade over the top. Turn steak to coat both sides. Cover and refrigerate 30 minutes, turning once. Remove steak and discard marinade. Grill steak, uncovered, for 17 to 21 minutes for medium rare to medium doneness, turning once. Baste occasionally with reserved marinade. Slice steak on diagonal across the grain. Pour any remaining marinade in a small saucepan and bring to a boil. Spoon hot marinade over steak slices. Garnish with orange slices and rosemary sprigs.

Yield: 4 to 6 servings

Flank Steak: A boneless cut of beef from the lower hindquarters. Long, thin and fibrous, it is usually tenderized by marinating, then broiled or grilled whole. London Broil is flank steak that has been cut into large pieces, marinated, grilled or broiled and thinly sliced across the grain.

Grilled Flank Steak Marinade

⅓ cup Japanese soy sauce
⅓ cup honey
1 clove garlic, crushed
½ cup dry sherry
1 teaspoon ground ginger
2 tablespoons thinly sliced lemon rind
1½-2 pounds flank steak

Combine all ingredients except steak for a marinade. Place steak in a plastic zip-top bag. Pour marinade over steak. Marinate 3 to 4 hours or overnight. Drain marinade and save. Grill steak 5 minutes on each side. Cook only to rare; further cooking will cause the steak to be tough. Cut into thin, diagonal slices. Bring remaining marinade to a boil and serve on the side.

~

For a quick barbecue cleanup, wrap the still warm grill rack in several layers of newspapers. Saturate with water from the garden hose. After a couple of hours, burned on food will wipe off easily.

Stroganoff Steak Sandwiches
A delicious use of flank steak

Marinade and Beef
⅔ cup beer
⅓ cup vegetable oil
1 teaspoon salt
¼ teaspoon black pepper
¼ teaspoon garlic powder
1 (2-pound) flank steak, about 1-inch thick

Topping
2 tablespoons butter or margarine
½ teaspoon paprika
Dash of salt
4 cups sliced onions
1 loaf French bread, sliced
1 cup sour cream
½-1 teaspoon prepared horseradish

Combine beer, oil, salt, pepper and garlic powder to make a marinade. Pour over flank steak, cover and refrigerate overnight. Remove steak from marinade. Broil or grill 5 to 7 minutes on each side for medium rare. Thinly slice meat on the diagonal across the grain.

To make topping, melt butter. Blend in paprika and salt. Add onions and cook until tender but not brown. For each serving, arrange meat slices over 2 slices of French bread. Top with onions. Combine sour cream and horseradish and spoon over onions.

Yield: 6 servings

Garlic Stuffed Sirloin
Garlic lovers will adore this.

¼ cup finely chopped garlic cloves
1 tablespoon olive oil
½ cup thinly sliced green onions
½ teaspoon salt
½ teaspoon black pepper
1-2 tablespoons Worcestershire sauce (optional)
1½-2 pounds sirloin steak, 2-inches thick, well trimmed

Sauté garlic in oil in a nonstick skillet over low heat until tender. Add onions and cook 5 minutes or until tender. Stir in salt, pepper and Worcestershire sauce. Cool. Make a pocket in the center of the steak by cutting horizontally into one side of the steak. Cut to but not through the opposite side. Spread garlic mixture evenly over inside of pocket. Secure opening with wooden picks. Cover and refrigerate for several hours or overnight. Grill over medium-low coals to desired degree of doneness. Remove picks and cut into ½-inch thick slices.

Yield: 6 to 8 servings

Grilled Sirloin and Vegetable Kebabs

Cook most of your meal outside so there's no cleanup.

1 pound lean, boneless beef top sirloin, trimmed	2 cloves garlic, crushed
4 ears corn, shucked and silked	1½ pounds red potatoes, cut into quarters
½ cup barbecue sauce	12 large cherry tomatoes
½ cup beer	

Cut beef into 1-inch cubes. Cut corn into 1-inch segments. Combine barbecue sauce, beer and garlic in a zip-top plastic bag. Add meat and corn to bag. Seal and shake to coat. Refrigerate up to 8 hours, turning occasionally. Cook potatoes in boiling water for 12 to 15 minutes or until just tender; drain. Remove beef and corn from bag. Pour marinade into a small saucepan and bring to a boil. Remove from heat and set aside. To assemble, thread beef, corn and potatoes onto long metal skewers, leaving some space at end of skewers for tomatoes. Coat grill rack with vegetable cooking spray. Place kebabs on rack and grill, covered, over medium hot coals for 10 minutes or until done. Turn and baste often with reserved marinade. Add cherry tomatoes to skewers during the last 2 minutes of cooking time.

Yield: 6 servings

Sirloin Steak: A cut of beef that lies between the very tender short loin and the tougher round. The closer the cut is to the short loin, the more tender the meat.

Never salt meat before grilling. Salt will draw moisture from the meat causing it to be dry.

~

Remove meat from refrigerator 20 to 30 minutes before placing on grill.

~

Only turn meat once while grilling.

Mini Beef Wellingtons

As elegant as it gets

Marinades and Rubs

Marinades and rubs are used to add unique flavor to meats, poultry or seafood. A marinade is highly seasoned liquid used to give flavor and, in some cases, to tenderize. A rub is a highly concentrated blend of herbs and spices which flavors the exterior of the meat as it grills.

Always marinate meat, poultry or fish in a heavy duty plastic freezer bag with a zip-top seal. Set the bag in a baking dish to catch any leakage.

Lemon Basil Marinade

¼ cup lemon juice
¼ cup water
1 tablespoon finely chopped fresh basil, or 1 teaspoon dried
1 teaspoon vegetable oil
½ teaspoon lemon zest
¼ teaspoon black pepper

Combine all ingredients, stirring until blended.

3   tablespoons olive oil, divided
8   (5-ounce) tenderloin fillets, 1-inch thick
1   pound mushrooms, finely chopped
⅓ cup dry red wine
⅓ cup finely chopped green onions
½ teaspoon dried thyme
½ teaspoon salt
¼ teaspoon black pepper
1   (17-ounce) package frozen puff pastry sheets
1   egg, beaten with 1 tablespoon water

Heat 2 tablespoons oil in a large skillet until hot. Add fillets and sear 3 minutes over medium-high heat, turning once. Steak will only be partially cooked at this point. Remove from heat and drain steaks on paper towel. Chill. Thaw pastry 20 minutes. Heat remaining 1 tablespoon oil in the same skillet. Add mushrooms and stir until tender. Add wine and cook 2 to 3 minutes. Stir in green onions, thyme, salt and pepper. Cook 1 minute longer. Remove from heat and cool. On a lightly floured surface, roll each pastry into a 14-inch square. Cut each sheet into four (7-inch) squares. Place about 2 tablespoons of mushroom mixture in the center of each square. Place a fillet on top of each. Brush pastry edges with egg wash and wrap around each steak, pinching edges to seal. Place on an ungreased baking sheet, seam-side down. Decorate tops with pastry trimmings, if desired. Bake for 20 to 25 minutes or until pastry is golden. If necessary, cover loosely with foil during last 5 minutes to prevent overbrowning.

Yield: 8 servings

Tenderloin: One of the most tender cuts of beef which comes from the short loin in the middle of the back. It is tender because the muscles in this area do little that could toughen them.

Salt Encrusted Rib-Eye Roast

The salt crust seals moisture in for the juiciest roast imaginable.

Preheat oven to 425°.

1 (3-pound) box coarse (Kosher) salt	4-6 pound beef rib-eye roast, small end, well trimmed
1-1¼ cups water	1 tablespoon vegetable oil
	2-3 teaspoons cracked black pepper

Combine salt and water and mix well. Mixture may appear dry, but do not add more than 1¼ cups water. Spoon 1½ cups of salt mixture into a foil-lined shallow roasting pan. Pat mixture into a rectangle one-half to one inch larger than the size of the beef roast. Brush roast with oil, using extra if needed to adequately cover. Pat pepper evenly over the surface of the roast. Insert a meat thermometer into the thickest part of the roast, being sure it is not into fat. Center roast on salt layer. Starting at the base of the roast, pack remaining salt mixture over roast to completely cover. (Some salt mixture may fall off, but this will not affect cooking. Do not add water to pan; do not cover pan.) Bake for 1 hour, 30 minutes to 1 hour, 45 minutes or until thermometer reaches 130° for medium rare, or a bit longer to 145° for medium doneness. Remove from oven and let stand 10 to 15 minutes. Temperature will continue to rise about 15 degrees to reach desired doneness. Remove salt crust from roast and discard. Brush off any remaining salt and cut into ½-inch thick slices.

Yield: 6 to 8 servings

Rib-Eye Roast: A roast cut from the rib section between the short loin and the chuck. The 3 most popular cuts are the standing rib, rolled rib and rib-eye. The boneless rib-eye is cut from the center of the rib section, which is the most tender and desirable, and there-fore, the most expensive.

Southwestern Rub

1½ teaspoons chili powder
1 teaspoon garlic salt
½ teaspoon dried oregano, crushed
¼ teaspoon ground cumin

Combine all ingredients. Use on meat or poultry.

~

Rosemary Garlic Rub

1½ teaspoons lemon zest
1 teaspoon dried rosemary
¼ teaspoon salt
¼ teaspoon thyme
¼ teaspoon black pepper
2 large cloves garlic, minced

Combine all ingredients.

~

Creole Seasoning Rub

1 tablespoon salt
1½ teaspoons garlic powder
1½ teaspoons onion powder
1½ teaspoons paprika
1¼ teaspoons dried thyme
1 teaspoon cayenne pepper
¾ teaspoon black pepper
¾ teaspoon dried oregano
½ teaspoon ground bay leaves
¼ teaspoon chili powder

Combine all ingredients.

Marinated Roast Tenderloin

May also be used as an appetizer for a cocktail buffet

Beef tenderloin is available trimmed or untrimmed, meaning a difference of about 1½ to 3 pounds of meat, fat and connective tissue. There is very little price savings unless the untrimmed meat is on sale. Keep in mind that one-third of untrimmed tenderloin will not be usable. An average untrimmed tenderloin weighs 5 to 7 pounds; an average trimmed tenderloin weighs 3½ to 4 pounds.

Preheat oven to 450°.

5-8 pounds beef tenderloin	**1½-2 cups soy sauce**
Coarsely ground black pepper	**½-¾ cup bourbon**
2 cloves garlic, crushed	**3-4 strips bacon, uncooked**

Sprinkle beef with pepper and place in a large plastic zip-top bag. Combine garlic, soy sauce and bourbon and pour over beef. Seal bag and turn several times to coat meat. Marinate 2 hours or overnight in refrigerator, turning occasionally. When ready to cook, place beef on a rack inside a broiler pan. Place bacon over the roast. Pour marinade over the top. Place in preheated 450° oven. Immediately reduce heat to 400° and roast for 35 to 50 minutes, depending on size of roast. Internal temperature of meat should be 135° for a rare, juicy roast.

Yield: 6 to 8 servings

Best Ever Company Meatloaf

What better way to describe this — best ever!

Preheat oven to 325°.

2 pounds ground sirloin	**1 tablespoon Worcestershire sauce**
1 cup grated carrots	**1 teaspoon salt**
1 cup sour cream	**1 teaspoon black pepper**
1 sleeve round buttery crackers, crushed	**1 cup grated cheddar cheese**
¼ cup chopped onions	**3 slices bacon, cooked and crumbled**

Combine sirloin, carrots, sour cream, crushed crackers, onions, Worcestershire sauce, salt and pepper. Mix well and form into a loaf shape. Place in a 9x13-inch baking pan. Bake for 1 hour, 10 minutes or until done. Ten minutes before done, sprinkle with cheddar cheese. Just before serving, top with bacon.

Yield: 6 to 8

Cuban Roast Beef
Unique combination of flavors

Preheat oven to 350°.

4	ounces smoked ham, finely chopped
4	ounces raw bacon, finely chopped
1	cup minced onions
1	tablespoon minced capers
1	clove garlic, minced
2	tablespoons coarsely chopped green olives

1	tablespoon minced green chiles
1	(3-pound) eye of round beef roast
	Salt and pepper to taste
2	tablespoons bacon fat
1	cup beef broth
½	cup tomato sauce
1	tablespoon vinegar

Combine ham, bacon, onions, capers, garlic, olives and chiles to make a stuffing. Make a cut 1½ to 2 inches deep along the length of the roast. Place stuffing in the cut. Secure the opening with wooden picks, if needed. Season roast with salt and pepper. Brown the roast on all sides in bacon fat in a Dutch oven. Combine broth, tomato sauce and vinegar and pour over roast. Bake for 2 hours, 30 minutes or until meat is very tender. Add water or extra broth to pan during cooking if needed so that dish is not totally dry.

Yield: 8 to 10 servings

Capers: The small buds of a bush native to the Mediterranean and parts of Asia. Buds are picked, sun-dried and pickled in a vinegar brine. They are used to add flavor to many sauces and condiments.

To clarify beef or chicken stock: Use 1 egg for each quart of stock. Separate eggs and set yolks aside for another use. Beat whites slightly. Crush egg shells. Add whites and shells to soup. Bring to a boil, stirring constantly. Boil 3 to 4 minutes. Reduce heat, cover and simmer 15 minutes. Remove from heat and let stand 15 minutes. Strain mixture through several layers of cheesecloth.

~

The most flavorful type of ground beef is chuck. Unfortunately, it also has the highest fat content. Ground round or ground sirloin can be used interchangeably in most dishes, as well as ground lamb or veal or a combination of any of these. Since they all contain different amounts of fat and juices, shrinkage will vary.

Beef Brisket with Apple Glaze

An old favorite with a delicious new taste

Marinade for Beef Brisket

2 tablespoons liquid smoke

1 teaspoon garlic salt

2 teaspoons celery salt

1 teaspoon onion salt

½ teaspoon salt

1 tablespoon black pepper

2 tablespoons Worcestershire sauce

2 tablespoons soy sauce

½ cup brown sugar

1 tablespoon prepared mustard

½ cup ketchup

Mix all ingredients. Pour over a 2½- to 3-pound brisket. Marinate in refrigerator 48 hours.

4-5 pounds boneless beef brisket
1 medium onion, quartered
2 large cloves garlic
10 whole cloves
1 (10-ounce) jar apple jelly
⅓ cup dry white wine
3 tablespoons minced green onions
1½ teaspoons salt
¾ teaspoon cracked black peppercorns
¾ teaspoon curry powder

Place brisket, onions, garlic and cloves in a large Dutch oven. Add water to cover. Bring to a boil. Reduce heat and cover. Simmer 2 hours, 30 minutes to 3 hours or until tender. Drain brisket, cover and refrigerate 24 hours. Prepare glaze by combining jelly, wine, green onions, salt, peppercorns and curry powder in a small saucepan. Heat until jelly melts, stirring occasionally. Place brisket in a shallow roasting pan and brush with glaze. Heat for 45 minutes at 325°, basting frequently with glaze. Cut brisket into thin slices and serve with remaining glaze.

Yield: 8 servings

Variation: Heat cooked brisket on a charcoal grill for 30 minutes. Baste often with glaze.

Brisket: A cut of beef taken from the breast section under the first 5 ribs. Brisket is best cooked slowly over a long period of time.

Beef Burgundy

Full-bodied and rich tasting

Preheat oven to 450°.

6 ounces bacon or salt pork	2 teaspoons finely chopped garlic
1 tablespoon olive oil	2 teaspoons tomato paste
3 pounds top sirloin, cut into 2-inch cubes	¼ teaspoon dried thyme
1 onion, sliced	1 bay leaf, crumbled
1 carrot, sliced	2-3 cups beef broth
1 teaspoon salt	2 cups burgundy wine
Black pepper to taste	18 small white onions
3 tablespoons all-purpose flour, divided	1 tablespoon sugar
¼ cup brandy or cognac	¾ pound mushrooms, quartered
5 tablespoons butter, divided	1 teaspoon lemon juice
	2 tablespoons chopped fresh parsley

If using salt pork, trim rind. Dice bacon or pork and place in a saucepan. Cover with cold water and bring to a boil. Drain. Sauté in oil until lightly browned. Set bacon aside, reserving drippings. Pat beef cubes dry thoroughly with paper towel. Sauté beef in pan drippings until brown. Transfer beef to a large casserole dish. Add sliced onions and carrots, and sauté until brown. Add to casserole dish. Add 1 teaspoon salt and pepper to taste. Sprinkle with 2 tablespoons flour. Bake in center of oven for 4 minutes. Toss to mix, return to oven for 4 minutes. Remove from oven. In a separate pan, heat brandy and ignite. Pour brandy over meat. Remove contents of casserole dish. Melt 2 tablespoons butter in casserole dish and add garlic. Remove from heat and add tomato paste, thyme, bay leaf and remaining 1 tablespoon flour. Mix until smooth. Stir in beef broth and wine. Bring to a simmer. Add beef back into casserole and cover. Bake at 325° for 2 hours, 30 minutes to 3 hours. Baste occasionally. While cooking, skin the white onions and blanch. Melt 2 tablespoons butter in a skillet. Add onions and shake skillet over medium heat until brown. Sprinkle with sugar; salt and pepper to taste. Set aside. Melt remaining 1 tablespoon butter in skillet. Add mushrooms and lemon juice; salt and pepper to taste. Sauté 3 minutes and set aside. Fifteen minutes before beef is done, add bacon, onions and mushrooms to casserole. Serve with parsley sprinkled on top.

Yield: 6 servings

> "When I was a child, my mother had hot biscuits and cornbread waiting for me on the stovetop every day after school. Good country cooking is always worth coming home to."
>
> *Honorable Louise McBee Georgia State Senator*

Beef Stroganoff with Portobella Mushrooms

Good enough for company

1	pound sirloin steak, about 1-inch thick	8	ounces portobella or white mushrooms, sliced
½	teaspoon white pepper, divided	1	(10½-ounce) can beef gravy
2	tablespoons butter or margarine, divided	2	tablespoons balsamic vinegar or 1 tablespoon red wine vinegar
6	green onions	⅓	cup sour cream

Slice steak into thin strips across the grain. Cut strips in half to make bite-size pieces. Sprinkle with ¼ teaspoon white pepper. Melt 1 tablespoon butter in a large skillet over medium heat. Cut the white of the onions into slices, reserving the green tops for garnish. Add onion slices, mushrooms and remaining ¼ teaspoon white pepper to skillet. Cook, stirring often, until mushrooms are tender. Transfer to a bowl using a slotted spoon. Wipe skillet clean and add remaining 1 tablespoon butter. Heat until sizzling over high heat. Add beef strips and stir-fry 2 minutes or until browned. Stir in gravy and vinegar and bring to a boil. Remove from heat and stir in sour cream. Serve over cooked egg noodles or rice. Garnish with reserved chopped green onion tops.

Yield: 4 servings

Scallion: A name applied to several members of the onion family including a distinct variety called scallions, green onions, young leeks and sometimes the tops of young shallots. All are used interchangeably, although true scallions are milder in flavor than green onions.

California Burgers

1 pound
ground turkey

2 tablespoons soy sauce

2 green onions, thinly sliced

Black pepper to taste

1 tablespoon
grated ginger, or
1 teaspoon ground

Combine all ingredients. Form into 4 patties. Grill over high heat for 1 to 2 minutes on each side. Reduce heat or move patties to a cooler part of grill and cook 5 minutes longer on each side or until they spring back to the touch. Ideal to serve with pita bread.

Yield: 4 servings

Slow Cooker Orange-Glazed Short Ribs
with Rice and Green Peas
Imagine coming home to a dish like this!

1 large orange	1 cup dry long-grain rice
1 cup teriyaki basting sauce or marinade	1 cup frozen green peas
½ cup water	1 teaspoon dark sesame oil
2 cloves garlic, crushed	2 teaspoons cornstarch, dissolved in 1 tablespoon water
½ teaspoon black pepper	
2½ pounds boneless beef short ribs, well trimmed, or 3¾ pounds bone-in	Toasted slivered almonds

Use a vegetable peeler to peel three (3x1-inch) strips of orange rind. Squeeze juice from orange to yield ½ cup and set aside. In a small bowl, combine orange rind, teriyaki sauce, water, garlic and pepper. Cut short ribs into 2x2x4-inch pieces and place in a slow cooker. Pour teriyaki mixture over the top and cover. Cook on low for 7 hours, 30 minutes to 8 hours, 30 minutes or until beef is tender. You do not need to stir while cooking. Fifteen minutes before meat is done, prepare rice following package directions. When rice is almost done cooking, stir in peas. Cover and keep warm. Remove meat from slow cooker and keep warm. Strain cooking liquid and skim off fat. Combine 1 cup cooking liquid, reserved ½ cup orange juice, sesame oil and cornstarch. Bring to a boil. Cook and stir 1 minute or until thick and bubbly. To serve, spoon rice and pea mixture onto a platter. Arrange meat over rice. Pour some of the orange glaze over the meat and sprinkle with almonds. Serve remaining glaze in a gravy boat.

Yield: 6 to 8 servings

Short Ribs: Rectangles of beef about 2x3-inches taken from the chuck cut and containing layers of fat, meat and pieces of rib bone. Very tough requiring long, slow and moist heat cooking methods.

Grilled Crab Burgers

6 ounces fresh crabmeat, or 1 (6-ounce) can, drained
1½ cups fresh white breadcrumbs, divided
½ cup chopped green onions
4½ tablespoons mayonnaise, divided
1 teaspoon seafood seasoning
1 egg yolk
1½ tablespoons Dijon mustard
Salt and pepper to taste

Mix together crabmeat, 1 cup breadcrumbs, green onions, 2 tablespoons mayonnaise and seafood seasoning. Stir in egg yolk. Form mixture into four 2½-inch diameter patties. Place remaining ½ cup breadcrumbs in a shallow bowl. Dip patties into crumbs, coating completely. Meanwhile, mix remaining 2½ tablespoons mayonnaise with mustard. Cook crabmeat patties on a greased grill over medium heat for 4 minutes on each side or until golden brown. Place on your favorite toasted buns to which mustard mixture has been added.

Yield: 2 servings

Easy Beef Stir-Fry with Couscous

A good way to introduce an unfamiliar food to your family

Lemon Couscous

1½ cups water or
chicken broth
½ teaspoon salt
½ teaspoon black
pepper
Juice and zest of 2 lemons
1 cup dry couscous
4 green onions, sliced
1 tablespoon finely
chopped fresh basil

Bring water to a boil in
a medium saucepan.
Add salt, pepper,
lemon juice and zest.
Stir in couscous, cover
and remove from heat.
Let stand 5 minutes.
Just before serving, add
green onions and basil
and fluff with a fork.

~

*Stir-frying is a
versatile quick-
cooking method used
with meat, poultry and
seafood. One of the
advantages of stir-
frying is that much of
the slicing and
chopping can be done
in advance. Cook your
rice while you stir-fry
and it will be done at
the same time.*

1¼ pounds boneless beef top
sirloin, 1-inch thick
1 (14½-ounce) can beef broth
1 cup dry couscous
1 tablespoon olive oil
1 medium red bell pepper, cut
into ¼-inch slices

½ cup coarsely chopped Vidalia
or other sweet onions
½ cup prepared honey mustard
barbecue sauce
1 tablespoon chopped fresh
parsley
Parsley sprigs and red pepper
rings for garnish

Cutting diagonally across the grain, slice beef into strips. Set aside. In a medium saucepan, bring beef broth to a boil. Stir in couscous, cover and remove from heat. In a large nonstick skillet, heat oil over medium heat until hot. Add half of beef strips and stir-fry 1 to 2 minutes or until no longer pink. Remove from skillet and keep warm. Repeat with remaining strips. In the same skillet, stir-fry red peppers and onions 2 to 3 minutes or until crisp-tender. Add beef back to skillet and stir in barbecue sauce. Cook 1 to 2 minutes or until heated through. Spoon couscous onto platter. Top with beef mixture and garnish with parsley sprigs and red pepper rings.

Yield: 4 servings

Couscous: (KOOS koos) Granular semolina with a mild flavor and grain-like texture similar to grits. May be served with milk for breakfast, used with a dressing as a salad or sweetened and mixed with fruit for dessert.

Grillade (Beef and Grits) Casserole

You must try this! You'll be so glad you did.

Preheat oven to 350°.

1	pound boneless lean sirloin steak, trimmed and cut into thin strips
½	teaspoon salt
	Black pepper to taste
2	cloves garlic, minced
½	cup thinly sliced green bell peppers
½	cup thinly sliced red bell peppers

1	medium onion, cut into thin strips
1	(6-ounce) can tomato paste
2	teaspoons Italian seasoning
2¾	cups water, divided
⅔	cup dry quick cooking grits
½	cup grated mozzarella cheese
2	egg whites
¼	cup grated Parmesan cheese

Spray a skillet with cooking spray. Add steak and cook and stir 3 minutes or until brown on all sides. Transfer to a bowl and sprinkle with salt and pepper. Add garlic to skillet and sauté until tender. Add garlic to meat. Coat skillet again with cooking spray. Add bell peppers and onions and sauté until tender. Add tomato paste, Italian seasoning, meat mixture and ¾ cup water. Stir well. Transfer meat mixture to a greased 11x7x1½-inch baking dish. Bring remaining 2 cups water to a boil in a saucepan. Add grits and cover. Reduce heat and simmer 5 minutes or until thickened. Remove from heat, stir in mozzarella cheese. While grits are cooking, beat egg whites with an electric mixer at high speed until stiff peaks form. Stir a fourth of egg whites into grits mixture, then fold in remaining egg whites. Spread grits over meat mixture. Bake for 35 minutes or until puffy and golden. Let stand 10 minutes before serving.

Yield: 6 servings

Grillade: (gruh LAHD; gree YAHD) a French term meaning grilled or broiled food, usually meat. Customarily served with grits.

Portobella Mushroom Burgers with Basil Mustard Sauce

1½ cups mesquite chips for grilling
1 cup mayonnaise
⅓ cup chopped fresh basil
2 tablespoons Dijon mustard
1 teaspoon lemon juice
Salt and pepper to taste
⅓ cup olive oil
3 red onions, sliced
6 portobella mushrooms, stems removed
6 whole-grain hamburger buns, split and grilled
6 large leaves romaine lettuce
6 large slices tomato

Soak 1½ cups mesquite chips in cold water for 60 minutes. Combine mayonnaise, basil, mustard, lemon juice, salt and pepper. Set aside. Heat grill to medium-high heat. Drain chips and scatter over coals. Brush oil over both sides of onion slices and mushroom caps. Grill onions and mushrooms 4 minutes per side or until tender and golden brown. Place an onion slice, a mushroom cap, a lettuce leaf and a tomato slice on bottom half of each bun. Add a dollop of mayonnaise mixture to inside of top half of bun and serve.

Yield: 6 servings

Layered Taco Pie

A huge hit with teenagers - fills them up, too

Preheat oven to 400°.

For a quick and effective way to cook ground beef without the fat, crumble meat into a plastic (do not use metal) colander. Set colander in a shallow glass casserole dish and place in the microwave. Cook on high for 2 to 3 minutes. Stir and cook 2 to 3 minutes more or until done, depending on wattage of microwave and amount of meat. Grease from the ground beef will drain into the casserole dish, leaving the ground beef cooked and greatly reduced in fat content.

Another method is to cook ground beef in ½ cup water for each pound of meat. When brown, rinse beef with hot tap water and drain in a colander. Then rinse a second time. This method reduces the amount of fat in the beef by 50 to 60 percent and has very little effect on the taste.

1   pound ground beef
1   medium onion, chopped
1   (1¼-ounce) package taco seasoning mix
¾   cup water
1   (16-ounce) can refried beans
1   (8-ounce) jar taco sauce, divided

1   (9-inch) pie crust, baked
2   cups grated cheddar cheese, divided
1   cup crushed corn chips
    Shredded lettuce
    Chopped tomatoes
    Sour cream

Cook and stir beef and onions until browned. Add taco seasoning and water. Mix well. Bring to a boil. Reduce heat and simmer 20 minutes, stirring occasionally. Combine beans and ⅓ cup taco sauce. Spoon half of bean mixture into bottom of pie crust. Top with layers of half the meat mixture, 1 cup of cheese and all of corn chips. Repeat layers, using remaining beans, meat and cheese. Bake for 20 to 25 minutes. Cut into wedges and serve with lettuce, tomatoes, sour cream and remaining taco sauce.

Yield: 6 servings

Fruit Stuffed Pork Loin

Elegant dinner entrée

Preheat oven to 350°.

4	pounds boneless pork loin roast
	Salt and pepper to taste
1	clove garlic, sliced
1	tablespoon dried thyme
1	cup pitted prunes
1	cup dried apricots

¼	cup all-purpose flour
2	tablespoons paprika
4	tablespoons butter, softened
1	tablespoon molasses
1	cup Madeira wine
½	cup heavy cream

Make a horizontal cut in roast to, but not through, the opposite side. Season inside pocket with salt and pepper and place garlic and thyme in pocket. Pack prunes and apricots into pocket and secure shut with string. Rub the outside surface with salt and pepper. Combine flour and paprika in a shallow dish. Dredge roast in flour mixture. Brown in butter in a roaster or heavy oven pan. Combine molasses and wine and pour over meat. Cover and bake for 1 hour, 30 minutes or until done. Remove roast from pan and keep warm. Add cream to pan and heat and stir for about 3 minutes. Slice roast and pour cream mixture over top.

Yield: 8 to 10 servings

Honey Mustard Glazed Tenderloin

Sweet, tangy and full of flavor

Preheat oven to 350°

2	(12-ounce) pork tenderloins, trimmed
¼	cup honey

2	tablespoons apple cider vinegar
1	tablespoon Dijon mustard
½	teaspoon paprika

Place tenderloins on a cooking spray-coated rack set in a broiler pan. Combine honey, vinegar, mustard and paprika. Spoon a third of mixture over tenderloins. Bake for 30 minutes or until a meat thermometer inserted into the thickest part reads 160°. Baste occasionally with remaining honey mixture. Cut into thin slices and serve.

Yield: 6 servings

Quick and Easy Glazed Pork Roast

4-5 pounds boneless pork loin roast (double loin, rolled and tied)

1 (12-ounce) jar apricot preserves

¼ cup light corn syrup

3 tablespoons cider vinegar

½ teaspoon dry mustard

Place roast on a rack in a shallow pan. Roast, uncovered, in pre-heated 325° oven for 2 hours, 30 minutes to 3 hours or until a meat thermometer inserted in thickest part reaches 160°. To make a glaze, combine preserves, corn syrup, vinegar and mustard in a saucepan. Simmer 2 to 3 minutes. Brush glaze over roast during final 30 minutes of cooking.

Yield: 8 to 10 servings

Smoked Pork Loin Mahogany

The smoker gives it such a wonderful flavor.

For those messy barbecued ribs or chicken, your guests will appreciate having a moist hot towel to wipe their hands on. The towels needn't be fancy — colorful, inexpensive tea towels or napkins, even mismatched ones, work great. Stack towels in a container along with a few lemon slices and pour some hot water over them — just enough to soak through the stack. Or dampen the towels and place in the microwave for a couple of minutes. For a dressier occasion, you can even offer them to your guests in a shallow silver bowl.

Roast

1   (3- to 4-pound) boneless rolled pork loin roast
½   teaspoon black pepper
½   teaspoon garlic salt
    Mesquite or hickory chips for grilling
4   (12-ounce) cans beer

Mahogany Sauce

3   slices bacon, finely chopped
½   cup chopped onions
1   cup grape jam
1   cup ketchup
2   tablespoons cider vinegar

Sprinkle roast evenly with black pepper and garlic salt. Soak mesquite chips in water for 30 minutes; drain. Prepare a charcoal fire in a smoker. Let burn 20 minutes before adding mesquite chips to coals. Place empty water pan in smoker. Add beer and enough hot water to fill pan. Place roast on food rack and cover with smoker lid. Cook 2 hours, 30 minutes to 3 hours or until a meat thermometer reads 160°.

Meanwhile, prepare sauce. Cook bacon and onions over medium-high heat until onion is tender; drain. Stir in jam, ketchup and vinegar. Cook over low heat for 10 to 15 minutes, stirring occasionally. Serve roast with sauce on the side.

Yield: 8 to 10 servings, 2 cups sauce

Marinated Pork Tenderloin
with Roasted Vegetables

Perfect for the working person - most of the work's done the night before

2 tablespoons dry mustard	2 tablespoons chopped basil
2 tablespoons black pepper	½ cup wine vinegar
2 cloves garlic, minced	¼ cup chopped cilantro
2 tablespoons lime juice	3 pounds pork tenderloin
¾ cup soy sauce	3 large carrots, chopped
¼ cup vegetable oil	2-3 stalks celery, chopped
2 tablespoons Worcestershire sauce	1 medium onion, chopped
	Strips of bacon
	2 tablespoons all-purpose flour

Combine mustard, pepper, garlic, juice, soy sauce, oil, Worcestershire sauce, basil, vinegar and cilantro. Marinate pork in mixture overnight in the refrigerator. Remove tenderloins, reserving marinade. Grill pork 10 to 15 minutes to brown meat on each side. Transfer pork to a pan. Add reserved marinade, carrots, celery and onions. Top with strips of bacon. Cover and bake in preheated 325° oven for 45 minutes. Remove pork and pour pan drippings into a saucepan. Add flour to saucepan, cook and stir over low heat until thickened. Add chicken broth if needed for extra sauce. Pour sauce over sliced pork and serve.

Yield: 6 servings

Zesty Grilled Ham

Easy to fix — no cleanup

1 cup brown sugar	1 (1- to 1½-pound) fully cooked
⅓ cup prepared horseradish	ham steak, 1-inch thick
¼ cup lemon juice	

Bring brown sugar, horseradish and lemon juice to a boil. Brush over both sides of ham. Grill over medium coals, turning once, for 20 to 25 minutes or until heated through and well glazed.

Yield: 3-4 servings

Pork tenderloins are usually packaged in pairs. When putting tenderloins in a baking dish, place fat and skinny sides opposite each other for more even cooking.

~

Cutting into a pork tenderloin to check doneness allows too many good juices to escape. Use a meat thermometer by inserting it in the thickest section of the tenderloin. Make sure the internal temperature reaches 160°. This temperature ensures that the meat is safe to eat but not dry and overcooked.

Bourbon and Praline Ham A La Epting

A specialty of Lee Epting - Athens caterer extraordinaire

6-8 pounds precooked ham, untrimmed	½ cup brown sugar
1½ cups bourbon	½ cup ground or finely chopped pecans
2 tablespoons butter	½ cup pecan halves
1 cup maple syrup	

Score the skin and fat of the ham and rub surface liberally with bourbon. Place in the smallest baking pan that will hold it and pour remaining bourbon over the top. Marinate 2-3 hours, basting every 30 minutes. Pour off excess bourbon and reserve. Bake ham, skin-side up, in preheated 325° oven for 2 hours. Melt butter in a saucepan. Stir in reserved bourbon, maple syrup, brown sugar and ground pecans. Bring to a boil. Brush bourbon glaze over ham. Decorate with pecan halves and bake 15 to 20 minutes longer.

Yield: 12 servings

Polish Potato Casserole

Satisfying and so good

Preheat oven to 350°.

1 tablespoon margarine	4 large potatoes, thinly sliced
2 tablespoons all-purpose flour	1 large onion, sliced
2 cups milk	2 cups grated green cabbage
¼ teaspoon salt	½ pound kielbasa sausage, thinly sliced
¼ teaspoon black pepper	

Melt margarine and stir in flour. Cook and stir 1 minute. Gradually add milk, stirring constantly until smooth. Cook and stir over low to medium heat until mixture is the consistency of buttermilk. Add salt and pepper to sauce and set aside. Spread a third of potatoes in the bottom of a greased 2½- to 3-quart casserole dish. Add, in layers, half the onions, half the cabbage, half the sausage and a third of the sauce. Repeat layers with a third of potatoes, remainder of onions, cabbage and sausage, and a third of sauce. Top with remaining potatoes and sauce. Cover and bake for 60 minutes. Uncover and bake 15 minutes longer.

Yield: 6 to 8 servings

In the old days, every Southern farm had a smoke-house, an out building where hams were salted down and left to cure over the long winter months. When ham was needed, they would go out to the smokehouse, slice off a slab or two, soak it overnight to remove some of the saltiness and fry it up for breakfast. Afterwards, strong coffee was poured over the pan drippings to make what we in the South call Redeye Gravy.

~

William Tate was Dean of Men at the University of Georgia for many years. A true institution, he ruled the students with an iron hand. If any property was "innocently" removed from a local residence as a prank, Dean Tate always knew where to find it and made sure that it was returned to its owner. He didn't know much about cooking other than how to boil water for coffee, but his favorite foods were country ham and home-cooked green beans.

Sunday Brunch Glazed Canadian Bacon

Serve something a little different at your next brunch

Preheat oven to 350°.

1 (2½-pound) piece Canadian bacon, rind removed	½ cup firmly packed dark brown sugar
2 tablespoons cloves	3 tablespoons Dijon mustard

Score top and sides of bacon lightly into diamonds. Stud center of each diamond with a clove. Place in a shallow roasting pan. Combine brown sugar and mustard and pour over the bacon. Bake for 30 minutes, basting several times with the brown sugar glaze. Cover with foil and let stand at least 10 minutes and up to 60 minutes before slicing.

Yield: 6 servings

Canadian Bacon: More like ham than bacon, Canadian bacon comes from the tender eye of the loin, which is located in the middle of the back. It costs more than bacon, but because it is leaner and pre-cooked, it offers more servings per pound. It is available in tubular chunks that can be sliced or cut however desired.

Peach Glazed Baby Back Ribs

A different way to fix ribs

1 (10-ounce) jar peach preserves	¼ teaspoon ground cardamom or cinnamon
2 tablespoons lemon juice	4-5 pounds meaty baby back ribs
1 teaspoon Dijon mustard	

In a small saucepan, combine preserves, lemon juice, mustard and cardamom. Cook and stir over medium heat until preserves melt. Remove from heat. Grill pork over medium heat, brushing occasionally with preserves glaze, until tender.

Yield: 4 to 6 servings

Country Ham with Redeye Gravy

2 (¼-inch thick) slices uncooked country ham

2 tablespoons vegetable oil

1 cup strong black coffee

2 tablespoons all-purpose flour

Using a knife, cut gashes in the fat around the ham to keep the edges from curling. Cook ham in oil in a heavy skillet over low heat until browned. Add a small amount of water to the skillet and simmer for a few minutes. Remove ham from skillet and keep warm, reserving pan drippings. Stir together coffee and flour and add to skillet with pan drippings. Cook and stir constantly until thickened. Serve gravy with ham.

Yield: 2 servings

~

To remove some of the salt and add moisture to the ham, soak overnight in water before cooking.

Honey Glazed Pork Chops and Apples

Pork and apples - always good together

Preheat oven to 325°.

6 center cut pork chops	1 large cooking apple, peeled
½ cup honey	and sliced
3 tablespoons cider vinegar	¼ cup raisins
1 teaspoon salt	2 tablespoons dark brown
¼ teaspoon dry mustard	sugar

Place pork chops in a shallow 2-quart baking dish. Combine honey, vinegar, salt and mustard and pour over chops. Top with apple slices and raisins. Sprinkle with brown sugar. Bake for 60 minutes, basting twice while cooking.

Yield: 6 servings

Cookouts are popular in the South almost year round. Go to any outside event, be it a concert in the park, a Georgia football game or a day at the beach and you're sure to get a whiff of that intoxicating smell — somebody's grilling something somewhere!

Alabama Bar-B-Que Sauce

¾ cup ketchup
¼ cup cider vinegar
2 teaspoons Worcestershire sauce
¼ teaspoon hot pepper sauce, or to taste
2 tablespoons prepared yellow mustard
¼ cup molasses or dark brown sugar
½ teaspoon salt
1 teaspoon celery seed (optional)

Combine all ingredients in a small saucepan. Heat to combine flavors. Good for chicken or ribs. Do not start basting with sauce until almost done; ketchup burns quickly.

Yield: about 1½ cups

Hoedown Ribs and Chicken

Delicious even as leftovers

5 pounds pork spareribs	2 cups unsweetened
2 (3½- to 4-pound) chickens,	pineapple juice
quartered	2 cups dry red wine
Salt and pepper	1 tablespoon salt
2 cups ketchup	¼-½ cup Worcestershire sauce
	1 teaspoon hot pepper sauce

Lightly season pork and chicken with salt and pepper. Combine ketchup, juice, wine, 1 tablespoon salt, Worcestershire sauce and hot pepper sauce to make a marinade. Pour over pork and chicken, cover and refrigerate overnight. Grill pork and chicken over medium-hot coals for 60 minutes, turning and basting with marinade often.

Yield: 8 to 10 servings

Wedge's Old Fashioned Brunswick Stew

An old family recipe perfected over the years

Part One

6   chicken breasts
1   package chicken thighs
5   (14½-ounce) cans chicken broth, divided
1   cup chopped celery, divided
1   cup chopped onions, divided

½   cup chopped carrots, divided
2   tablespoons finely minced garlic, divided
2   bay leaves, divided
3-4 pounds beef roast
3-4 pounds pork roast
1   (14½-ounce) can beef broth

Part Two

1   (16-ounce) package frozen white shoe peg corn
1   (16-ounce) package frozen white cream-style corn
½   cup white vinegar
¼   cup Worcestershire sauce
1   teaspoon poultry seasoning
¼   teaspoon allspice
1   teaspoon white pepper
1   teaspoon black pepper
¼   cup smoky flavored barbecue sauce

¼   teaspoon cayenne pepper
1   teaspoon hot pepper sauce
3   (14½-ounce) cans diced tomatoes
2   (15-ounce) cans tomato sauce
2   large Vidalia or other sweet onions, chopped
1   stick butter
¼   cup brown sugar
    Juice of 2 lemons
    Juice of 1 lime
    Salt to taste

To prepare first part of recipe, combine chicken breasts and thighs with 3 cans chicken broth, adding enough water to cover in a large pot. Add ½ cup celery, ½ cup onions, ¼ cup carrots, 1 tablespoon garlic and 1 bay leaf. Bring to a boil and cook until tender. Remove chicken to cool, reserving broth and vegetables. Remove bay leaf from broth and skim fat. Debone chicken and chop meat. Cut beef and pork roasts into 1-inch cubes. Place cubes in a second large pot with beef broth and remaining 2 cans chicken broth. Add water to cover. Add remaining celery, onions, carrots, garlic and bay leaf. Bring to a boil and cook until tender. Remove meat to cool, reserving broth and vegetables. Remove bay leaf from broth and skim fat. Working in small batches at a time, place some of all cooked meats in a food processor. Add a small amount of broth and vegetables from both pots. Process until no large pieces remain. Repeat until all meat and vegetables are processed. Save any remaining broth. Place processed meat mixture in a very large pot.

Add all ingredients from Part Two of recipe. Stir well and cook slowly for several hours. Stir often while cooking to prevent sticking or burning. Add remaining broth and water as needed if stew is too thick.

Yield: 24 (1-cup) servings

Carolina Bar-B-Que Sauce

Western North Carolina, that is

3 tablespoons sugar
1 cup cider vinegar
⅔ cup ketchup
½ cup water
⅛ teaspoon cayenne pepper
¾ teaspoon salt
¼ teaspoon black pepper
Dash of Tabasco

Mix sugar and vinegar together and heat until sugar dissolves. Add ketchup, water, cayenne pepper, salt, black pepper and Tabasco. Simmer 10 minutes. If too thick, thin with warm water. Use warm over grated cole slaw as in Western North Carolina.

~

Sergeant Perry's Pig-Picking Sauce

1 quart cider vinegar
2 tablespoons salt
2 tablespoons black pepper
1 tablespoon crushed red pepper flakes
1 tablespoon sugar

Combine all ingredients in a saucepan. Bring to a boil. Reduce heat and simmer 60 minutes. Baste meat of choice with sauce frequently while grilling.

Veal has a delicate and distinctive flavor. Milk-fed veal is the best; top-quality veal should be tender and succulent with a white or very pale pink color.

~

Veal is lower in fat than beef, so it may toughen quickly. It should never be broiled; long, slow, covered cooking is best.

Easy Veal Piccata

Double the vermouth, butter and lemon juice and serve on the side as a sauce for the meat.

8	veal cutlets, about 1½ pounds	¼	cup vermouth or dry white wine
⅓	cup all-purpose flour	3	tablespoons butter
½	teaspoon salt	3	tablespoons lemon juice
¼	teaspoon black pepper	4	teaspoons lemon zest
2	tablespoons peanut or vegetable oil		Lemon slices and parsley for garnish

Place cutlets between 2 sheets of plastic wrap. Pound with a rolling pin until flattened to ⅛-inch thickness. Combine flour, salt and pepper. Dredge cutlets in flour mixture. Cook in oil in a skillet over medium heat for about 1 minute on each side. Remove from skillet and keep warm. Add vermouth to skillet and cook until thoroughly heated. Add butter and lemon juice and heat just until butter melts. Return veal to skillet and cook another 2 to 3 minutes. Sprinkle with lemon zest and garnish with lemon slices and parsley.

Yield: 4 servings

Veal Stew

A delicious slow cooker recipe

4	slices bacon, chopped	1	cup converted rice (no substitutions)
2	pounds veal, cut into 1-inch cubes	1½	teaspoons salt
2¼	cups water	4	tomatoes, peeled and quartered
2	onions, coarsely chopped	2	bell peppers, cut into strips
2	cloves garlic, minced		Dash of Tabasco sauce
6	carrots, sliced	2	tablespoons chopped fresh parsley

Cook bacon in a large skillet until transparent. Add veal and brown well. Place in a slow cooker. Add some of the 2¼ cups water to the skillet and stir to pick up brown bits from bottom. Add to slow cooker along with remainder of water. Stir in onions, garlic, carrots, rice and salt. Cover and cook on low heat for about 8 hours. Add tomatoes, bell peppers and Tabasco sauce during last 10 minutes of cooking. Serve with parsley sprinkled on top.

Yield: 6 to 8 servings

Converted Rice: a term used to describe par-boiled rice. Unhulled grains are soaked and dried before milling which produces grains that are separated and fluffy when cooked.

Barbecued Leg of Lamb

Such an easy way to cook lamb

5 pounds leg of lamb	1 tablespoon Worcestershire
Vegetable oil	sauce
Salt	¼ cup lemon juice
½ teaspoon black pepper	1 teaspoon dry mustard
½ cup water	Dash of hot pepper sauce
½ cup dry red wine	¼ teaspoon paprika
2 tablespoons red wine vinegar	1 clove garlic, pressed
	1 medium onion, grated

Rub lamb with 1 tablespoon oil. Season with salt and pepper. Place on a grill over low heat and cook for about 60 minutes, turning occasionally and brushing with oil. Combine water, wine, vinegar, Worcestershire sauce, lemon juice, mustard, hot sauce, paprika, garlic, onions, 1 tablespoon oil and ½ teaspoon salt in a medium saucepan. Bring to a boil. Brush lamb with the sauce and continue to cook 60 minutes or until done, occasionally basting with sauce.

Yield: 8 to 10 servings

Lamb Chops Roquefort

The Roquefort sets it apart.

4 ounces Roquefort cheese	4 (2-inch thick) lamb chops
1 teaspoon Worcestershire	1 clove garlic, sliced
sauce	⅛ teaspoon salt
Few drops of hot pepper sauce	⅛ teaspoon black pepper

Combine cheese, Worcestershire sauce and hot sauce. Blend well and set aside. Rub chops with garlic and season with salt and pepper. Broil chops 3 inches from the heat source for 10 to 14 minutes per side, depending on desired degree of doneness. About 5 minutes before chops are done, spread entire surface of each chop with 2 tablespoons of cheese mixture. Complete broiling. Serve with mint jelly.

Yield: 4 servings

Vidalia-Mint Butter

⅓ cup fresh mint
¼ cup chopped Vidalia onions
Salt and pepper to taste
1 stick butter, softened

Combine all ingredients in a food processor or blender. Process until smooth. Chill at least 60 minutes. Add 1 to 2 teaspoons of mint butter to the top of lamb chops that have been grilled or pan-seared.

~

Red Pepper Jelly Sauce

½ cup red pepper jelly
¼ cup port wine
¼ cup ketchup
2 tablespoons butter or margarine
½ tablespoon Worcestershire sauce

Combine all ingredients in a saucepan. Heat over low-medium heat. Serve with pork, lamb or wild game.

Aunt Estelle's Oyster Casserole

Nice change from scalloped oysters

1	(8-ounce) package thin spaghetti, cooked al dente and drained	1	sleeve saltine crackers, crushed
2	cups grated sharp cheddar cheese	1	pint fresh oysters, juice reserved Butter Salt and pepper
		1	pint half-and-half

In a greased casserole dish, layer a third each of spaghetti, cheese, cracker crumbs and oysters. Dot with butter and sprinkle with salt and pepper. Repeat layers twice. Pour reserved oyster juice and half-and-half over the top. Refrigerate overnight. Bake, uncovered, in preheated 350° oven for 30 to 45 minutes or until hot and bubbly.

Yield: 6 to 8 servings

Crabmeat Au Gratin

Cook and serve in individual au gratin dishes for a special occasion.

Preheat oven to 350°.

1	large onion, chopped	2	egg yolks
3	stalks celery, chopped	2	pounds crabmeat
2	sticks butter or margarine		Salt and pepper to taste
¼	cup all-purpose flour	2½	cups grated cheddar cheese
1	(12-ounce) plus 1 (5-ounce) can evaporated milk		

Sauté onions and celery in butter until soft. Add flour and stir until flour is blended and cooked but not burned. Stir in milk. Remove from heat and cool. Add egg yolks and crabmeat. Season with salt and pepper. Pour into individual casserole dishes or one large casserole dish. Top with cheese. Bake for 20 minutes or until cheese is melted.

Yield: 6 servings

Variation: If desired, small fresh shrimp may be added.

Salmon Bake with Pecan Crumb Coating

Can be prepared before guests arrive and cooked right before eating

Preheat oven to 450°.

2 tablespoons Dijon mustard	2 teaspoons chopped fresh
2 tablespoons butter, melted	parsley
4 teaspoons honey	4 (4- to 6-ounce) salmon fillets
¼ cup fresh breadcrumbs	Salt and pepper to taste
¼ cup finely chopped pecans	Lemon wedges for garnish

Combine mustard, butter and honey in a small bowl. Set aside. Mix together breadcrumbs, pecans and parsley in a separate bowl. Set aside. Season salmon fillets with salt and pepper. Place fillets on a greased baking sheet. Brush fillets with mustard mixture. Pat breadcrumb mixture onto top of each fillet. Bake for 10 minutes or until salmon just begins to flake easily. Serve with lemon wedges.

Yield: 4 servings

Celebration Seafood Casserole

So rich you'll want to save for a very special occasion

Preheat oven to 400°.

1½ sticks butter, divided	1 cup sliced mushrooms
6 tablespoons all-purpose flour	1 pound small shrimp, cooked
2 teaspoons salt	8 ounces crabmeat
¼ teaspoon white pepper	¼ cup sherry
4 cups light cream	6 tablespoons fine breadcrumbs
1 pound scallops	Chopped pimento
½ cup finely chopped onions	

Melt 1 stick plus 1 tablespoon butter in a saucepan. Blend in flour until smooth. Cook over low heat for several minutes, stirring frequently. Season with salt and white pepper. Gradually stir in cream. Cook and stir until sauce begins to bubble. Simmer over low heat for 5 minutes. In a skillet, sauté scallops and onions in remaining 3 tablespoons butter until onions are golden. Remove scallops and onions and set aside. In same skillet, sauté mushrooms for 3 minutes. Add mushrooms, scallops and onions to cream sauce. Stir in shrimp, crabmeat and sherry. Spoon mixture into a casserole dish or individual scallop shells and sprinkle with breadcrumbs. Bake for 10 minutes or until breadcrumbs are slightly browned. Garnish with pimento and serve immediately.

Yield: 10 to 12 servings

Several varieties of salmon are available in the grocery store. The Chinook and sockeye varieties have the highest fat content at about 10 grams per 4 ounces. The coho and Atlantic are moderately fatty, containing about 6 grams of fat per 4 ounces. The chum and pink salmon varieties are leanest at about 4 grams of fat per 4-ounce portion. Keep in mind, however, that even the fat content of the higher fat salmons is comparable to that of lean ground beef. Also, the type of fat in seafood has been shown to be beneficial to one's health.

~

"Being from the coast, we ate a lot of seafood. What I remember best is my mother's crab omelet sandwiches. We would eat them on Friday, when being Catholic, you don't eat meat."

Vince Dooley, former Head Football Coach and current Athletic Director, UGA

147

Poached Scallops in Wine Sauce

Scallops prepared this way are so tender and flavorful.

Preheat oven to 350°.

1	pound bay scallops	3	tablespoons butter, divided
1	cup white wine	3	tablespoons all-purpose flour
1	tablespoon lemon juice	¼	cup chicken broth
⅓	pound mushrooms, thinly sliced	½	cup light cream
1	small onion, diced		Salt and pepper to taste
		¼	cup Parmesan cheese

Wash and drain scallops and place in a saucepan. Add wine and lemon juice. Bring almost to a boil and cover. Reduce heat and simmer 2 minutes. Drain, reserving 1 cup of poaching liquid. Sauté mushrooms and onions in 1 tablespoon butter in a skillet until soft but not brown. Remove mushroom mixture and set aside. Melt remaining 2 tablespoons butter in same skillet. Blend in flour. Add mushroom mixture and reserved cup of poaching liquid. Cook and stir until thickened. Stir in broth and cream until smooth. Add scallops and season with salt and pepper. Place in individual baking dishes. Sprinkle with Parmesan cheese. Bake until lightly browned.

Yield: 2 entrée servings, 4 to 6 appetizer servings

Scallop: A bivalve mollusk. Bay scallops are tiny and found only on the East Coast. Sea scallops are much larger and more readily available. Bay scallops are sweet and more succulent than sea scallops and are also more expensive.

Tortilla Crusted Tilapia with Mango Butter

Healthy, colorful, and tasty

4	tilapia fillets	1	mango, chopped
4	tablespoons olive oil, divided	2	tablespoons butter
	Salt and pepper to taste	2	cloves garlic, minced
½	cup finely crushed multi-colored tortilla chips		

Brush fillets lightly on all sides with 2 tablespoons of oil. Salt and pepper both sides. Dredge fillets in crushed chips to lightly coat. Heat remaining 2 tablespoons oil in a heavy skillet over medium-high heat. Add fillets and sauté 2 to 2½ minutes on each side, depending on thickness of fillets. Sauté mango in butter until tender. Add garlic and cook, being careful not to burn. Serve fish over cooked leaf spinach and top with mango butter.

Yield: 4 servings

Fresh or cooked scallops can be refrigerated 1 to 2 days in a sealed container. Frozen scallops will keep for up to 3 months. No special preparation is needed to freeze scallops once they have been removed from their shell. To thaw, place frozen scallops into boiling milk that has been removed from the heat, or thaw in refrigerator. Scallops will retain more of their flavor if they are cooked while still frozen.

~

Tilapia was originally a small African fish that could live in fresh water. New hybrids are being developed worldwide. This fish is moist and mild; a light meunière sauce would complement its sweet flavor.

Easy Pan-Fried Tilapia

Couldn't be easier to prepare

All-purpose flour
Salt and pepper to taste
4   tilapia fillets
2   tablespoons butter

2   tablespoons olive oil
**¼   cup freshly squeezed lemon
       juice**

Season flour with salt and pepper. Lightly coat fillets with seasoned flour. Pan-fry fillets in butter and oil until brown on each side. Sprinkle lemon juice evenly over fillets.

Yield: 4 servings

Crusted Horseradish Salmon
with Orange Vodka Sauce

A creation of Executive Chef Christopher McCook, Athens Country Club

Preheat oven to 350°.

Salmon
4   (5-ounce) salmon fillets
2   sticks butter, softened
**½   loaf bread, crusts removed,
       cubed**

¼   cup horseradish
Juice of 1 lemon
Salt and pepper to taste
Worcestershire sauce to taste
Tabasco sauce to taste

Sauce
2   shallots, minced
1   teaspoon olive oil
¼   cup vodka
1   teaspoon saffron

1   cup orange juice
**1   teaspoon caraway seeds,
       toasted**
1   tablespoon butter

Place salmon in a baking pan. Combine butter, bread cubes, horseradish, lemon juice, salt, pepper, Worcestershire sauce and Tabasco sauce. Divide mixture evenly over top of fillets. Bake for about 20 minutes.

To make sauce, sauté shallots in oil until transparent. Add vodka and cook to reduce for 2 to 3 minutes. Add saffron, juice and caraway seeds. Cook to reduce for another 2 to 3 minutes. When ready to serve, whip in butter and pour sauce over salmon.

Yield: 4 servings

Meunière Sauce

**¼ cup clarified
butter**
**1 tablespoon finely
chopped fresh parsley**
1 teaspoon lemon juice
Salt to taste

Heat butter in a saucepan slowly until light brown in color. Stir in parsley, juice and salt.

~

Clarified Butter

Melt unsalted butter slowly, allowing milk solids to separate to the bottom. Skim off any foam that has formed on the surface. Pour off clear or clarified butter, leaving milky residue in pan. Use clarified butter for frying or sautéing foods. Its higher smoke point, a result of the milk solids being removed, allows for cooking foods at a higher temperature than regular butter.

Jiffy Salmon Patties with Creamed Peas
Makes a good weeknight meal

Salmon

1	(15½-ounce) can pink salmon	2	eggs, beaten
½	cup chopped green onions	1	teaspoon prepared mustard
¼	cup chopped fresh parsley	2	tablespoons lemon juice
2	cups fine breadcrumbs, divided	2	tablespoons vegetable oil

Creamed Peas

1	(10-ounce) package frozen green peas	½	teaspoon salt
			Dash of white pepper
2	tablespoons butter or margarine	1½	cups milk
2	tablespoons all-purpose flour	1	tablespoon minced fresh parsley (optional)

Drain salmon, reserving one-third cup of liquid. Remove skin and bones and flake salmon with a fork into a bowl. Add onions, parsley and 1 cup breadcrumbs. Mix well. Stir in eggs, mustard, lemon juice and reserved salmon liquid. Shape mixture into patties and dredge in remaining cup of breadcrumbs to coat lightly. Heat oil over medium heat and add patties. Cook until lightly browned on both sides.

To make creamed peas, cook green peas as directed on package. Melt butter in a medium saucepan. Blend in flour, salt and pepper. Gradually add milk and cook over low heat, stirring until thickened. Add drained peas and parsley. Heat thoroughly. Serve hot over salmon patties.

Yield: 6 servings

"As native Georgians, Nell and I were surrounded by the tradition of family and friends enjoying good food. We fondly recall sampling delicious offerings that came from the kitchens of people who nurtured the idea of sharing their special culinary skills with others. Our children share in this rich heritage as they remember their favorite dishes prepared lovingly for them by their grand-parents and aunt. In Georgia, visiting and eating are a way of life!"

J. Robert Chambers, Jr.
Headmaster,
Athens Academy

Trout Amandine à la Brennan's

Brennan's — one of New Orleans' famous restaurants

1 egg	⅓ cup slivered almonds
1 cup milk	2 tablespoons freshly squeezed
All-purpose flour	lemon juice
Salt and pepper to taste	2 tablespoons Worcestershire
8 (4-ounce) trout fillets	sauce
1 stick unsalted butter	1 tablespoon minced fresh parsley

Whisk together egg and milk in a shallow bowl. Season flour with salt and pepper. Dip fillets in egg mixture, allowing excess to drip off. Dredge in seasoned flour and shake off excess. Heat butter in a large heavy skillet over medium-high heat until foam subsides. Cook fillets in 2 batches. Cook 3 to 4 minutes on each side or until fish flakes easily with a fork. Transfer fillets to a platter and keep warm in a 200° oven. Add almonds to the skillet and cook over medium heat, stirring for 1 minute, until light golden. Add lemon juice, Worcestershire sauce and parsley. Cook and stir until heated throughout. Spoon sauce over fillets to serve.

Yield: 4 servings

Pan-Seared Blackened Snapper

*Fresh snapper is available most of the year,
but is at its peak during the summer.*

4 (10-ounce) red snapper fillets	1 teaspoon dried thyme
½ teaspoon salt	½ teaspoon dried oregano
1 onion, thinly sliced	¼ teaspoon cayenne pepper
4 large cloves garlic, coarsely chopped	2 sticks butter, melted and cooled
1½ teaspoons black pepper	2 lemons, cut into wedges

Season fillets with salt and place in a shallow dish. Cover with onions and garlic. Cover dish with plastic wrap and refrigerate 3 to 4 hours. Combine black pepper, thyme, oregano and cayenne pepper. Take fish out of refrigerator and remove onion and garlic. Brush fillets with some of butter and sprinkle pepper mixture evenly over both sides. Heat a cast iron skillet over high heat. Add half the fillets, skin-side down, and cook 3 minutes or until completely charred. Drizzle more butter on top and turn. Cook 2 minutes longer. Transfer to a platter and keep warm. Wipe out skillet and repeat with remaining fish and butter. Serve with lemon wedges.

Yield: 4 servings

This recipe creates a lot of smoke. Make sure your kitchen is well-ventilated and your smoke alarm is temporarily disengaged. Please remember to reconnect smoke alarm when done cooking.

When frying fish, oil should be kept at a temperature of 365° to 375°. Always let oil reach this temperature before adding more fish.

~

If a finer cornmeal texture is desired, process cornmeal in a blender until pulverized. Or try a "fish fry" breading mix available at most grocery stores.

Fried Catfish

Brings back memories of fish frys on the river banks

Peanut oil for frying
½   cup cornmeal
1   teaspoon salt
½   teaspoon black pepper

¼   teaspoon cayenne pepper, or
      to taste
3   pounds catfish or other white
      fleshed fish fillets

Pour oil into a heavy Dutch oven to a depth of at least 1½ inches. Heat oil to 375°. Combine cornmeal, salt, black pepper and cayenne pepper. Dip fish in seasoned cornmeal to coat, shaking off any excess. Carefully lower fish into hot oil, being careful not to overcrowd the container. The hot oil should bubble up around each fillet. Cook 2 to 3 minutes per side or until golden, depending on the thickness of the fillets. Remove from oil using a wire mesh strainer that allows excess oil to drain back into the pot. Place on a cooling rack to drain or lay on paper towels or brown paper bags. Keep warm in a 200° oven while other fillets cook.

Yield: 6 to 8 servings

Just Plain Old Fried Shrimp

"So named because this is what my children always requested when they were home. Nothing fancy — just plain old fried shrimp, which they still claim are the best!" Patricia Maxwell

2-3 pounds large shrimp, peeled
      and deveined
      Salt to taste
2   eggs
⅛   teaspoon black pepper
1   (14-ounce) container cracker
      meal

Vegetable oil for frying
Cocktail sauce (see sidebar on
      page 153))
Tartar sauce (see sidebar on
      page 153)

Rinse shrimp and pat dry. Lightly season with salt. Beat together eggs and black pepper. Dredge shrimp in cracker meal, then dip in egg wash. Dip again in cracker meal. Heat oil over medium-high heat in a heavy skillet or Dutch oven. Add shrimp and fry until golden brown. Serve with cocktail sauce and tartar sauce on the side.

Yield: 6 servings

Henry's Famous Shrimp Marinade

A Five Points favorite

1   (10-ounce) bottle low-
    sodium soy sauce
    Juice of 3 lemons
2   cloves garlic, crushed

3   tablespoons olive oil
3   dashes hot pepper sauce
2   pounds large shrimp, peeled
    and deveined

Combine all ingredients except shrimp. Pour marinade over shrimp. Refrigerate 3 to 4 hours. Grill shrimp over hot coals for 2 to 3 minutes per side.

Yield: 4 to 6 servings

Note: For an attractive presentation, thread shrimp on individual wooden skewers that have been soaked in water. Serve cooked shrimp on skewers with small bowls of clarified butter for dipping.

Grilled Fish Marinade

Fast and easy

½   cup virgin olive oil
1   tablespoon grated onion
¼   cup lemon juice
2   teaspoons Worcestershire
    sauce

½   teaspoon salt
½   teaspoon white pepper
½   teaspoon garlic powder
6   small fish fillets of choice
    (about 2 pounds)

Combine all ingredients except fish fillets in a 1-gallon plastic zip-top bag. Add fish to bag. Marinate 30 minutes, turning once. Grill fillets as desired.

Yield: 6 servings

Basic Cocktail Sauce

½ cup thick
chili sauce
2 tablespoons
horseradish
2 tablespoons lemon
juice
1 teaspoon
Worcestershire sauce
½ teaspoon dried onion
flakes (optional)
Tabasco sauce to taste
(optional)

Combine all
ingredients. Chill well.

~

Homemade Tartar Sauce

1 cup mayonnaise or
salad dressing
2 tablespoons finely
chopped dill pickle
1 tablespoon snipped
fresh parsley
1 teaspoon grated onion

Mix all ingredients.
Cover and refrigerate.

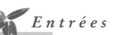

Tips for Grilling Fish

To keep fish from sticking, lightly coat the clean cooking surface with nonstick cooking spray or cooking oil.

~

Seafood cooks best over a moderately hot fire with no active flames present.

~

Whole fish should be cooked over indirect heat. Fill the cavity with fresh herbs and lemon slices, bank the coals to the sides of the grill and place fish in the center.

~

Follow the 10-minute rule when grilling fish; cook for about 10 minutes per inch of thickness, 5 minutes per side. Remove from grill just before it's done.

~

Steaks or fillets at least ¾-inch thick are easiest to grill. Thinner pieces grill best if wrapped in foil with a few holes punched in it.

~

Testing for Doneness: poke a fork into the thickest portion of the fish at a 45° angle and twist gently. If the fish flakes easily and looks opaque, it's done. Fish cooks quickly, so test it frequently.

Grilled Tuna Steak

Almost no preparation needed

1½ sticks butter	2½ teaspoons lemon juice
1 teaspoon minced garlic	2 pounds tuna steaks, patted
1 tablespoon soy sauce	dry

Melt butter over medium heat. Add garlic and sauté briefly. Remove from heat and add soy sauce and lemon juice. Place tuna steaks in a greased shallow baking dish. Pour butter marinade over fish and let stand 30 minutes. Broil 7 minutes on each side or until fish starts to flake.

Yield: 4 to 6 servings

Italian Swordfish Parmesan

A nice change from grilled

1 clove garlic, halved	½ cup black olives
1 tablespoon olive oil	2 tablespoons chopped fresh
1 pound swordfish, cut into	parsley
bite-size pieces	1 tablespoon lemon juice
¼ cup all-purpose flour	2 teaspoons Parmesan cheese
1 cup coarsely chopped plum	
tomatoes	

In a large skillet, sauté garlic in oil over medium-high heat for 1 minute. Press garlic with the back of a fork, remove and discard. Dredge fish in flour, coating evenly. Add fish to skillet and sauté 8 to 10 minutes or until browned on all sides. Stir in tomatoes, olives, parsley and lemon juice. Cover and cook 1 minute. Serve topped with Parmesan cheese.

Yield: 4 servings

PASTA, RICE, EGGS AND CHEESE

Bertelsmann Foundation Building

Sautéed Lobster Medallions with Red Bells, Onions, Artichoke Hearts and a Sambal Oelek Mascarpone Cream

A blending of hot, sweet, and creamy with the best of Indonesian, Italian, Island, and Chinese culinary history

3	medium new potatoes, thinly sliced	¼	cup flour
¼	cup olive oil	½	teaspoon salt
3	tablespoons butter	½	teaspoon black pepper
½	teaspoon grated garlic	½	cup heavy cream
½	teaspoon grated ginger	½	cup mascarpone cheese
1	medium-size red bell pepper, diced	1	tablespoon sambal oelek
½	yellow onion, diced		Juice of ½ a lime
10	artichoke hearts, quartered	6	large fresh basil leaves
8	ounces sea scallops	5	ounces dry Chinese wide rice noodles
8	ounces lobster tail meat		or rice sticks

Sauté potatoes in oil until lightly browned. Add butter and stir until melted. Add garlic, ginger, peppers and onions and cook on medium-high heat until softened. Add artichoke hearts and cook 1 minute. Dust scallops and lobster in flour. Add scallops to vegetable mixture and cook until outer flesh turns white. Stir in lobster and increase heat to high. Season mixture with salt and pepper. Cook 2 minutes. Pour off and reserve excess liquid for cream sauce. Prepare cream sauce in a separate pan. Pour cream into pan and heat until warm. Add cheese and stir until melted. Add sambal, lime juice, and reserved excess liquid. Cook until slightly thickened. Pour sauce into vegetable/seafood mixture and stir to combine. Add basil leaves and cook until thickened. Soften noodles by placing in very hot water. Let stand about 10 minutes, stirring about half-way through. Drain noodles and stir into vegetable/lobster mixture. Continue to heat on low for about 2 minutes or until sauce is thick and mixture is completely warm. Pour onto a platter and serve.

Yield: 4 servings

Variation: Alternate additions to this recipe include broccoli and wild mushrooms, or even a medley of exotic fruits such as carambola, guava, and papaya. Oranges or tangerines, sweet apples, or Bosc pears will also work well. The excitement of this dish is the combination of heat and sweet.

Note: Sambal oelek is a Vietnamese chili. It is composed of Thai bird chili peppers and vinegar. If you cannot find this item, use a similar mixture such as Mexican Chalula sauce and crushed red peppers.

East-West Bistro

A fusion of Mediterranean and Pacific Rim cuisine in a Bistro setting located "uptown downtown."

Valerie's Famous Cheese Grits

It's Southern, after all!

Preheat oven to 325°.

2	cups quick cooking grits	4	eggs, beaten
½	cup milk	1	stick butter or margarine, melted
⅓-½	pound processed cheese loaf, grated or chopped		Salt to taste
⅓-½	pound sharp cheddar cheese, grated or chopped		Parmesan cheese
			Paprika

Cook grits as directed on package. Add milk, processed cheese and cheddar cheese. Add a bit of hot grit mixture to eggs. Add egg mixture and butter to grits. Season with salt. Pour into a shallow 3-quart greased casserole dish. Sprinkle with Parmesan cheese and paprika. Bake for 30 to 35 minutes.

Yield: 10 to 12 servings

Grits: Coarsely ground dry corn that is cooked in water or milk and served as a cereal or a side dish.

Sausage, Eggs and Grits Soufflé

A delicious one dish meal

Preheat oven to 350°.

1	pound hot sausage	½	teaspoon black pepper
1	cup quick grits	4	tablespoons margarine
7	eggs, well beaten	2	cups grated sharp cheddar cheese, divided
1½	cups milk		
½	teaspoon salt		

Cook sausage until done. Drain well and set aside. Cook grits in a large Dutch oven according to package directions. Combine eggs, milk, salt and pepper. Slowly stir egg mixture into grits. Add margarine and 1½ cups cheese, stirring until cheese melts. Add sausage and mix well. Transfer to a 3-quart round casserole dish. Bake for 1 hour to 1 hour, 30 minutes. Sprinkle remaining cheese on top and bake 5 minutes longer.

Yield: 10 to 12 servings

It's hard to imagine anything more Southern than grits. Grits are to the South what pasta is to the Italians and rice is to China. It's a staple, as much a part of our Southern heritage as fried chicken and sweet iced tea.
If you've never eaten "real grits", you've missed one of the South's greatest treasures. We're talking the real thing — not the bland, instant, watery version so often found in restaurants. These grits are cooked slowly over low heat and stirred often so they don't stick to the pan. True grits are seasoned with just the right amount of salt and pepper and, dare we say it, butter. Serve with hot biscuits, country ham with redeye gravy, scrambled eggs, and homemade jam. Could anything be any better?

Grits and Greens

It's Southern, after all!

3 cups milk	1 pound greens, chopped (kale,
1 cup heavy cream	spinach, turnip, mustard or
1 cup quick grits	a mixture)
6 tablespoons butter, divided	½ cup Parmesan cheese

Combine milk and cream in a heavy, nonstick saucepan. Bring to nearly a boil. Stir in grits and cook 5 to 10 minutes, stirring as needed. Remove from heat and stir in 2 tablespoons butter. Place greens, still wet from washing, in a large skillet. Cook over medium-high heat for 5 minutes or until wilted. The water clinging to the greens should be sufficient, but add a few tablespoons of water if needed to cook. Drain the greens and refresh with cold water. Drain again and squeeze to remove all water. Melt remaining 4 tablespoons butter in skillet. Add greens and sauté briefly. Add greens to grits. Stir in cheese. Season to taste.

Yield: 6 servings

Pecan Grits Balls

Excellent with ham or serve with a favorite
dipping sauce for an unusual appetizer.

3 cups cooked grits	2 eggs, beaten
1 cup heavy cream	1 tablespoon milk
½ teaspoon Worcestershire sauce	Breadcrumbs
2 cups crushed pecans	Oil for deep-fat frying

Mix grits, cream, Worcestershire sauce and pecans together thoroughly. Form into balls and chill. When ready to serve, combine eggs and milk. Dip balls in egg wash, then roll in breadcrumbs. Fry in oil and drain on paper towels.

Grits are easy to cook if you follow the package directions. Quick cooking or instant grits must be served immediately after cooking. Regular grits can be cooked and placed in a double boiler over warm water until time to serve.

~

Grits lend themselves to many variations. Try adding any of the following to your grits: crumbled bacon or sausage, chopped ham or various cheeses - bleu, feta, Swiss or cheddar.

~

For leftover grits, should there be any, spread grits (not too thick) in a small baking dish. Chill several hours. Cut into desired size and shape. Combine flour, salt and pepper. Dip grits patty in flour mixture. Fry in a small amount of vegetable oil or bacon drippings until golden on both sides. Use as a side dish for breakfast, lunch or dinner.

Baked Spaghetti Frittata

A big hit with kids

Preheat oven to 350°.

2 tablespoons butter	Salt and pepper to taste
4 ounces mushrooms, sliced	3½ ounces spaghetti, cooked and
1 bell pepper, chopped	chopped
4 ounces ham, sliced	2 tablespoons chopped fresh
½ cup frozen peas	parsley
6 eggs	¼ cup Parmesan cheese
1 cup cream or milk	

Melt butter in a skillet. Add mushrooms and cook over low heat for 2 to 3 minutes. Add bell peppers and cook 1 minute. Stir in ham and peas. Remove from heat and cool slightly. In a bowl, whisk together eggs, cream, salt and pepper. Stir in spaghetti, parsley and mushroom mixture. Pour into a greased 9-inch flan pan. Sprinkle with cheese. Bake for 25 to 30 minutes. Serve with grilled vegetables and a green salad.

Yield: 4 servings

Frittata: (frih TAH tuh) An Italian-style omelet in which the ingredients are mixed with the eggs instead of being folded inside.

The next time you make pasta, cook more than you need. Follow package directions, except omit salt and butter or margarine. Rinse and drain well. Line custard cups or small plastic food containers with plastic wrap. Fill with pasta and freeze until firm. Remove frozen pasta from containers, wrap individually, and store in a large freezer bag. When you need pasta, simply unwrap the amount you need and drop into a pot of boiling water. Return water to a boil and cook 1 minute. Drain and serve. Or, simply place in a microwave-safe dish and heat in the microwave oven until hot.

Fettuccine Carbonara

"Have served this many times. People love it."

1	(12-ounce) package fettuccine	½-1	teaspoon garlic powder
½	cup Parmesan cheese	4	tablespoons butter or
½	cup heavy cream		margarine, cubed
2	eggs	8	slices bacon, cooked and
2	tablespoons parsley		crumbled

Cook fettuccine in a pot according to package directions. Meanwhile, combine cheese, cream, eggs, parsley and garlic powder. Whisk well. When pasta is done, drain and return to pot. Add butter and carefully stir over low heat until melted. Add cheese mixture and bacon and lightly toss. Serve with a salad and French bread.

Yield: 6 servings

Fettuccine: (feht tuh CHEE nee) Egg noodles that have been cut into flat, narrow strips.

Puttanesca Sauce

Serve over tubular pasta with ridges to hold the sauce.

2 (35-ounce) cans tomatoes, drained and chopped	¼ cup chopped dry black olives in brine
¼ cup olive oil	¼ cup drained capers
¼ teaspoon crushed red pepper flakes	5 cloves garlic, chopped
1½ teaspoons oregano	8 small anchovy fillets, chopped
¼ cup coarsely chopped black olives	½ cup Italian parsley, chopped

Squeeze excess liquid out of tomatoes. Combine tomatoes and oil in a saucepan. Bring to a boil. Add remaining ingredients while keeping mixture at a full boil. Reduce heat and simmer until thickened.

Yield: 4 to 6 servings

Time was when we only had two choices in pasta: spaghetti or macaroni. Now the selection is almost limitless. Over 600 different pasta shapes are made today in Italy alone. If you have trouble deciding which pasta to use, remember this rule of thumb:

The thinner the sauce, the longer the pasta. Long pastas include spaghetti, linguine and vermicelli. The twists and turns of short pasta, such as penne, fusilli and farfalle, trap the thicker sauces. Fettuccine is perfect for Alfredo sauce, while penne or ziti work well with thick tomato sauce.

Rigatoni with Tomato Sauce, Cheese and Olives

Great with French bread and a salad

6 tablespoons olive oil, divided
1 onion, chopped
1 teaspoon minced garlic
3 (28-ounce) cans Italian plum tomatoes, drained
2 teaspoons dried basil
1½ teaspoons crushed red pepper flakes

2 cups chicken broth
Salt and pepper to taste
1 (16-ounce) package rigatoni, cooked and drained
2½ cups grated Havarti cheese
½ cup sliced brine-cured olives
⅓ cup Parmesan cheese
¼ cup finely chopped fresh basil

Over medium heat in a Dutch oven, heat 3 tablespoons oil. Add onions and garlic and sauté until tender. Mix in tomatoes, basil and pepper flakes. Bring to a boil, breaking up tomatoes with a spoon. Add broth and return to a boil. Reduce heat to medium and cook 60 minutes or until mixture is a chunky sauce. Season with salt and pepper. Add remaining 3 tablespoons oil to cooked pasta. Toss lightly. Pour tomato sauce over pasta and toss to mix. Blend in Havarti cheese. Transfer to a 9x13x2-inch glass baking dish. Sprinkle with olives and Parmesan cheese. Bake in preheated 375° oven for 30 minutes.

Yield: 6 servings

Rigatoni: Short, grooved tubes of macaroni.

Olives that are picked young are hard and green. They ripen and darken on the tree. Olives may be preserved in oil, often with herbs, or in brine. Kalamata olives are brine-cured Greek olives, dark in color with a rich and fruity flavor.

Angel Hair Pasta with Tomato Basil Sauce

Grilled chicken may be added for a more filling version.

1 pint cherry tomatoes, halved
1 cup chopped fresh basil
¼ cup olive oil
½ teaspoon salt

½ teaspoon black pepper
1 (9-ounce) package fresh angel hair pasta

Combine tomatoes, basil, oil, salt and pepper in a large bowl. Toss together to coat. Refrigerate 30 minutes. Cook pasta according to package directions. Serve tomato mixture over hot pasta.

Yield: 6 servings

Absolute Penne

Absolutely delicious!

1	tablespoon butter	¼	cup vodka
1	tablespoon olive oil	¼	teaspoon crushed red pepper flakes
1	small onion, finely chopped		
1	(28-ounce) can Italian plum tomatoes, drained and seeded	1	(16-ounce) package penne pasta, cooked and drained
1	cup heavy cream	¼	cup Parmesan cheese

Melt butter and oil together over medium heat. Add onions and sauté 8 minutes or until translucent. Add tomatoes and cook down 25 minutes or until almost all liquid is gone, stirring frequently. Add cream, vodka and pepper flakes. Cook until mixture is a sauce consistency. Pour over cooked pasta and sprinkle with Parmesan cheese.

Yield: 4 to 6 servings

Penne: (PEN nay) Large, straight tubes of macaroni that are cut on the diagonal.

Pancetta is an Italian bacon that has been cured with salt and spices but not smoked. The slightly salty flavor lends itself to Italian cooking where it's used to flavor pastas, sauces, meats and vegetables. If pancetta is unavailable, thinly sliced country ham or bacon may be substituted.

Peas and Bow Ties

The addition of pancetta adds a unique flavor to this dish.

1	(16-ounce) box farfalle (bow tie) pasta	2	tablespoons shredded fresh basil
1½	cups frozen green peas	1-2	tablespoons shredded fresh mint
8	thin slices pancetta, chopped		
½	stick butter		Cracked black pepper

Cook pasta in a large pot of boiling water until al dente. Drain and return to pot. While pasta cooks, cook peas until tender; drain. Do not overcook. Cook pancetta in butter over medium heat for 2 minutes. Add pancetta mixture, peas, basil and mint to pasta and toss. Season with black pepper.

Yield: 4 servings

Farfalle: (fahr FAH lay) Pasta that is shaped like a bow tie or small butterfly.

Beef Mozzarella Bake

Great for pot luck suppers

Preheat oven to 350°.

1½	pounds lean ground beef	1	(12-ounce) container cottage cheese
1	small onion, chopped		
2	(8-ounce) cans tomato sauce	2	cups grated mozzarella cheese
⅛	teaspoon garlic salt	⅛	teaspoon salt
⅛	teaspoon black pepper	1	(8-ounce) package thin spaghetti, cooked and drained
1	egg		
1	(8-ounce) container sour cream		
		3	ounces Parmesan cheese, grated

Brown beef and onions in a large skillet and drain. Add tomato sauce, garlic salt and pepper to skillet with beef. Cook over low heat for 15 to 20 minutes. Beat egg in a large bowl. Add sour cream, cottage cheese, mozzarella cheese and salt. Stir in spaghetti. Place half the spaghetti mixture into a greased baking dish. Top with half the ground beef mixture. Repeat layers. Sprinkle Parmesan cheese over the top. Bake for 20 to 30 minutes or until hot and bubbly.

Yield: 6 to 8 servings

Fettuccine with Low Fat Alfredo Sauce

With this, you can have your sauce and eat it too!

1½	cups low fat cottage cheese	⅛	teaspoon black pepper
3	tablespoons low fat milk	1	(8-ounce) package fettuccine or linguine pasta, cooked and drained
½	cup chopped red bell pepper		
1	clove garlic, minced		
1	tablespoon margarine	2	tablespoons Parmesan cheese
½	cup frozen green peas	1	tablespoon chopped fresh basil
⅛	teaspoon salt		

Combine cottage cheese and milk in a blender. Process until smooth. In a 2-quart saucepan, sauté bell peppers and garlic in margarine over medium-high heat until tender. Reduce heat and add milk mixture, peas, salt and pepper. Cook and stir sauce until heated, but do not bring to a boil. Add sauce to hot pasta. Sprinkle with Parmesan cheese and basil.

Yield: 4 servings

To reduce the fat and calories in this recipe by more than half, substitute:

2 egg whites for 1 egg

8 ounces reduced-fat sour cream for regular sour cream

12 ounces fat-free cottage cheese for the whole milk variety

8 ounces part-skim mozzarella for the full fat option

3 ounces grated fat-free Parmesan cheese for the traditional type

~

The ever-popular Fettuccine Alfredo was created in the 1920's by the Italian restaurateur Alfredo di Lello. The sauce for this divine creation is made of butter, Parmesan cheese, heavy cream and freshly ground black pepper. It is served over— what else but— fettuccine noodles.

Pasta, Pesto and Parmesan

The 3 P's of pasta

> There's a fine line between under-cooked and overcooked pasta. Undercooked pasta is hard and raw tasting. Overcooked pasta tastes doughy and gummy. Pasta that is cooked just right is completely tender, but still firm.
>
> ~
>
> When cooking pasta, it's always better to have too much water than too little. There should be enough so that the pasta can move about freely. Otherwise, pasta strands will stick together.
>
> ~
>
> To properly cook pasta, bring 4 quarts of water to a full boil. Add 2 tablespoons salt and drop in 1 pound of pasta. If desired, 1 teaspoon olive oil may be added to the water to help keep the noodles from sticking together. Fresh pasta will be done by the time the water again reaches a full boil. Dried pasta takes longer, depending on the size and shape.

1 (16-ounce) package linguine pasta	½ cup extra virgin olive oil
¼ cup pine nuts	Salt to taste
2 cups firmly packed fresh basil leaves	Freshly ground black pepper to taste
2 cloves garlic, chopped	Shavings of Parmesan cheese for garnish
¼ cup freshly grated Parmesan cheese	

Cook pasta in a large pot of boiling salted water until al dente. Drain and return to pot. While pasta cooks, place pine nuts, basil, garlic and cheese in a food processor. Process to a very fine consistency. With the motor running, add oil in a slow stream until a smooth paste forms. Season with salt and pepper. Add pesto to pasta and toss. Garnish with Parmesan cheese shavings.

Yield: 6 servings

Linguine: (lihng GWEE nee) Long, flat, narrow noodles often referred to as flat spaghetti.

Vegetarian Lasagna
Cook one for now, freeze one for later.

Preheat oven to 350°.

1	medium-size yellow onion, chopped	2	(32-ounce) jars spaghetti sauce
1	tablespoon vegetable oil	1	(16-ounce) container ricotta cheese
8	ounces mushrooms, chopped		
4	medium-size yellow squash, chopped	1	pound mozzarella cheese, grated
4	medium zucchini, chopped	1	pound sharp cheddar cheese, grated
2	bunches broccoli, chopped		
1	(8-ounce) can artichoke hearts, quartered	2	eggs, beaten
		1	(16-ounce) package lasagna noodles, uncooked

Sauté onions in oil. Add mushrooms, squash, zucchini, broccoli and artichoke hearts and sauté briefly. Stir in spaghetti sauce. In a separate bowl, mix together cheeses and eggs. Use one 9x13-inch baking pan and one 8-inch square baking pan, both sprayed with cooking spray. Form 2 layers in each pan in the following order: dry lasagna noodles, cheese mixture, sauce mixture. Be sure noodles are completely covered with sauce. Cover with foil and bake for 50 to 60 minutes.

Yield: 12 servings plus 8 servings between the two pans

Keeping pasta hot until everyone gets to the table can be a problem. Here are some tips that might help the next time you have stragglers who are late for dinner. Drain the pasta quickly. Don't let it stand in the colander any longer than necessary. Immediately place the pasta back into the cooking pan. The heat from the pan will help to keep the pasta warm. Always use a warm serving dish. Simply run hot water into the dish and let it stand for a few minutes. Then drain off the water and wipe dry. Add the cooked pasta and serve immediately.

Summer Bow Tie Pasta with Salmon, Sun-Dried Tomatoes, Spinach and Dill Cream

A specialty of Lance F. Jeffers Jr.,
Executive Chef, Jennings Mill Country Club

Extra virgin olive oil is made from the first pressing of the olives, during which time no heating of the fruit occurs and no chemicals are used. It has almost no acidity and is thick and rich in color. Extra virgin is generally considered to be the finest and fruitiest of all the oils, and therefore, the most expensive.

4	ounces salmon, cut into ¾-inch cubes	1	cup heavy cream
½	teaspoon olive oil	1½	tablespoons julienned sun-dried tomatoes in oil
	Pinch of coarse salt	1	(7-ounce) package farfalle (bow tie) pasta, cooked al dente
	Pinch of black pepper, plus ⅛ teaspoon, divided		
¼	teaspoon minced garlic		Salt to taste
¼	teaspoon minced shallots	1	ounce spinach, stemmed and shredded
2	tablespoons thinly sliced shiitake mushrooms	1	teaspoon chopped fresh dill
2	tablespoons dry white wine		Dill sprig for garnish

Marinate salmon in oil and a pinch of coarse salt and pepper for 5 to 10 minutes. In a very hot non-stick skillet, sear salmon on all sides, using no additional oil. Add garlic, shallots and mushrooms. Sauté 2 minutes or until mushrooms are softened. Add wine and reduce by half. Add cream and bring to a simmer. Stir in tomatoes and cooked pasta. Season with ⅛ teaspoon black pepper and salt to taste. Cook sauce until reduced by half. The sauce should be thick enough to coat the pasta well but thin enough to allow for the pasta to absorb some of the sauce. Add spinach and dill and toss with pasta. When spinach has wilted, serve in a pasta bowl. Garnish with a dill sprig.

Yield: 1 serving

Al Dente: (al DEN tay) An Italian phrase meaning "to the tooth". Used to describe pasta that is cooked only until it offers slight resistance when bitten into.

Seafood Lasagna

You'll be glad you made the effort.

Preheat oven to 350°.

1	(8-ounce) package oven ready lasagna noodles	2	cups milk
1	pound boneless fish fillets	2	cups dry white wine
4	ounces scallops, cleaned	1	cup grated cheddar cheese
1	pound shrimp, peeled and deveined		Salt and pepper to taste
1	stick butter	½	cup heavy cream
1	onion, chopped	½	cup freshly grated Parmesan cheese
⅔	cup all-purpose flour	2	tablespoons chopped fresh parsley

Line a greased, deep lasagna pan with noodles, breaking some if needed to fill gaps. Set aside. Chop fish, scallops and shrimp into even sized pieces. Melt butter in a skillet. Add onions and sauté 1 minute. Stir in flour and cook 1 minute. Gradually add milk and wine, stirring until mixture is smooth. Continue to cook and stir over medium heat until sauce begins to bubble and thicken. Reduce heat and simmer 3 minutes. Remove from heat and stir in cheddar cheese, salt and pepper. Return to heat, add seafood and simmer 1 minute. Remove from heat. Spoon half the seafood mixture over the noodles in the pan. Top with a second layer of noodles, the remainder of the seafood mixture and a final layer of noodles. Pour cream over the top. Combine Parmesan cheese and parsley and sprinkle over lasagna. Bake, uncovered, for 30 minutes or until bubbly and golden brown.

Yield: 6 servings

Lasagna: (luh ZAHN yuh) A wide, flat noodle sometimes with ruffled edges. Oven ready noodles do not require cooking in water prior to assembly of the lasagna.

Wedding Day Brunch at the Taylor Grady House

Dining at the Taylor Grady House is like stepping back in time. Why, there's even a special room called "The Bride's Room".

~

Menu

Cranberry Orange Blush

Sunday Brunch Glazed Canadian Bacon

Brie Mushroom Strata

Deliciously Different Hot Baked Fruit

Angel Biscuits

Sleepover Cinnamon Muffins

Cecilia's Jelly Roll with Custard Sauce

Iced Tea

Coffee

Pasta with Three Peppers and Chicken
A colorful chicken mixture

4 slices bacon, cut into ½-inch strips	1½ cups cubed cooked chicken
1 medium-size red bell pepper, cut into strips	¾ cup heavy cream
1 medium-size green bell pepper, cut into strips	½ teaspoon dried summer savory leaves
1 medium-size yellow bell pepper, cut into strips	¼ teaspoon salt
	¼ teaspoon black pepper
	1 (8-ounce) package linguine, cooked and drained

Cook bacon in a large skillet until crisp. Remove bacon and drain, reserving 1 tablespoon bacon drippings in skillet. Add bell peppers and stir-fry 3 to 5 minutes until crisp-tender. Reduce heat to low, stir in chicken, cream, savory, salt and black pepper. Cook, stirring constantly, over low heat until mixture boils and is slightly thickened. Pour over hot linguine. Sprinkle with bacon.

Yield: 6 servings

Savory: (SAY vuh ree) An herb closely related to the mint family. Summer savory is slightly milder than winter savory, but both are strongly flavored and should be used carefully.

Five Star Mac and Cheese
A specialty of Five Star Day Café

1 pound dry macaroni	1 cup grated smoked Gouda cheese
2 cups half-and-half	Pinch of salt
2 cups milk	Pinch of black pepper
½ cup Parmesan cheese	
1½ cups grated cheddar cheese	

Cook macaroni per package directions. Drain, return to pan and keep warm. Meanwhile, bring half-and-half and milk to a low boil. Add cheeses and whisk until melted. Stir cheese sauce into macaroni. Season with salt and pepper and serve.

Yield: 8 servings

The sweet green bell pepper has always been a favorite ingredient in salads, stir-frys and casseroles. Now there are many other colors available to substitute for or combine with the old favorite. These can add even more color, texture, and flavor to cooked dishes. Colors include golden or orange, red, yellow, and even chocolate brown.

~

Both onions and bell peppers can be chopped ahead and frozen for later use. Chop and spread in a single layer on a shallow baking pan. Place in freezer for 1 hour or until frozen. Store in freezer bags for up to 1 month. To use, measure and use as if they were fresh.

Garden Fresh Tomato Marinara

Make a big batch and keep on hand.

1-2 tablespoons olive oil
1   cup chopped onions
½   cup finely grated carrot
1   clove garlic, minced
2   pounds ripe tomatoes, cored
     and chopped, or 2 (14½-ounce)
     cans diced and undrained

2   tablespoons snipped fresh
     basil, or 2 teaspoons dried
½   teaspoon sugar
½   teaspoon salt or to taste
¼   teaspoon black pepper

Heat oil in a skillet. Add onions, carrots and garlic and sauté until tender. Stir in tomatoes, basil, sugar, salt and pepper. Simmer 20 minutes or until desired consistency. For a smoother sauce, purée in a blender.

Yield: 4 servings

Marinara: (mah ree NAHR uh) A highly seasoned tomato sauce made with tomato, onion, garlic and spices.

Divine Italian Pie

Children love this!

Preheat oven to 350°.

Crust
6   ounces vermicelli, cooked
     and drained
4   tablespoons butter

½   cup Parmesan cheese
1   egg, beaten
1   teaspoon dried basil

Filling
1   pound lean ground beef
¼   pound Italian sausage
     (optional)
1   medium onion, chopped

1   (15½-ounce) jar spaghetti
     sauce
1   (8-ounce) package grated
     mozzarella cheese, divided

Combine all crust ingredients in a bowl. Chop mixture and press into the bottom and sides of a 10-inch pie pan.

To make filling, brown beef, sausage and onions in a skillet. Drain. Stir sauce into meat mixture. To assemble pie, sprinkle ½ cup of mozzarella cheese on the crust. Pour meat mixture on top. Sprinkle with remaining cheese. Bake for 30 minutes or until brown.

Yield: 8 to 10 servings

Most pasta dishes can be easily reheated. If the dish contains a lot of sauce or has a dressing that contains oil, like pesto, place in a saucepan and stir over high heat until hot. You can also place the pasta in a casserole dish, cover with foil and bake in a 350° oven until hot. Pasta without sauce can simply be placed in a colander with boiling water poured over the top or immersed into a pot of boiling water for 30 seconds. And, of course, there is always the microwave.

Barley Casserole

Serve with tenderloin or use as a stuffing for tomatoes.

Preheat oven to 350°.

8 ounces fresh mushrooms, sliced	Salt and pepper to taste
1 large onion, chopped	2-3 cups beef broth
4 tablespoons butter	Toasted slivered almonds for garnish (optional)
1 cup dry barley	

Sauté mushrooms and onions in butter. Mix in barley, salt and pepper. Pour into a greased 1½-quart casserole dish. Add broth to half an inch above barley. Cover and bake for 45 minutes or until liquid is absorbed. Garnish with almonds.

Yield: 6 servings

Barley: A hearty grain dating back to the Stone Age. It is used in dishes ranging from cereals to soups and bread.

~

Lentils make a great tasting, high fiber dish. They do not need to be soaked before cooking, but should be washed and picked over carefully since they often contain small stones.

Herbed Lentils and Rice

Great tasting, low in fat and high in flavor

Preheat oven to 350°.

2⅔ cups chicken broth	¼ teaspoon salt
¾ cup dry lentils	½ teaspoon oregano
½ cup chopped onions	½ teaspoon thyme
½ cup dry brown rice	¼ teaspoon garlic powder
¼ cup dry red wine (optional)	¼ teaspoon black pepper
1 teaspoon basil	

Combine all ingredients in a 1½-quart casserole dish. Stir to mix. Bake, uncovered, for 1 hour, 30 minutes to 2 hours or until rice and lentils are tender.

Yield: 6 servings

Note: If not using wine, use an additional ¼ cup broth.

Lentils: The tiny, lens-shaped seed of the lentil, long used as a meat substitute.

Risotto with Pesto
A new classic

4-5 cups canned chicken broth	5 tablespoons butter
¼ cup fresh basil	1 medium onion, minced
1 tablespoon fresh parsley	1½ cups Arborio rice
2 tablespoons walnuts	1 cup freshly grated Parmesan
¼ cup olive oil	cheese
1 teaspoon salt	Salt and pepper to taste

In a medium saucepan, warm broth. In a blender, combine basil, parsley, walnuts, oil and salt. Process to form a paste. In another medium saucepan, heat butter until foamy. Add onions and sauté 2 minutes. Add rice and sauté 2 to 3 minutes. Add warm broth, ½ cup at a time, stirring constantly until each addition is absorbed. When all broth is absorbed, remove from heat. Stir in pesto paste and cheese. Season with salt and pepper and serve immediately.

Yield: 6 to 8 servings

Risotto: (rih SAW toh, ree ZAW toh) An Italian rice dish made by stirring hot broth into a mixture of rice and, sometimes, sautéed onion.

Arborio Rice: (ar BOH ree oh) An Italian grown rice with high starch kernels that are shorter and fatter than any other short grained rice. Traditionally used for risotto because of the creaminess it gives to the dish.

Barley Toasted with Apples and Raisins
Spicy and tasty

1½ cups quick cooking barley	½ teaspoon cinnamon
2 cups chicken broth	¼ teaspoon allspice
1 cup chopped peeled apples	¼ teaspoon salt
⅓ cup sliced green onions	⅛ teaspoon black pepper
3 tablespoons raisins	

Sauté barley over medium heat until toasted and golden brown. Add remaining ingredients and bring to a boil. Reduce heat, cover and simmer about 10 to 12 minutes or until barley is tender and most of liquid is absorbed. Remove from heat and let sit, covered, for 5 minutes.

Yield: 6 servings

The secret to this creamy concoction is adding the broth only ½ cup at a time, stirring continually until all the liquid is absorbed before adding more. Risotto may be flavored with any number of ingredients including shellfish, chicken, sausage, vegetables, cheese and herbs.

Arborio rice is traditionally used for risotto because of its ability to absorb large quantities of water without becoming soft and mushy.

~

Barley cooks quickly and adds a chewy texture and nutty flavor to dishes.

Black Beans, Sausage and Rice

A nutritious one-dish meal

⅓ cup chopped green bell peppers	Olive oil
⅓ cup chopped red bell peppers	1 bay leaf
⅓ cup chopped celery	1 (16-ounce) can black beans, undrained
⅓ cup chopped onions	1 beef bouillon cube
1 teaspoon ground cumin	½ pound andouille sausage, chopped
1 teaspoon oregano	
1 teaspoon chopped garlic	

Cook bell peppers, celery, onions, cumin, oregano and garlic in oil in a large skillet until tender. Add bay leaf, beans, bouillon cube and sausage. Simmer 30 minutes. Serve over a prepared long grain and wild rice mix.

Yield: 4 to 6 servings

Sausage is one of the oldest processed foods; meat was ground into sausage in the Mediterranean over 3000 years ago. Freshly ground sausage as links or patties has traditionally been a part of many a Southern breakfast or supper. Andouille is a highly spiced French sausage made from pork and veal and used in Creole dishes.

Vidalia Onion Rice Casserole

It's Southern, after all!

Preheat oven to 325°.

3 pounds Vidalia onions, thinly sliced	2 cups water
1 stick butter	1½ cups grated Swiss cheese
1 cup dry rice	1⅓ cups half-and-half

Sauté onions in butter in a large skillet for 10 minutes or until soft. Boil rice in 2 cups water in a saucepan for 5 minutes. Drain well. Combine onions, rice, cheese and half-and-half in a greased 10x13-inch casserole dish. Bake, uncovered, for 60 minutes.

Yield: 8 servings

Note: The flavor of this casserole actually improves when prepared and baked in advance. When ready to serve, simply reheat at 325° for 20 minutes.

Lynn's Green Rice

Great side dish

Preheat oven to 350°.

2 cups cooked rice
1 teaspoon salt
12 ounces Monterey Jack
   cheese, cubed

2 cups sour cream
1 (10-ounce) can chopped green
   chiles
1 small clove garlic, minced

Combine all ingredients in a casserole dish. Bake, uncovered, for 20 minutes.

Yield: 6 servings

Buttered Baked Rice

A family favorite—goes well with everything

Preheat oven to 325°.

2 teaspoons salt
2 cups water
1 cup dry long-grain rice
1 stick butter

Dash of garlic salt
1 (14-ounce) can chicken broth,
   or 1¾ cups
¼ cup slivered almonds

Combine salt and water in a saucepan. Bring to a boil. Add rice and remove from heat. Let stand 30 minutes and drain. Rinse with cold water and drain again. Melt butter in a skillet. Add rice and garlic salt. Cook over medium heat, stirring frequently, for 5 minutes or until butter is absorbed. Combine rice and broth in a greased 2-quart casserole dish. Bake for 45 minutes. Sprinkle almonds over top during last 5 minutes of baking.

Yield: 4 to 6 servings

White rice is rice that has been milled to completely remove the hull and bran layers. Brown rice has had only the hull removed. The bran layers that are left give the grain its characteristic tan color. Cooked brown rice has a nutty flavor and slightly chewy texture. Brown rice takes about 35 minutes to cook; white rice cooks in about 15 minutes.

~

To toast almonds, place in a small, nonstick skillet sprayed with nonstick spray. Cook, stirring constantly, for 2 to 3 minutes. This will develop the rich flavor of the nuts.

Brie Mushroom Strata
Elegant entrée for brunch

The Brie cheese in this recipe sets it apart from other casseroles of this type. Brie has long been acclaimed as one of the world's great cheeses. It has an edible, white rind and a creamy, buttery soft interior that should ooze at the peak of ripeness. When shopping for Brie, look for one that is plump and resilient to the touch — a sign that it is ripe. The rind might actually show some pale brown edges. Once ripened, Brie has a short shelf life and should be used within a few days.

~

"Unlike my life now, when I was growing up, our biggest meal was always breakfast. Every morning we had eggs (prepared different ways), grits, toast or biscuits, and ham, bacon, steak or sausage. It was great!"

Marianne Rogers Alias

6 cups sliced mushrooms (about 1 pound)	2½ cups finely chopped Brie cheese, rind removed
4 tablespoons butter	1 tablespoon chopped fresh tarragon, or 1 teaspoon dried
1 loaf French bread, sliced 1-inch thick	½ teaspoon salt
2 tablespoons Dijon mustard	¼ teaspoon black pepper
9 eggs, lightly beaten	
3 cups milk	

Sauté mushrooms in butter until just tender. Spread evenly in a greased 3-quart rectangular casserole dish. Set aside. Trim crusts from bread. Spread mustard on 1 side of each bread slice. Cut slices into 1-inch cubes and arrange over mushrooms. Combine eggs, milk, cheese, tarragon, salt and pepper. Pour over bread and press gently to moisten each piece. Cover and refrigerate 2 to 24 hours. Bake, uncovered, in a preheated oven at 350° for 40 to 50 minutes or until a knife inserted in the center comes out clean. Let stand 10 minutes before serving.

Yield: 6 to 8 servings

Strata: A dish popular at breakfast or brunch, containing either sliced or cubed bread, cheese and eggs. Meat such as ham, bacon or sausage and sautéed vegetables may also be included for added flavor.

Breakfast Sausage Bake
Sausage and eggs all in one

Preheat oven to 350°.

5	cups crispy rice cereal, divided	6	eggs
2	pounds bulk sausage	1	(10¾-ounce) can condensed cream of mushroom soup
1	onion, minced	1	(10¾-ounce) can condensed cream of celery soup
2	cups cooked rice	½	cup milk
2	cups grated sharp cheddar cheese		

Spread 4 cups cereal in a greased 9x13x2-inch baking dish. Brown sausage and onions in a skillet. Drain and spread over cereal. Layer rice over sausage. Sprinkle cheese over top. In a bowl, combine eggs, soups and milk. Mix thoroughly and pour over cheese. Sprinkle remaining 1 cup cereal on top. Bake for 45 to 60 minutes or until center is bubbly.

Yield: 8 to 10 servings

Note: If preparing ahead, refrigerate after adding soup mixture. Sprinkle cereal over the top just before baking.

A brunch is a great way to start the day. Whether it's a lazy Saturday at the lake or a more structured affair before the big game, brunch always suggests a more relaxed, casual atmosphere. Plan the menu around the activities, if any, that will follow. If the big game will last all afternoon, a heartier fare will be needed. A bridesmaid's brunch before an early afternoon wedding would most likely resemble a light but elegant luncheon. Regardless, it's a thoughtful gesture to offer something refreshing upon arrival, like juice, for those who have not had breakfast.

Hash Brown Quiche

Even "real men" like this quiche.

If you are trying to reduce the amount of fat in your diet, there are simple ways to cut the amount of cheese you use without sacrificing flavor:

Substitute ½ cup grated cheese for four 1-ounce slices of cheese

~

Substitute a strong flavored cheese, like Cheddar, for a mild one, such as Colby. Reduce the amount used by a third to a half.

~

Use one of the low fat cheeses that are on the market. Just remember, they take longer to melt and aren't as smooth as regular cheeses.

Preheat oven to 425°.

3   cups frozen shredded hash browns, thawed
5   tablespoons butter or margarine, melted
1   cup diced cooked ham
1   cup grated Cheddar cheese
¼   cup diced bell peppers
2   eggs, lightly beaten
½   cup milk
½   teaspoon salt
¼   teaspoon black pepper

Press hash browns between paper towels to remove excess moisture. Press into the bottom and up the sides of an ungreased 9-inch pie pan to form a crust. Drizzle with butter. Bake for 25 minutes. Combine eggs, ham, cheese and bell peppers and spoon over crust. Stir together eggs, milk, salt and pepper. Pour egg mixture over top. Reduce heat to 350° and bake for 20 to 25 minutes or until a knife inserted in center comes out clean. Let stand 10 minutes before cutting.

Yield: 6 servings

Quiche: (KEESH) A pastry shell filled with a custard made of eggs, cream, seasonings and various other ingredients including mushrooms, herbs, meats and vegetables.

Surprise Casserole

You'll be surprised when you see what's in it!

Preheat oven to 350°.

1	pound sausage	1	cup buttermilk
1	medium onion, chopped	½	cup vegetable oil
1	cup regular cornmeal	½	cup chopped green bell peppers
½	cup all-purpose flour		
½	teaspoon baking soda	½	cup chopped red bell pepper
1	teaspoon salt	¾	cup cream-style corn
⅛	teaspoon white pepper	2	cups grated Cheddar cheese
2	eggs, beaten	2	cups cooked black-eyed peas

Brown sausage in a skillet. Remove from skillet and drain, reserving a small amount of drippings in the skillet. Add onions to skillet and sauté. Add onions to sausage; set aside. In a bowl, combine cornmeal, flour, baking soda, salt and white pepper. In a separate bowl, beat together eggs, buttermilk and oil. Add dry ingredients and mix until just moistened. Stir in sausage mixture, bell peppers, corn, cheese and black-eyed peas. Spread in a greased 9x13x2-inch baking pan. Bake for 50 minutes or until golden brown.

Yield: 6 to 8 servings

"In the mid 1950's we had a chance to move to Athens, Georgia. We took it with enthusiasm! This gave us great new friends, a wonderful climate, peaceful living conditions, community involvement and high on the list… 'southern cooking'! I feel sorry for those who have not experienced the above, but there aren't enough collards to go around! Athens is so much more. What a wonderful experience!"

Bob Marion,
Life Trustee member of the Athens Academy Board of Trustees and Annual Fund chairman for many years.

Country Soufflé

Make the day before and it's ready to go in the morning.

16	slices bread, crusts trimmed	6	eggs
4	tablespoons butter, softened	3	cups milk
10	slices cheddar cheese	½	teaspoon Worcestershire
10	thin slices cooked ham or		sauce
	Canadian bacon	½	teaspoon finely chopped
1½	cups sliced mushrooms		chives
1	large onion, minced	½	teaspoon dry mustard
1	cup chopped black olives	1	cup dry breadcrumbs
1	cup chopped bell peppers	½	cup melted butter
1	cup chopped tomato		

Spread 1 side of each bread slice with softened butter. Place 8 slices, buttered-side down, in a greased 9x13-inch baking dish. Layer cheese, ham, mushrooms, onions, olives, bell peppers and tomatoes over bread. Place remaining bread slices, buttered-side up, on top. In a bowl, beat together eggs, milk, Worcestershire sauce, chives and mustard. Pour mixture over bread. Cover and refrigerate overnight. When ready to bake, mix together breadcrumbs and melted butter. Sprinkle over soufflé. Bake in preheated 350° oven for 60 minutes.

Yield: 12 servings

Deviled Bacon and Eggs

Two favorites in one

1 dozen eggs, hard-cooked and halved lengthwise	¼ tablespoon dry mustard
1 pound lean bacon, cooked and crumbled	2 tablespoons sweet pickle relish, plus a little relish juice
¾ cup mayonnaise	Parsley for garnish

Place egg yolks in a bowl, reserving egg white shells. Combine yolks with bacon, mayonnaise, mustard and relish. Spoon or pipe yolk mixture into egg white shells. Garnish with parsley.

Yield: 12 servings

Church has always played a major role in the lives of Southern families. In many rural communities, it was the center of all social as well as religious life. Summertime brought all-day singings, week long revivals, and camp meetings, always accompanied by "dinner on the ground". Long tables were set up outside under the trees and covered with platters of fried chicken, fresh vegetables, salads, pickles and relishes of all kinds, biscuits, rolls, cornbread, cakes, pies, cookies and gallons and gallons of sweet iced tea and lemonade. And, oh yes, let's not forget deviled eggs, or as we like to call them, "stuffed eggs". At least a half dozen platters of them, all of which would go home empty.

Baked Deviled Eggs

Is there anyone who doesn't like deviled eggs?

Preheat oven to 350°.

1   dozen eggs, hard-cooked and
      halved lengthwise
      Prepared mustard
      Mayonnaise
3   cups medium white sauce
1   (2½-ounce) package dried
      chipped beef

1   teaspoon minced onions
      Salt to taste
      White pepper to taste
      Parmesan cheese
      Paprika

Place egg yolks in a bowl, reserving egg white shells. Combine yolks with mustard and a small amount of mayonnaise until creamy. Spoon or pipe yolk mixture into egg white shells. Place eggs in a flat 8x11-inch glass baking dish. Prepare white sauce. Mix in beef, onions, salt and pepper and pour sauce over the eggs. Sprinkle generously with cheese and enough paprika to add color. Bake for 20 minutes.

Yield: 8 servings

White Sauce: A basic sauce made by stirring milk into a butter/flour mixture. The thickness of the sauce depends on the proportion of flour and butter to milk. Also called béchamel (bay shah MEHL, BEH shah mehl) sauce.

Mother's Crab Stuffed Eggs

Fancy enough for your next dinner party

1 dozen eggs, hard-cooked and
      halved lengthwise
1 cup flaked crabmeat
1 cup finely chopped celery
2 tablespoons chopped bell
      peppers

2 tablespoons chopped pimento
1 tablespoon French salad
      dressing
¼ cup mayonnaise or sour cream
      Salt and white pepper
      to taste

Place egg yolks in a bowl, reserving egg white shells. Combine yolks with remaining ingredients. Spoon or pipe yolk mixture into egg white shells. Chill.

Basic
White Sauce

Thin
(makes 1½ cups)
1 tablespoon butter or
margarine
1 tablespoon all-
purpose flour
¼ teaspoon salt
Dash of white pepper
1½ cups milk

Medium
(makes 1 cup)
2 tablespoons butter or
margarine
2 tablespoons all-
purpose flour
¼ teaspoon salt
Dash of white pepper
1 cup milk

Thick
(makes 1 cup)
3 tablespoons butter or
margarine
4 tablespoons all-
purpose flour
¼ teaspoon salt
Dash of white pepper
1 cup milk

Melt butter in a
saucepan over low
heat. Blend in flour,
salt and pepper. Add
milk and cook, stirring
constantly, until
mixture thickens and
bubbles. Add cheeses
and other flavors as
desired or as called for
in a recipe.

179

Walnut Egg Salad

Delightfully different

1	(8-ounce) package cream cheese, softened	¼	cup chopped sweet pickles
¼	cup finely chopped onions	1	cup finely chopped walnuts
¼	cup finely chopped bell peppers	3	eggs, hard-cooked and chopped

Beat cream cheese until smooth. Add onions, bell peppers, pickles and walnuts. Mix well. Blend in eggs. Serve on toast points or bread with crusts removed for finger sandwiches. (24 pieces of bread = 12 regular-size sandwiches or 48 finger sandwiches.)

Yield: 48 servings

Mock Egg Salad

A delicious, healthy alternative to traditional egg salad

Mash 8 ounces tofu with a fork on a glass pie pan. Add several tablespoons fat-free mayonnaise to moisten and bind. Sprinkle with about 3 tablespoons nutritional yeast (a yellow powder sold in health food stores — not the same as brewer's yeast) until tofu turns a pale yellow hue. Season with tamari (soy) sauce and your favorite condiment. Serve as a sandwich filling or a dip with crackers.

Yield: 2 servings

Lee's Pimento Cheese

Even pimento cheese haters love this.

¾	pound New York State extra sharp cheese, coarsely grated	4	ounces pimentos, sliced
		¾	cup or more Duke's mayonnaise

Combine all ingredients and mix.

Note: This mixture gets better after it sits a while. Do not make any substitutions from the above ingredients.

Tofu, a soybean curd made from soymilk, is packed with protein and vitamin B, low in sodium and saturated fat and cholesterol free. Although virtually tasteless by itself, tofu easily absorbs other flavors and lends itself to many different cooking techniques. Soft tofu is good for whipping, blending and crumbling, and a good substitute for creamy ingredients in dips, puddings, soups and salad dressings. Firm tofu can be cubed, sliced or crumbled for use in salads, stir-frying and pasta. Extra firm tofu is a good choice for stir-frying.

State
Botanical
Garden

Zim's Best Summer Squash Casserole

Preheat oven to 400°.

2 tablespoons olive oil	2 cups drained canned Italian plum tomatoes, shredded by hand
2 onions, coarsely chopped	
4 medium cloves garlic, finely minced	⅓ cup tomato paste
2 teaspoons chopped fresh oregano or thyme or a combination, or 1 teaspoon dried	Salt and pepper to taste
	⅔ cup Parmesan cheese
9 medium yellow summer squash, sliced into ¼-inch rounds	⅔ cup fresh breadcrumbs
	Butter

Heat oil over medium-high heat in a sauté pan. Add onions and cook until just wilted. Add garlic and oregano and cook 2 minutes longer. Add squash and cook and stir briefly. Add tomatoes, tomato paste, salt, and pepper. Transfer mixture to a greased 9x13-inch casserole dish. Bake, uncovered, for 20 minutes. Blend cheese and breadcrumbs. Gently stir half of breadcrumb mixture into cooked casserole. Reduce heat to 350° and cook 15 minutes longer. Sprinkle with remaining breadcrumb mixture and dot with butter. Bake 45 minutes.

Yield: 10 servings

Zim's Bagel Bakery

A popular eatery for breakfast, brunch and lunch favored by students and townspeople alike.

Marinated Asparagus

Welcome spring with tender, fresh asparagus

3	pounds fresh asparagus
2	(14-ounce) cans hearts of palm, drained
½	cup cider vinegar
1	cup canola oil
1½	teaspoons salt
1	teaspoon black pepper
3	cloves garlic, crushed
	Cherry tomatoes for garnish

Trim tough ends from asparagus and remove scales from stalks with a knife. Place asparagus in a steamer and cook 4 minutes. Drain, submerge in ice water until cool and drain again. Cut hearts of palm into ½-inch slices. Combine asparagus and hearts of palm in a zip-top plastic bag. Combine vinegar, oil, salt, black pepper and garlic in a jar. Cover and shake. Pour dressing over vegetables and seal bag. Refrigerate 8 hours, turning occasionally. When ready to serve, transfer to a serving bowl and garnish with cherry tomatoes.

Yield: 12 servings

Hearts of palm: the edible inner portion of the stem of the cabbage palm tree. They are often used in salads or main dishes.

Stir-Fried Asparagus with Walnuts

The walnuts make the difference.

1½	pounds fresh asparagus, trimmed
2	tablespoons peanut or vegetable oil
2	teaspoons minced fresh ginger or ½ teaspoon ground
1	clove garlic, minced
⅛	teaspoon crushed red pepper flakes
¼	cup chopped walnuts
¼	cup red bell pepper, cut into thin strips
2	tablespoons soy sauce
2	tablespoons dry sherry
½	teaspoon sugar
½	teaspoon salt

Cut asparagus diagonally into short pieces. Heat oil in a large skillet and add asparagus. Stir-fry 2 minutes or until crisp-tender. Remove from skillet and set aside. Add ginger, garlic, pepper flakes, walnuts and bell peppers to skillet. Cook and stir 1 minute. Combine soy sauce, sherry, sugar and salt and add to skillet. Add asparagus back to skillet. Toss and cook until heated throughout.

Yield: 6 servings

Southerners have eaten vegetables since long before we knew they were good for us. Our grand-fathers consulted the Farmer's Almanac as fervently as their grandsons read the stock quotes. Planting was done by the book following the signs of the moon. Their workday lasted from sunup to sundown taking breaks only for water or a glass of sweet tea and a big spread at lunch. But, oh to be lucky enough to reap the fruits of their labor: beans so tender they didn't have strings, corn so juicy it spattered you when you cut it off the cobs, enough peas, butterbeans, cucumbers, squash and okra to feed a small army, and, of course, tomatoes—baskets and baskets of the most delicious tomatoes imaginable. Words just can't do them justice!

Mrs. Cobb's Casserole

Mrs. Henry Cobb was a local caterer
whose culinary talents were legendary.

Preheat oven to 350°.

2 sticks butter	2 cups grated New York State
1 cup all-purpose flour	cheese
2 (16-ounce) cans asparagus	¼ cup sherry
spears, liquid reserved	Salt and pepper to taste
2 (14-ounce) cans artichoke	Nutmeg to taste
hearts, liquid reserved	Sliced almonds for garnish
1 (5-ounce) can water	
chestnuts, liquid reserved	

Melt butter in a skillet. Stir in flour and cook until browned. Add reserved liquid from canned vegetables. If mixture seems too thick, add a small amount of water. Stir in cheese and sherry. Season with salt, pepper and nutmeg. Combine cheese sauce with asparagus, artichoke hearts and water chestnuts in a casserole dish. Top with sliced almonds. Bake for 30 minutes. Serve hot.

Yield: 10 to 12 servings

Artichoke hearts: the center portion of the artichoke. Tender and tasty.

Fresh Asparagus with Easy Hollandaise Sauce

Use the sauce over any steamed vegetable.

1 pound fresh asparagus	7 tablespoons hot water, or
1 stick butter, softened	less as needed
4 egg yolks	Salt and white pepper to taste
3 tablespoons lemon juice	

Steam asparagus in microwave for 2 to 3 minutes or until tender-crisp and bright green in color. Cream butter in a food processor or mixer. While processing, add egg yolks, one at a time. Add lemon juice and water. Mix well. Transfer mixture to a double boiler and cook a few minutes or until thickened. Season with salt and pepper. Serve over asparagus, broccoli or steamed vegetable of your choice.

Yield: 1 cup

When buying asparagus, size does not count. Thin stalks are not necessarily more tender than thick ones. Tightly closed flower buds are the best indicator of fresh, flavorful asparagus. If asparagus must be purchased days ahead, refrigerate upright in a container with ½-inch of water in the bottom, or lying on a refrigerator shelf in a plastic bag with ends wrapped in wet paper towels.

~

It's an old wives tale that stalks will readily snap where they change texture. You will lose a lot of expensive asparagus if you snap it off. Use a knife to cut the stalk where the hard fibrous portion begins.

Sweet and Sour Green Beans

Tart, tangy and so tasty

Preheat oven to 350°.

2 (15.5-ounce) cans French green beans, drained	½ cup slivered almonds
1 small red onion, cut into rings	6 tablespoons sugar
8 slices bacon	6 tablespoons raspberry vinegar

Place green beans in a greased 1½-quart casserole dish. Place onion rings over beans. Fry bacon, reserving drippings in pan. Quarter bacon strips and place over onions. Sprinkle almonds on top. Add sugar and vinegar to bacon drippings and heat. Pour over casserole and refrigerate several hours or overnight. Bake for 40 to 45 minutes.

Yield: 8 servings

Garden Green Beans

A traditional favorite in Southern homes

4 cups water	1½ pounds fresh green beans, snipped and strung
4 ounces salt pork or ham hock, diced	Salt and pepper to taste
	½ teaspoon sugar

Place water and pork in a 2-quart saucepan. Add beans, salt, pepper and sugar. Cover and cook over medium heat 30 to 35 minutes or until tender.

Yield: 6 servings

Vinegar used to come in only two types: white and cider. Today, they are flavored with everything from tarragon to raspberries and are used in recipes ranging from salad dressings to desserts. Thanks to these great vinegar flavors, you can add new life to vinaigrettes for green salads. Just add a little oil to one of these and make your low-fat salad a taste sensation.

~

Discover some new vinegar-food pairings: tarragon vinegar and chicken, balsamic vinegar with beef, red wine vinegar on grilled vegetables, raspberry vinegar on fresh strawberries. Any way you try them, vinegars add flavor without fat.

Green Bean Bundles

A wonderful complement to pork and beef entrées

**New Year's Day
Lunch at
The President's
Home**

*Scarlett O'Hara never
had it this good!*

Menu

*Sally Ann's
Tangy Wings*

*Honey Mustard
Pork Tenderloin*

*Anita's Sweet
Potato Casserole*

Hoppin John

*Mama's Old Fashioned
Turnip Greens
with Alabama
Tomato Topping*

Southern Fried Apples

*Granny's Buttermilk
Cornbread*

Never Fails Pecan Pie

Iced Tea

Coffee

2	pounds fresh green beans, trimmed
1	pound bacon
1	cup light brown sugar
2	tablespoons soy sauce
½	teaspoon garlic powder
1	stick butter
	Salt and pepper to taste

Cook green beans in boiling water for 5 minutes. Drain. To make bundles, wrap 10 to 12 beans with 1 strip of bacon, twisting the ends of the bacon and then securing with a toothpick. Place bundles in a greased glass baking dish. Combine sugar, soy sauce, garlic powder and butter in a saucepan. Heat until butter melts. Season with salt and pepper. Pour mixture over bundles and refrigerate several hours or overnight. Allow dish to reach room temperature before baking. Bake in preheated 350° oven for 30 minutes.

Yield: 8 servings

Broccoli with Almonds

A great side dish for a dinner party

Preheat oven to 375°.

2	pounds fresh broccoli
1	teaspoon salt
1	beef bouillon cube
¾	cup hot water
1	cup half-and-half
4	tablespoons butter
¼	cup all-purpose flour
2	tablespoons sherry
2	tablespoons lemon juice
⅛	teaspoon black pepper
½	cup grated cheddar cheese
¼	cup slivered almonds

Cut broccoli into florets. Cook with salt in boiling water and drain. Transfer broccoli to a greased 8x12-inch baking dish. Dissolve bouillon cube in hot water. Stir in half-and-half and set aside. In a heavy saucepan, melt butter over low heat. Blend in flour until smooth. Cook 1 minute, stirring constantly. Gradually add bouillon mixture. Cook and stir over medium heat until thick and bubbly. Stir in sherry, lemon juice and pepper. Pour sauce over broccoli. Sprinkle cheese and almonds on top. Bake for 25 to 30 minutes.

Yield: 6 servings

Broccoli Supreme

You can't go wrong with artichoke hearts.

Preheat oven to 350°.

2 cups coarsely chopped fresh broccoli	2 eggs, lightly beaten
3 carrots, sliced	1 tablespoon fresh lemon juice
1 (14-ounce) can artichoke hearts, drained and quartered	1 tablespoon Worcestershire sauce
1 (10¾-ounce) can condensed cream of mushroom soup	1 cup grated sharp cheddar cheese
½ cup mayonnaise	1 cup herb-seasoned stuffing mix
	4 tablespoons butter, melted

Cook broccoli and carrots in boiling water or steam until crisp-tender. Drain and set aside. Place artichoke hearts in bottom of a greased 8-inch square baking dish. Combine soup, mayonnaise, eggs, lemon juice and Worcestershire sauce in a bowl and mix well. Stir in broccoli and carrots. Pour mixture over artichoke hearts. Sprinkle with cheese and stuffing mix. Drizzle butter over the top. Bake for 25 minutes or until heated through.

Note: For a lower fat version of this recipe, substitute reduced-fat soup, mayonnaise, cheese and margarine.

Yield: 6 servings

Cabbage Au Gratin

Just like the one at the Dillard House in Dillard, Georgia

Preheat oven to 350°.

4-5 cups coarsely chopped cabbage	½ teaspoon black pepper
2 teaspoons salt, divided	1½ cups milk
2 tablespoons butter	1½ cups grated sharp cheddar cheese
2 tablespoons all-purpose flour	

Cook cabbage in boiling water with 1 teaspoon salt until crisp-tender. Do not overcook. Drain well. Melt butter in a saucepan. Add flour, remaining 1 teaspoon salt and pepper and stir until a paste forms. Add milk, cook and stir until thick. Cover bottom of a greased 2-quart casserole dish with some of the cabbage. Add a layer of white sauce and sprinkle with some of the cheese. Repeat layers until all ingredients are used. Bake for 15 to 20 minutes or until hot and bubbly.

Yield: 6 to 8 servings

Broccoli with Caper Sauce

Cook 2 pounds fresh broccoli in salted water until just crisp-tender. Drain thoroughly. Place in a heated serving dish and pour melted butter over all. Spoon bottled capers, along with a little of the juice, over the broccoli!

Yield: 6 servings

~

Broccoli is loaded with nutrients and fiber that may help in the prevention of cancer. When preparing broccoli, peel the stems directly from under the flower bud to the end of the stem. Cook until barely tender to retain nutrients. To microwave, cook in water 7½ to 10½ minutes on full power. Good with hollandaise sauce or lemon butter.

Tailgate Baked Beans

A must have for cookouts and tailgates

Preheat oven to 300°.

6	slices bacon	½	cup ketchup
1	large onion, chopped	½	cup brown sugar
½	bell pepper, chopped	1	tablespoon Worcestershire
½	pound ham, slivered		sauce
2	(28-ounce) cans pork and beans		Salt and pepper to taste

Cook bacon until crisp. Remove bacon, crumble and set aside; reserve bacon drippings in pan. Sauté onions and bell peppers in drippings for 5 minutes. Add ham and cook 2 to 3 minutes longer. Stir in crumbled bacon, pork and beans, ketchup, brown sugar and Worcestershire sauce. Season with salt and pepper. Transfer to a bean pot. Bake, uncovered, for 1 hour.

Yield: 8 to 10 servings

Note: Recipe may be prepared ahead and frozen, adding all ingredients except the beans. When ready to eat, add beans to thawed mixture and bake as directed above.

Brussels Sprouts and Baby Carrots

Cut the stems from Brussels sprouts and halve lengthwise. Cook in chicken broth or water for 5 to 7 minutes or until bright green and crisp-tender. Drain well. Cook 1 to 2 pounds of baby carrots in boiling water just until tender; drain. Add 1 tablespoon butter and 1 teaspoon sugar and quickly cook down until carrots are tender and glazed. Add to Brussels sprouts and season to taste with salt and pepper.

Carrot Soufflé

Shhhhh! Don't tell them it's carrots; they'll love it!

Preheat oven to 350°.

Soufflé

1	pound carrots, cooked	1	teaspoon vanilla
3	eggs	1	stick butter, melted
⅓	cup sugar		Dash of nutmeg
3	tablespoons all-purpose flour		

Topping

¼-½	cup crushed corn flakes	2	teaspoons butter, softened
3	tablespoons brown sugar		

Place carrots and eggs in a blender. Do not use a food processor. Add sugar, flour, vanilla, butter and nutmeg. Blend until smooth. Pour into a 1½-quart pan or a soufflé dish. Bake for 40 minutes. To make topping, blend together corn flakes, brown sugar and butter. Spread over baked soufflé and cook 5 to 10 minutes longer.

Yield: 6 servings

Zesty Carrots

For people who don't like their carrots sweet

Preheat oven to 375°.

6-8 carrots, cut lengthwise
2 tablespoons bottled
   horseradish
2 tablespoons grated onion
½ teaspoon salt
¼ teaspoon black pepper

½ cup mayonnaise
¼ cup fine breadcrumbs or
   cracker crumbs
1 tablespoons butter, melted
   Dash of paprika

Cook carrots in a small amount of water until tender. Drain, reserving ¼ cup of cooking liquid. Arrange carrots in a shallow baking dish. Combine reserved cooking liquid, horseradish, onions, salt, pepper and mayonnaise and pour over carrots. Combine crumbs, butter and paprika and sprinkle over top. Bake for 15 to 20 minutes.

Yield: 6 servings

Bottled horseradish: a condiment made from grated horseradish root. Its "bite" makes it a popular accompaniment to sauces, meat and fish.

Colcannon

A wonderful marriage of flavors

1 medium head cabbage,
   coarsely grated
6 medium potatoes, peeled and
   cut into eighths

4 tablespoons butter or
   margarine
1½ cups milk
1 teaspoon salt
¼ teaspoon black pepper

Cook cabbage, covered, in a small amount of boiling salted water for 5 to 7 minutes or until tender. Drain well and set aside. Cook potatoes in enough boiling salted water to cover for 15 minutes or until tender. Drain and mash with butter, milk, salt and pepper. Add cabbage and mix well. Serve immediately.

Yield: 8 to 10 servings

Colcannon: (kuhl KAN uhn) An Irish peasant dish made of mashed potatoes, cabbage or kale, and onions.

Pickled Carrots

1½ cups
cider vinegar
1½ cups water
1 cup sugar
2 tablespoons dill seed
3-4 cloves garlic, minced
2 pounds baby carrots

Combine vinegar, water and sugar in a large saucepan. Bring to a boil, stirring until sugar dissolves. Add dill seed, garlic and carrots. Bring to a boil over medium heat. Reduce heat, cover and simmer 6 to 10 minutes. Remove from heat and cool. Chill 8 hours or overnight. Strain, discarding liquid. Store refrigerated in a plastic bag.

***Makes a
good side dish.***

Curried Baked Cauliflower

Once you try this, you may never go back to cheese sauce.

Preheat oven to 350°.

1 large head cauliflower	⅓ cup mayonnaise
½ teaspoon salt	1 teaspoon curry powder
1 (10½-ounce) can condensed cream of chicken soup	¼ cup dry breadcrumbs
1 cup grated cheese	2 tablespoons butter or margarine, melted

Break cauliflower into florets. Place in a saucepan and add boiling water to a depth of 1 inch; do not cover cauliflower. Add salt and bring to a boil. Cook 10 minutes; drain well. Transfer cauliflower to a 2-quart casserole dish. Combine soup, cheese, mayonnaise and curry powder. Pour mixture over cauliflower. Toss breadcrumbs with butter and sprinkle over casserole. Bake for 30 minutes or until hot and bubbly.

Yield: 8 to 10 servings

Note: This dish can be prepared ahead and frozen up to 1 month. Thaw overnight in refrigerator. Bake at 350° for about 40 minutes or until hot and bubbly. For a delicious change, use canned onion rings crumbled over the top instead of breadcrumbs.

So Easy Salt Roasted Potatoes

So easy and different

Preheat oven to 450°.

18 small new potatoes, about uniform in size	2 tablespoons vegetable oil
	2 teaspoon coarse (Kosher) salt

Scrub potatoes and pat dry. Place potatoes, unpeeled, in a 9x13-inch baking dish. Bake for 20 minutes, turning once half way through. Drizzle oil over potatoes and stir gently to coat. Sprinkle with salt and stir again. Bake 10 minutes longer or until tender.

Yield: 4 to 6 servings

To prepare cauliflower for cooking, use a fork to scrape off any brown spots. Cutting these spots off causes unnecessary loss of the vegetable. Use a paring knife to separate florets from the core, breaking along the naturally occurring divisions. Trim any stems that seem too large.

~

"New" potatoes are not a variety of potato at all; they are simply any newly harvested potato with a skin so tender it can be scraped off. For this recipe, look for small, immature potatoes that are uniform in size so they will all cook at the same rate.

Southern Fried Corn

It's Southern, after all!

12 ears fresh corn	2-4 teaspoons sugar, or to taste
8 slices bacon	2 teaspoons salt, or to taste
4 tablespoons butter or margarine	½ teaspoon black pepper, or to taste

Using a sharp knife or corn cutter, cut away corn kernels from the ear and place in a large bowl. Use the back of the knife to scrape corn milk and remaining pulp from each ear. Add to corn kernels and set aside. Cook bacon in a heavy skillet, preferably cast iron, until crisp. Remove bacon and discard all but 2 tablespoons drippings. Add corn mixture, butter, sugar, salt and pepper to reserved drippings. Cook over medium to low heat until corn loses its "raw" look and taste and mixture thickens. Stir often to prevent sticking. Adjust seasonings as desired. Serve immediately with bacon crumbled over the top.

Yield: 4 to 6 servings

Note: The sweetness and juiciness of corn can vary depending on growing conditions and time of year. If the corn appears dry, add a little water to the mixture. Adjust seasonings as needed.

Best Ever Corn Pudding

Absolutely the best corn pudding — no lie!

Preheat oven to 350°.

¼ cup sugar	6 eggs
3 tablespoons all-purpose flour	2 cups heavy cream
2 teaspoons baking powder	1 stick butter or margarine, melted
2 teaspoons salt	6 cups fresh or frozen corn

Combine sugar, flour, baking powder and salt in a small bowl. Beat eggs with a fork in a large bowl. Stir in cream and butter. Gradually add sugar mixture, stirring until smooth. Stir in corn and mix well. Pour into a greased 13x9x2-inch baking dish. Bake for 45 minutes or until deep golden brown and set.

Yield: 8 servings

If you've never eaten fried corn made from corn fresh out of the field, you've missed one of the best of all Southern dishes. The name is somewhat misleading since the corn is not actually fried in the truest sense of the word, but it is cooked in a skillet — preferably a heavy, well-seasoned, cast iron skillet. Use the freshest corn you can find and apply the thumb nail test to make sure it isn't dry. You need lots of "corn milk" to make good fried corn. Stir often and watch carefully. Because it is starchy, corn sticks easily. Once you've had the "real thing", you'll never want anything less.

~

So-called canned or frozen "creamed corn" is not really creamed at all. It has no added fat - just sugar and cornstarch.

Collards and Ham Hocks

It's Southern, after all!

2	pounds smoked ham hocks	2	teaspoons salt
1	cup chopped onion	2	cups dry white wine
1	tablespoon finely chopped garlic	2	pounds collard greens, washed and chopped
	Hot sauce or cayenne pepper to taste	2	tablespoons soy sauce

Combine ham hocks, onion, garlic and hot sauce in an 8-quart pot with enough water to cover. Cover and cook over medium-high heat until water comes to a boil. Remove lid and boil 5 more minutes. Stir in salt, wine and collard greens. Add soy sauce and stir again. Cover, reduce heat to low and cook 1½ to 2 hours, stirring occasionally. Add water as needed to prevent greens from sticking to bottom of pan.

Yield: 4 to 6 servings

In other places, "greens" may refer to salad makings or vegetables. To a Southerner, it means collard and turnip greens, mustard and kale — the leaves of certain vegetables that are simmered for a long time with some type of smoked pork for seasoning. Cooked the traditional way, Southern greens are truly "soul food" with earthy aromas and strong flavors - a taste that, to the uninitiated, might take some getting used to. But add some candied sweet potatoes, a juicy pork chop, crisp hot cornbread and, of course, sweet iced tea and you have the makings of a feast. And, oh yes, never throw out the "pot likker" — that's the best part of all!

Mama's Old Fashioned Turnip Greens

It's Southern, after all!

4-5	pounds fresh turnip greens	¼	teaspoon black pepper
½-1	pound salt pork, including streaks of lean		Salt to taste
3	quarts water		Sugar to taste (optional)

Carefully pick through greens, discarding stems and damaged leaves. Wash thoroughly, especially if greens are dirty or gritty. Drain. Tear larger leaves from tough center stem. Set aside. Slash salt pork at intervals, cutting to, but not through, skin or rind. Combine salt pork, water and pepper in a large Dutch oven and bring to a boil. Reduce heat, cover and simmer 60 minutes. Add greens and cook, uncovered, 20 minutes or until tender. Season as desired with salt and sugar. Serve with hot pepper sauce or vinegar.

Yield: 4 to 6 servings

Note: When choosing turnip greens, young tender leaves are best. You may also use a mixture of greens, including collards, mustard or kale.

Alabama Tomato Topping

Best when served over turnip greens or collards

2	(14½-ounce) cans tomatoes, chopped	Sugar to taste
		Salt and pepper to taste

Place tomatoes in a heavy saucepan. Add sugar, salt and pepper. Cook over low heat to a semi-paste consistency. Adjust seasonings as needed. Spoon over greens.

Yield: 4 to 6 servings

Although turnip greens may be boiled, sautéed, steamed or stir-fried, Southerners like them best prepared very simply. Sometimes we cut the turnip roots into chunks and cook them along with the greens. (They are also delicious boiled and mashed like potatoes to be served as a side dish with greens.) Some Southerners like their greens topped with a tomato sauce that has been cooked down to a semi-paste consistency. However you like your greens, they are so good and so good for you.

~

Portia opened a paper sack she had placed on the kitchen table. "I done bought a nice mess of collard greens and I thought maybe we have supper together. I done bought a piece of side meat, too. These here greens need to be seasoned with that."

Carson McCullers,
The Heart Is A Lonely Hunter

Creamed Mushrooms in Wild Rice Ring

Elegant side dish for prime rib

Preheat oven to 350°.

To substitute canned mushrooms for fresh:

1 (6 to 8-ounce) can is equivalent to 1 pound of fresh.

To substitute fresh for canned: 1 quart (20 to 24 medium mushroom caps) is equivalent to 1 (6 to 8-ounce) can.

Wild Rice Ring

1	cup wild rice		Salt and pepper to taste
1	cup chopped chicken livers	1½	teaspoons cornstarch
3	tablespoons butter	½	cup chicken broth

Creamed Mushrooms

1	pound fresh mushrooms, sliced		Dash cayenne pepper
2	tablespoons butter, melted	3	tablespoons butter
½	teaspoon salt	3	tablespoons all-purpose flour
½	teaspoon chives	2	cups half-and-half
¼	teaspoon soy sauce	½	teaspoon salt
		2	egg yolks

Cook wild rice as directed on the package. Sauté livers in butter until brown and add to rice. Season with salt and pepper. Mix cornstarch into broth, stirring until smooth. Add broth to rice mixture and mix well. Pack mixture into a greased 8-inch ring mold. Place mold in a shallow pan containing an inch of water. Bake for 30 minutes. Cool 10 minutes before unmolding onto a serving plate.

Meanwhile, place mushrooms on a jelly-roll pan. Pour 2 tablespoons melted butter over mushrooms. Sprinkle with salt, chives, soy sauce and cayenne pepper. Broil 5 minutes. Melt 3 tablespoons butter in a heavy saucepan over low heat. Add flour and cook 1 minute, stirring constantly. Gradually add half-and-half and cook over medium heat, stirring constantly, until thick. Stir in salt. Beat egg yolks until thick and lemon colored. Gradually stir about one-fourth of creamed mixture into yolks. Add back into remaining cream mixture. Cook and stir over low heat for 2 minutes. Stir in mushrooms and mix well. Spoon mushrooms into center of rice ring. Serve immediately.

Yield: 8 servings

Wild Rice: not rice at all but actually a long-grain marsh grass known for its nutty flavor and chewy texture.

Pan Fried Okra, Potatoes and Green Tomatoes
It's Southern, after all!

¾ cup yellow cornmeal
¼ cup all-purpose flour
2 teaspoons sweet paprika (optional)
½ teaspoon sugar
½ teaspoon black pepper
¼ teaspoon salt
1 egg
2 tablespoons milk

3 medium potatoes, peeled, cut into small cubes, and parboiled
4 medium green (unripe) tomatoes, cut into small cubes
1 pound fresh okra, cut into ½-inch pieces
3-4 tablespoons butter, divided
3-4 tablespoons vegetable oil, divided

In a shallow dish, combine cornmeal, flour, paprika, sugar, pepper and salt. Set aside. Whisk together egg and milk. Combine potatoes, tomatoes and okra in a bowl. Pour egg mixture over vegetables and stir to coat. Drain off excess liquid and dredge in cornmeal mixture. In a large, heavy skillet, heat 1 tablespoon each of butter and oil over medium-high heat until foam subsides. Add about a third of vegetable mixture and cook 3 to 4 minutes per side or until golden brown. Remove from skillet and keep warm in a 200° oven. Cook remaining vegetables in 2 batches using remaining butter and oil. Serve hot.

Yield: 6 to 8 servings

Okra à la Creole
A fancy dish from a very humble veggie

2 tablespoons olive oil
1 cup finely chopped onion
1 cup finely chopped green onions
1 cup finely chopped fresh parsley
1 cup finely chopped bell peppers
2 cups chopped tomatoes
1 cup tomato sauce

2 tablespoons minced garlic
2 tablespoons soy sauce
1 cup dry white wine
1 pound smoked sausage, sliced ¼-inch thick
5 cups sliced okra
Salt to taste
Hot sauce or cayenne pepper to taste

Heat oil in a large, high-walled skillet over medium heat. Add onions, parsley and bell peppers and sauté until onions are translucent. Stir in tomatoes, tomato sauce, garlic, soy sauce, wine and sausage. Cover and bring to a boil over medium heat, stirring occasionally. Stir in okra, salt and hot sauce. Reduce heat to low and cover. Simmer, stirring occasionally, for 45 minutes or until okra is tender.

Yield: 6 to 8 servings

Fried green tomatoes were popular in the South long before the movie hit the screen. It has always been a good way to use up nature's bounty before they rot on the vine. This recipe combines several traditional Southern favorites. If you prefer only green tomatoes, slice instead of cube, and leave out the okra and potatoes. For fried okra, simply leave out the tomatoes and potatoes. Yellow squash is also delicious sliced and prepared following these directions.

~

Cooking okra with tomatoes, bell peppers and onions helps to counteract the gumminess of the okra.

Hoppin' John

It's Southern, after all!

Hoppin' John is an old Southern dish that is traditionally eaten, along with turnip greens, on New Year's Day. As the legend goes, greens are for money, peas are for coins. The more you eat, the richer you'll be.

~

Southerners love to top their peas with relish.

Pepper Relish

2 pounds green bell peppers, finely chopped
2 pounds red bell peppers, finely chopped
6 medium onions, finely chopped
1 cup sugar
1 cup cider vinegar
½ cup water
1½ teaspoons salt
1½ teaspoons dill seed
10 (½-pint) empty jars with lids

Combine peppers and onions in a pan. Add boiling water to cover and let stand 5 minutes. Drain and return vegetables to pan. Add sugar, vinegar, ½ cup water, salt and dill seed. Bring to a boil and cook 5 minutes. Transfer to hot jars, filling to within ½-inch of top. Put lids on and cool. Refrigerate until ready to use.

Yield: 10 cups

1 cup dried black-eyed peas	1 onion, chopped
3½ cups water	½ cup dry long-grain rice
¼ pound slab bacon, lean salt pork or smoked pork, chopped	1 teaspoon salt
	½ teaspoon black pepper

Bring peas and water to a boil in a 2-quart saucepan. Cook 2 minutes. Remove from heat, cover and let stand several hours. Stir bacon and onions into peas. Bring to a boil; reduce heat. Cover and simmer 1 to 2 hours or until peas are tender. Stir in rice, salt and pepper. Cook, stirring occasionally, until rice is tender. Add extra water if needed.

Yield: 6 to 8 servings

Note: Be sure to only simmer the beans. Cooking too fast will cause peas to pop open.

Saucy Green Pea Casserole

The sauce sets it apart.

Preheat oven to 350°.

1 tablespoon butter	1 (16-ounce) package frozen green peas, cooked and drained
4 teaspoons grated onions	
2 tablespoons all-purpose flour	
1 teaspoon salt	1 (4-ounce) can mushrooms, drained
2 teaspoons sugar	
1 cup sour cream	20-25 buttery crackers, crushed
1 (4-ounce) package grated Swiss cheese	

Melt butter in a double boiler. Add onions and cook until tender. Combine flour, salt and sugar; stir into cooked onions. Add sour cream and cheese and cook until cheese melts. Remove from heat. Add peas and mushrooms. Pour into a greased 1½-quart casserole dish. Top with crushed crackers. Bake for 25 minutes.

Yield: 6 to 8 servings

Note: If preparing ahead, do not add crackers until ready to bake.

Vidalia Onion Casserole

It's Southern, after all!

3 medium Vidalia onions
2 tablespoons butter
2 (4½-ounce) cans mushrooms, drained
2 cups grated Swiss cheese, divided
1 (10¾-ounce) can cream of chicken soup

1 (5-ounce) can evaporated milk
1 tablespoon soy sauce
6 (½-inch thick) French bread slices
⅓ cup chopped parsley

Cut onions into thick slices. Sauté in butter until tender. Combine onions and mushrooms in a 2-quart casserole dish. Sprinkle with 1 cup cheese. Combine soup, milk and soy sauce and pour over onion mixture. Top with French bread and then remaining 1 cup cheese. Sprinkle with parsley. Cover and chill 8 hours. When ready to serve, remove from refrigerator and let stand at room temperature 30 minutes. Cover and bake in preheated 375° oven for 30 minutes. Uncover and bake 15 minutes longer.

Yield: 6 servings

Note: Best if made the day before serving.

Vidalia Onion Sauté

Makes a great side dish

5 medium Vidalia onions, sliced
4 tablespoons butter
½ teaspoon sugar
½ teaspoon salt

½ teaspoon black pepper
½ cup dry sherry
2 tablespoons Parmesan cheese

Sauté onions in butter in a heavy Dutch oven for 6 to 8 minutes or until crisp-tender. Sprinkle with sugar, salt and pepper and stir. Add sherry and simmer 2 minutes. Spoon into a serving dish and sprinkle with cheese.

Yield: 4 servings

Vidalia onions are the namesake of Vidalia, Georgia and a source of pride for the entire state. These sweet, yellow onions derive their distinctive taste from the soil in which they're grown. They are available from May through June.

~

Vidalia Onion Rings

1¼ cups all-purpose flour
¼ teaspoon salt
1 egg, lightly beaten
1¼ cups milk
1 teaspoon vegetable oil
5 large Vidalia onions, cut into ¼-inch slices
Vegetable oil for frying

To make a batter, combine flour and salt in a bowl. Blend in egg, milk and 1 teaspoon vegetable oil. Batter will be slightly lumpy. Separate onion slices into rings. Dip rings in batter. Drop rings, a few at a time, into 375° vegetable oil. Fry until rings are golden brown and float to the surface. Remove from oil and drain on paper towels.

Yield: 4 servings

Baked Mashed Potato Casserole

An excellent make-ahead dish for a hungry crowd

Preheat oven to 350°.

4	large potatoes, peeled and quartered	1	egg, beaten
¼	cup milk	1	(8-ounce) container sour cream (1 cup)
½	teaspoon salt	1	cup small curd cottage cheese
2	tablespoons butter or margarine, melted, divided	5	green onions, finely chopped
		½	cup crushed buttery crackers

Cook potatoes in a small amount of water until tender. Drain. Place in a large bowl and add milk, salt and 1 tablespoon butter. Beat until light and fluffy. Fold in egg, sour cream, cottage cheese and onions. Spoon into a greased 1½-quart casserole dish. Combine crackers and remaining 1 tablespoon butter and sprinkle over potatoes. Bake, uncovered, for 20 to 30 minutes or until crumbs are lightly browned.

Yield: 4 to 6 servings

Note : If preparing ahead, do not add crackers until ready to bake.

Gourmet Scalloped Potatoes

A sophisticated change from the ordinary

Preheat oven to 350°.

1	large garlic clove, minced	½	teaspoon salt
½	teaspoon crushed red pepper flakes	¼	teaspoon black pepper
3	tablespoons butter	2½	pounds red potatoes, unpeeled and sliced
1¼	cups milk	1	cup grated Gruyère cheese
1½	cups heavy cream	¼	cup Parmesan cheese

Sauté garlic and pepper flakes in butter until tender. Add milk, cream, salt and pepper, stirring well. Add potatoes and bring to a boil over medium heat. Spoon mixture into a greased 9x13-inch baking dish. Sprinkle cheeses on top. Bake for 60 minutes. Remove from oven and let stand 30 minutes before serving.

Yield: 8 servings

Variation: Swiss or cheddar cheese may be used instead of Gruyère.

Gruyère cheese: (groo-YEHR, gree-YEHR) A firm, moderate-fat cheese with small holes and a rich, sweet, nutty flavor.

Mock Sour Cream

2 cups low-fat cottage cheese
¼ cup plain low-fat yogurt
1 egg
1 tablespoon lemon juice
1 tablespoon water
½ teaspoon dry mustard
¼ teaspoon white pepper
⅛ teaspoon hot sauce

Combine all ingredients in a blender. Process until mixture is smooth. Chill. Serve as a topping for baked potatoes or as a base for dips and spreads.

Yield: 2 cups

About 14 calories per tablespoon.

Yukon Gold Potatoes and Mushroom Gratin

Buttery good

Preheat oven to 400°.

5 ounces blue cheese, crumbled	1 pound fresh mushrooms, thinly sliced
2½ cups heavy cream, divided	1½ teaspoons fresh thyme, or ¾ teaspoon dried
1 teaspoon salt	
½ teaspoon black pepper	2 pounds Yukon Gold potatoes, peeled and thinly sliced into rounds
1½ tablespoons butter	

Place cheese in a medium bowl. Add ½ cup cream and mash until a paste forms. Add salt and pepper. Mix in remaining 2 cups cream. Melt butter over medium heat. Add mushrooms and thyme and sauté 8 minutes or until mushrooms are tender and liquid cooks off. Cover bottom of a greased 9x13x2-inch dish with half of the potato slices. Add a layer using half the mushrooms. Cover with ¾ cup of cheese sauce. Add another layer each using remaining potatoes and mushrooms. Pour remaining cheese sauce over the top. Bake, covered, in the top third of the oven for 30 minutes. Uncover and bake until top is golden brown. Let stand 10 minutes before serving.

Yield: 6 to 8 servings

Gratin: (GRAH-tn) Any dish that is topped with cheese or breadcrumbs and heated until golden and crispy. Sometimes referred to as au gratin or gratinée.

Gwen's Fried Potatoes

Okay, you can call them hash browns!

2 tablespoons shortening	8 medium potatoes, peeled and grated
1 tablespoon margarine	Salt and pepper to taste

Melt shortening and margarine in a 10-inch non-stick skillet until hot. Add potatoes and season with salt and pepper. Cover and cook over medium heat until brown on the bottom. Turn potatoes, breaking up clumps, and reduce heat slightly. Cook until brown on the other side; do not overbrown. Serve immediately.

Yield: 4 to 6 servings

Yukon Gold potatoes have a buttery yellow to golden colored skin and flesh. Their moist, almost succulent texture makes outstanding mashed potatoes.

~

To prevent leftover mushrooms from turning brown, refrigerate in a non-recycled paper bag.

Spicy Black-eyed Peas

It's Southern, after all!

3¼ cups frozen black-eyed peas	2 tablespoons low sodium soy sauce
2½ cups water	
4 slices bacon	2 teaspoons dry mustard
1¼ cups chopped onions	1 teaspoon chili powder
1¼ cups chopped bell peppers	1 teaspoon black pepper
2 (14½-ounce) cans no salt added stewed tomatoes, undrained and chopped	2 teaspoons liquid smoke
	¼ teaspoon cayenne pepper

Combine peas and water in a saucepan and bring to a boil. Reduce heat and cover. Simmer 20 minutes. Drain and set aside. Cook bacon until crisp. Remove bacon, reserving drippings in skillet. Crumble bacon and set aside. Add onions and bell peppers to drippings and sauté until crisp-tender. Add tomatoes, soy sauce, mustard, chili powder, pepper, liquid smoke, cayenne pepper, cooked peas and bacon. Bring to a boil. Reduce heat and cook 20 minutes or until peas are tender.

Yield: 6 to 8 servings

Spinach and Artichoke Casserole

Two favorites in one dish

Preheat oven to 350°.

3 (10-ounce) packages frozen chopped spinach	2 (3-ounce) packages cream cheese, softened
1 (14-ounce) can artichoke hearts, halved or quartered	Parmesan cheese to taste
1 small onion, minced	1 teaspoon lemon juice
1 stick margarine, melted	Garlic salt to taste (optional)
½ cup sour cream	1½ cups buttery cracker crumbs
	Melted butter

Cook and drain spinach. Line bottom of a greased 9x13x2-inch casserole dish with artichoke hearts. Sauté onions in margarine in a skillet. Add spinach, sour cream, cream cheese, Parmesan cheese, lemon juice and garlic salt. Spread mixture over artichoke hearts. Toss crumbs with melted butter and sprinkle over casserole. Top with more Parmesan cheese. Bake, uncovered, for 20 minutes or until bubbly.

Yield: 6 to 8 servings

Artichokes make wonderful table decorations, either used alone in a vegetable centerpiece, or as candleholders. Place a votive candle in the top of an artichoke by spiraling upper leaves open and inserting candle. After using, allow the artichoke to dry, then spray with gold or silver paint for the holidays.

~

Spinach Casserole

3 (10-ounce) packages chopped spinach
1 (8-ounce) container sour cream
1 envelope dry onion soup mix
Parmesan cheese or cheese of choice

Cook spinach and drain well. Combine spinach, sour cream and soup mix. Transfer to a baking dish. Sprinkle with cheese. Bake in preheated 350° oven for 20 to 25 minutes.

Yield: 4 to 6 servings

Baked Spinach with Creamed Vegetable Sauce

Elegant for a buffet

Preheat oven to 325°.

Soufflé

2	(10-ounce) packages frozen chopped spinach
½	cup breadcrumbs
½	teaspoon salt

⅛	teaspoon black pepper
½	cup milk
2	eggs, beaten
¾	cup slivered almonds
5	tablespoons butter, melted

Vegetable Sauce

4	tablespoons butter
⅓	cup diced onions
¼	cup all-purpose flour
2	cups milk

½	cup diced carrots, cooked
½	cup green peas, cooked
½	cup diced celery, cooked

Cook spinach per package directions. Drain. Combine spinach and remaining soufflé ingredients and place in a greased 1-quart round casserole dish. Bake for 45 to 60 minutes or until a knife inserted in the center comes out clean. Cool slightly before unmolding onto a serving platter.

To make sauce, melt butter in a saucepan. Add onions and cook until tender but not brown. Blend in flour. Gradually stir in milk. Cook, stirring constantly, until smooth and thickened. Add carrots, peas and celery and heat thoroughly. Pour over soufflé and serve.

Yield: 6 to 8 servings

Grilled Sweet Potatoes

"Baked" sweet potatoes on the grill

3	medium sweet potatoes
5	tablespoons butter

¼	cup brown sugar
1	tablespoon cinnamon

Halve potatoes lengthwise. Place each half on foil. Dot with butter. Combine brown sugar and cinnamon and sprinkle over potatoes. Wrap well. Grill 25 to 30 minutes, turning once.

Yield: 6 servings

Skillet Sweet Potatoes

Peel 2 pounds sweet potatoes; cut into ½-inch thick slices. In a 12-inch non-stick skillet over medium heat, melt 2 teaspoons butter or margarine. Add potato slices. Cover and cook 20 minutes, turning once, or until potatoes are golden and tender.

Serves 6.

~

"I have never forgotten the wonderful fried sweet potatoes my mother made me for breakfast every day."
Dan Magill, "Mr. Tennis", former UGA men's tennis coach and Tennis Hall of Famer, founder of UGA Bulldog Club.

Anita's Sweet Potato Casserole

It's Southern, after all!

Preheat oven to 350°.

Casserole

3	cups cooked and mashed sweet potatoes	1	tablespoon vanilla
1	cup sugar	2	tablespoon orange juice
1	(5-ounce) can evaporated milk	2	eggs
6	tablespoons butter, melted	½	teaspoon salt

Topping

½	cup brown sugar	1	stick butter
½	cup all-purpose flour	½	cup chopped pecans

Combine all casserole ingredients and pour into a greased 9x13-inch baking dish. Combine all topping ingredients and sprinkle over casserole. Bake for 45 minutes or until golden brown.

Yield: 6 to 8 servings

Sweet Potato Surprise

The surprise is apricots!

Preheat oven to 375°.

6	sweet potatoes, cooked and halved, or canned	1	teaspoon orange zest
1	cup brown sugar	1	(16-ounce) can apricot halves, drained, juice reserved
1½	tablespoons cornstarch	2	tablespoons butter
¼	teaspoon salt	½	cup pecan halves
⅛	teaspoon cinnamon	¼	cup orange juice

Place sweet potatoes in a greased 11x7-inch baking dish. Combine sugar, cornstarch, salt, cinnamon and orange zest in a saucepan. Stir in 1 cup reserved apricot syrup. Bring to a boil, stirring constantly, over medium heat. Cook 2 minutes. Add apricots, butter, pecans and orange juice. Pour mixture over sweet potatoes. Bake, uncovered, for 25 minutes.

Yield: 8 servings

Sweet potatoes and yams, though used interchangeably in print, are not the same at all. They are not even from the same plant species. The sweet potato is actually a root from the morning glory family. In the South, sweet potatoes are often called yams and canned sweet potatoes are frequently labeled as such. True yams, however, are seldom grown in the United States and would most likely be found in Latin American markets. The flesh of sweet potatoes can range from pale yellow to a rich, dark orange. Generally, the darker variety is sweeter and moister. This versatile tuber is good simply baked in its own skin and served with butter, just like a regular potato. But it can also be used for puddings, pies, cakes, breads, as a vegetable and even in ice cream.

Fresh Tomato Pie

Made ever so good with fresh tomatoes from the garden

Preheat oven to 325°.

1 (14½-ounce) can diced tomatoes	½ teaspoon seasoned salt
3 fresh tomatoes, chopped	½ teaspoon dried basil
1¼ cup herb stuffing mix, divided	1 (9-inch) deep-dish pie crust
1 medium onion, chopped	1 cup mayonnaise
	1 cup grated cheddar cheese

Combine tomatoes, ¾ cup stuffing mix, onions, seasoned salt and basil. Pour into pie crust. Mix mayonnaise, cheese and remaining ½ cup stuffing and spread over top of tomato mixture. Bake for 40 to 45 minutes.

Yield: 6 to 8 servings

Cheese Stuffed Tomatoes

Makes a beautiful addition to a meat platter or a buffet

Preheat oven to 350°.

6 medium tomatoes	½ teaspoon dried marjoram
2 cups grated Swiss cheese	1 teaspoon dry mustard
½ cup light cream	1½ teaspoons salt
2 egg yolks, lightly beaten	⅓ cup breadcrumbs
2 tablespoons chives	2 tablespoons butter, melted
3 tablespoons grated onion	

Halve tomatoes crosswise and scoop pulp into a bowl, reserving tomato shells. To pulp in bowl, add cheese, cream, egg yolks, chives, onions, marjoram, mustard and salt. Mix well. Spoon mixture into tomato shells. Toss breadcrumbs with butter and sprinkle over tomatoes. Place tomatoes in a greased 9x13x2-inch casserole dish. Bake, uncovered, for 25 minutes.

Yield: 6 servings

Chives: related to the onion and leek family. Slender, vivid green, hollow stems. Add near end of cooking time to retain their flavor.

Our long, hot days make growing tomatoes soooo easy. And grow them we do! Everything from sweet little cherry tomatoes to varieties so large it only takes one slice to cover a hamburger bun. There's just nothing better or more versatile. We use tomatoes in just about everything: soups, salads and sauces; jellies, jams and relishes; breads and beverages; in entrées and as sides. One of our favorite summer treats is a fresh tomato sandwich. You only need three basic ingredients: fresh, fresh sandwich bread, real mayonnaise and the biggest, juiciest tomato you can find. Just slather on the mayo, add the sliced tomato, salt and pepper to taste and there you have it: one of the best sandwiches you'll ever sink your teeth into.

Summertime Zucchini Tomato Casserole

Sensational together

Preheat oven to 350°.

4-5 zucchini, unpeeled and sliced lengthwise	6 slices American cheese
1 medium onion, thinly sliced	6-8 slices bacon, partially cooked and torn into pieces
2 medium tomatoes, thinly sliced	Parsley to taste
	Oregano to taste

In a 9x13-inch glass baking dish, layer zucchini, onions, tomatoes, cheese and bacon. Sprinkle with parsley and oregano. Bake for 35 minutes. Cut into squares and serve.

Yield: 6 to 8 servings

Note: To decrease fat in this dish, substitute reduced-fat cheese and cooked "Sizzlean" bacon. Microwave layered vegetables until tender, then add cheese, bacon, parsley and oregano. Bake at 350° until cheese melts.

Squash Casserole

"This recipe has been a favorite of both adults and children in our family for 3 generations."

Preheat oven to 350°.

4-6 medium yellow squash, sliced	2 eggs, lightly beaten, or 3 egg whites
1 medium onion, chopped	½ cup milk
4 tablespoons butter	8-10 saltine crackers, crushed, plus extra for topping
Salt and pepper to taste	
1 cup grated cheese	

Cook squash and onions until tender. Mash with a fork. Add butter, salt, pepper, cheese, eggs, milk and crackers. Mix well and transfer to a baking dish. Sprinkle a few extra crushed crackers over the top. Bake for 30 minutes or until edges turn brown.

Yield: 4 to 6 servings

Rice Stuffed Tomatoes

8 medium tomatoes
4 ounces long grain rice
1 large onion, chopped
1 large bell pepper, chopped
4 teaspoons butter
1 teaspoon salt
¼ teaspoon black pepper
Parmesan cheese

Halve tomatoes crosswise and scoop out and discard pulp, reserving tomato shells. Cook rice according to package directions. Sauté onions and bell peppers in butter. Add cooked rice, salt and pepper. Stuff mixture into tomato shells. Sprinkle with cheese. Bake in preheated 350° oven for 30 minutes.

Yield: 8 servings

~

Large zucchini tend to be pulpy and often bitter. Smaller ones are usually sweeter and more tender. Choose zucchini that have shiny, firm unblemished skin.

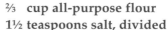

Italian Style Eggplant and Zucchini

Saucy and spicy

Preheat oven to 350°.

⅔ cup all-purpose flour
1½ teaspoons salt, divided
1 medium eggplant, peeled
    and cut into ¼-inch rounds
⅓ cup milk
2 tablespoons vegetable oil
2 medium zucchini, thinly sliced
1 medium onion, chopped

⅛ teaspoon red pepper
2 cups cottage cheese
2 eggs, beaten
½ cup dry breadcrumbs
8 ounces mozzarella cheese,
    diced
1 (15½-ounce) jar spaghetti
    sauce with mushrooms

Combine flour and 1 teaspoon salt; mix well. Dip eggplant slices in milk. Drain off excess and dredge in flour mixture. Heat oil in a skillet until hot. Add eggplant and cook until golden brown. Drain on paper towels and set aside; reserve drippings in skillet. Add zucchini and onions to skillet and sauté until crisp-tender. Stir in red pepper. Combine cottage cheese, eggs, and remaining ½ teaspoon salt in a small bowl. Mix well and set aside. Arrange half the eggplant in a greased 9x13-inch baking dish. Spoon half of zucchini mixture over eggplant. Top with half each of breadcrumbs, cottage cheese mixture and mozzarella cheese. Spread half of spaghetti sauce over all. Repeat layers. Bake for 60 minutes or until bubbly.

Yield: 6 to 8 servings

Summertime Succotash

So good!

1½ cups fresh corn
1 (10-ounce) package frozen
    baby lima beans
4 slices bacon

1 medium onion, chopped
1 tablespoon all-purpose flour
3-4 large fresh tomatoes, chopped,
    or 1 (16-ounce) can, undrained

Cook corn and lima beans in a small amount of boiling water until tender. Drain. Cook bacon until crisp. Remove from pan and crumble, reserving drippings in pan. Sauté onions in drippings until tender. Remove onions and add flour to pan. Stir until smooth. Cook 1 minute, stirring constantly. Add tomatoes, corn, lima beans, bacon and onions. Cook until heated.

Yield: 6 servings

Succotash: a traditional Southern dish made of lima beans, corn kernels and sometimes chopped red and green peppers.

"I was living in Miami, and I told a friend I wanted to go home, that I was tired of living away. He said, 'What's home?', and I said 'The South: if a man is what he eats, I'm pure Deep South.' After some of the places I've lived, Athens is a veritable banquet."

William U. Eiland,
Director,
Georgia Museum of Art

Easy Grilled Vegetables

Delicious accompaniment for grilled chicken

Use leftover grilled vegetables to make vegetable fajitas. Place vegetables and cheese in flour tortillas. Roll up and serve with salsa and sour cream.

~

Vegetable Marinade
¼ **cup olive or vegetable oil**
½ **cup apple cider**
2 teaspoons fines herbes
½ **teaspoon black pepper**

Combine all ingredients in a jar. Cover tightly and shake vigorously. Brush vegetables with marinade before and during grilling.

Yield: ¾ cup

~

Portobella mushrooms are as versatile as they are good to eat. They are so large and flavorful, they can be served as a main course or as a meat substitute. Offer grilled portobellas on a hamburger bun to the vegetarians in your family. Add slices of yellow squash, zucchini, eggplant and bell peppers to the grill and use on thick slices of coarse bread for fabulous grilled veggie sandwiches. Portobellas can also be sliced and used as a side dish, in quesadillas or over pasta.

	Mushrooms (oyster, button and shiitake), sliced	8	sun-dried tomatoes, cut into strips
2	yellow squash, sliced	2	tablespoons fresh oregano or basil
1	zucchini, sliced		
2	small red onions, cut into wedges	2	tablespoons capers
½	cup olive oil	2	tablespoons balsamic vinegar

Combine mushrooms, squash, zucchini and onions in a bowl or zip-top bag. Add oil and toss. Drain vegetables and transfer to a grilling basket or the surface of a grill. Grill over medium heat for 18 minutes. Transfer to a bowl and toss with tomatoes, oregano, capers and vinegar.

Yield: 3 to 4 servings

Grilled Portobella Mushrooms

The "new" hamburger

	Salt	6	cloves garlic, finely chopped
4-6	(4-inch diameter) portobella mushrooms	4-6	tablespoons olive oil
			Black pepper to taste

Dampen a paper towel and dip in salt. Use towel to clean mushrooms. Remove stems and set aside for another use. Combine garlic, oil and pepper in a zip-top bag. Add mushroom caps and seal. Marinate 60 minutes, turning occasionally. Remove mushrooms from marinade. Grill, stem-side down, 4 minutes. Turn and cook 4 minutes longer or until slightly charred on the outside and creamy and tender on the inside.

Yield: 4 to 6 servings

Portobella Mushroom: (por toh BEHL luh) An extremely large, dark brown mushroom with a dense meaty texture and flavor. Often grilled and used in a sandwich or cut into thick slices for a salad or entrée.

Cranberry Surprise

"Even men and children who don't like cranberry salad request this at Thanksgiving and Christmas and usually go back for seconds."

Preheat oven to 325°.

4	apples, peeled and quartered	2-3	tablespoons lemon juice
1	(16-ounce) package cranberries, rinsed	2	sticks margarine
1	cup granulated sugar	1¼	cups brown sugar
		2	cups oatmeal
		1	cup chopped pecans

Combine apples and cranberries in a 1-quart casserole dish. Sprinkle with granulated sugar and lemon juice. Melt margarine in a saucepan. Add brown sugar, oatmeal and pecans. Mix well and sprinkle over fruit; do not press down. Bake for 45 to 50 minutes, covering the first 25 minutes.

Yield: 8 servings

Note: Fresh cranberries are available in stores in the fall from about Halloween to Christmas, but they can be purchased ahead and frozen for use throughout the year. To use, partially thaw berries and add to your favorite recipe.

Deliciously Different Hot Baked Fruit

The name says it all!

Preheat oven to 350°.

½	pound pitted prunes, chopped	1	(16-ounce) can cherry pie filling
½	pound dried apricots	1½	cups water
1	(13-ounce) can pineapple chunks, undrained	¼	cup dry sherry
		⅓	cup slivered almonds, toasted

Place prunes, apricots and pineapple in a deep, 9-inch round casserole dish. Combine pie filling, water and sherry and pour into casserole dish. Mix well. Stir in almonds and cover. Bake for 1 hour, 10 minutes to 1 hour, 20 minutes.

Yield: 8 to 10 servings

Cranberry and Sausage Stuffed Apples

1 pound bulk sausage
1 onion, chopped
1 teaspoon dried sage
1 teaspoon dried thyme, crushed
1 cup cranberries
Salt and pepper to taste
½ cup fresh breadcrumbs
3 stalks celery, chopped
½ cup minced fresh parsley
8 Golden Delicious apples

Crumble sausage into a large skillet and cook over moderate heat. Stir in onions, sage, thyme and cranberries. Season with salt and pepper to taste. Cook, stirring until berries begin to pop. Stir in breadcrumbs, celery and parsley. Remove from heat. Cut a ½-inch slice off the top of each apple; reserve the top slices. Scoop out and chop apple meat. Add chopped apple to stuffing and mix. Stuff apples and replace tops. Arrange apples in a baking dish. Pour an inch of hot water into pan and cover with foil.

Bake in preheated 375° oven for 1½ hours.

Yield: 8 servings

Hot Pineapple Bake

Sweet, chunky and delicious

Preheat oven to 450°.

1 (20-ounce) can pineapple chunks, juice reserved	12 large marshmallows
	½ cup sugar
1 (8-ounce) package cream cheese, cut into small squares	2 tablespoons all-purpose flour
	1 egg
	½ cup grated cheddar cheese

Combine pineapple, cream cheese and marshmallows in a 9x13-inch baking dish. In a heavy skillet or double boiler, combine reserved juice, sugar, flour and egg. Cook over low heat until thickened. Pour over pineapple mixture. Top with cheddar cheese. Bake for 10 to 15 minutes.

Yield: 8 servings

Southern Fried Apples

It's Southern, after all!

4 tablespoons butter	½ cup sugar
Cooking apples, peeled and sliced	1 tablespoon lemon juice

Melt butter in a heavy skillet. Turn heat to medium-high and add apple slices, sugar and lemon juice. Check for browning and tenderness every 2 to 3 minutes. Turn carefully with a spatula. Cooking time should be no more than 10 to 12 minutes. Serve immediately.

Yield: varies with size of apples

Clara's Pickled Peaches

It's Southern, after all!

½ cup apple cider vinegar	1 teaspoon pickling spices
¼ cup water	4 cups drained, canned peach halves
1¼ cups sugar	

Combine vinegar, water, sugar and spices in a saucepan. Bring to a boil. Add peach halves. Cool slightly and transfer peaches and liquid to hot jars. Cover and cool jars. Refrigerate at least 2 weeks before serving.

Yield: 4 to 6 pints

Sautéed Pineapple Rings

Fresh pineapple slices
Sugar for dipping
2-3 tablespoons butter

Dip pineapple slices in sugar. Sauté in butter until light brown. Serve immediately.

~

Broiled Apple Rings

Wash and core large cooking apples. Cut into ¼-inch slices. Place on a broiler rack. Brush apple slices with a mixture of 1 part lemon juice to 3 parts melted butter. Broil 4 to 5 minutes or until slices begin to soften. Turn and brush other side with butter mixture. Broil 3 to 5 minutes longer.

~

Spiced Peaches

2 (16-ounce) cans peach halves, undrained
½ cup brandy
¼ teaspoon cinnamon

Combine all ingredients. Cook over medium heat until heated.

208

DESSERTS

Taylor Grady House

Bread Pudding with Whiskey Sauce and Chantilly Cream

Preheat oven to 350°.

Bread Pudding

1	loaf French bread	½	teaspoon salt	
¾	cup sugar	3	cups milk, scalded	
½	cup raisins	1	stick butter, melted	
½	teaspoon nutmeg	½	teaspoon vanilla	
1	teaspoon cinnamon	4	eggs, beaten	
½	teaspoon ground cloves	1	(15¼-ounce) can peaches, drained and chopped	

Whiskey Sauce

5	egg yolks	¼	cup whiskey	
¼	cup sugar	4	tablespoons butter, melted	
	Dash of ground cloves	¼	teaspoon vanilla	
		⅓	cup heavy cream	

Chantilly Cream

1	cup heavy cream	1	teaspoon brandy	
¼	cup sugar	1	teaspoon triple sec	
½	teaspoon vanilla	1½	tablespoons sour cream	

Tear bread into 1-inch cubes and place in a large mixing bowl. Add sugar, raisins, nutmeg, cinnamon, cloves and salt. Stir in milk. Add butter and mix well. Add vanilla, eggs and peaches. Pour into a greased baking pan. Bake for 45 minutes. Serve with Whiskey Sauce and Chantilly Cream.

To make sauce, combine yolks, sugar, cloves and whiskey in saucepan. Whisk over medium heat until mixture doubles and thickens, being careful not to burn bottom. Remove from heat and slowly add butter and vanilla. Gradually stir in cream.

To make cream, whip heavy cream and sugar until peaks form. Fold in vanilla, brandy, triple sec and sour cream with a spatula.

Yield: 8 servings

Harry Bissett's New Orleans Café

Exceptional dining with the ambiance of old New Orleans located across the street from the campus of the University of Georgia.

Georgia Peaches and Cream Cake

It's Southern, after all!

1 (18-ounce) box butter flavor cake mix	½ cup water
1½ cups granulated sugar	2 cups heavy cream
4 tablespoons cornstarch	2-3 tablespoons powdered sugar
4 cups chopped peaches	1 cup sour cream, divided
	Fresh sliced peaches

Prepare cake mix according to package instructions. Bake in two 8-inch round cake pans. Cool and cut each cake horizontally to make 4 circles. Meanwhile, combine granulated sugar and cornstarch in a saucepan. Add peaches and water. Heat and stir until sauce is smooth and thickened. Cool completely. Combine cream and powdered sugar in a medium mixing bowl. Beat until stiff peaks form. Place one cake circle on a serving platter. Spoon a third of peach filling over cake. Spread ⅓ cup sour cream over filling. Top with another cake layer. Repeat layers, ending with a cake layer. Frost cake with whipped cream. Garnish with peach slices. Refrigerate until ready to serve.

Yield: 16 servings

Heavy Cream: Creams are categorized according to the amount of milk fat they contain. Light cream contains 30 to 36 percent milk fat while heavy cream has a fat content of 36 to 40 percent.

Nowhere is the use of sugar more evident than in the South. We Southerners are passionate about desserts. We like our fruit pies and cobblers so rich you need a scoop of ice cream to balance the flavors. Our famous pralines, peanut brittle and divinity are so sweet they can literally make your teeth hurt. Why, there will likely be as many, if not more, desserts at a family reunion or potluck dinner than there are meats and vegetables. But like everyone else, we have become more health conscious and try to save the best for special occasions. Perhaps that's why we like to entertain so much; it gives us a good excuse to cook and eat those desserts we love so dearly.

All American Lemon Cake

The most "lemony" cake ever

Preheat oven to 350°.

Citrus zest is one of those ingredients you never seem to have when you need it. It's a good idea to grate the peel of lemons, limes and oranges when you have them on hand and freeze the zest for use later on. Use a vegetable peeler to remove the colored part of the peel. Do not remove the white layer, as it is bitter. Drop the peeled zest into a food processor. Add 1½ teaspoons of sugar per fruit. Pulse 2 to 3 times, then process for 1 minute. Transfer to a zip-top freezer bag and freeze for later use.

~

1 teaspoon zest = 2 tablespoons fresh juice

Cake
3 tablespoons fine breadcrumbs	2 sticks unsalted butter, softened
3 cups all-purpose flour	2 cups sugar
2 teaspoons baking powder	4 eggs
½ teaspoon salt	1¼ cups milk
	1 tablespoon lemon zest

Glaze
⅓ cup fresh lemon juice	4 tablespoons butter, melted
⅔ cup sugar	

Garnish
1 lemon, thinly sliced	Sugar

Coat a greased 12-cup Bundt or tube pan with breadcrumbs. Shake out excess crumbs. Combine flour, baking powder and salt in a medium bowl. In a large bowl, cream butter and sugar with an electric mixer on medium speed. Beat in eggs, one at a time, on low speed. Alternately, add flour mixture and milk, using one-third of flour mixture at a time. Beat after each addition only until blended. Stir in lemon zest. Pour batter into prepared pan. Level batter with a spatula while rotating pan. Bake for 1 hour, 15 minutes. Remove from oven and cool in pan 5 minutes. Invert onto a cooling rack or a serving platter.

To make glaze, combine lemon juice and sugar in a small saucepan. Heat until sugar dissolves. Add butter and mix well. Brush glaze over warm cake. Cake will absorb the glaze. Cool completely before serving.

To make garnish, cover lemon slices with sugar and place on a paper towel. Let stand 2 hours. Arrange garnish on cake.

Yield: 12 servings

Apple Pie Cake with Rum Butter Sauce

"A favorite dessert with our visitors from New Zealand"

Preheat oven to 350°.

Cake

1½ sticks butter, softened	2 tablespoons hot water
1 cup sugar	1 teaspoon vanilla
1 egg	3 cups peeled and diced
1 cup all-purpose flour	cooking apples
1 teaspoon salt	½ cup chopped pecans
1 teaspoon cinnamon	

Rum Butter Sauce

½ cup brown sugar	½ cup heavy cream
½ cup granulated sugar	1 tablespoon rum
4 tablespoons butter, softened	

Cream butter with an electric mixer on medium speed. Gradually add sugar and beat well. Beat in egg until blended. In a separate bowl, mix flour, salt and cinnamon. On low speed, beat dry ingredients into creamed mixture until smooth. Stir in hot water and vanilla. Fold in apples and pecans. Spoon batter into a greased and floured 9-inch pie pan. Bake for 45 minutes.

To make Rum Butter Sauce, combine sugars, butter and cream in a saucepan. Bring to a boil and cook 1 minute. Stir in rum. Cake may be served warm or cold, topped with ice cream and drizzled with Rum Butter Sauce.

Yield: 8 servings

Family Reunion at Memorial Park

Picture tables laden with food, kids romping on the grass, grown-ups swatting flies, and gallons of iced tea and lemonade waiting to be had. It is as American as it gets!

Menu

Southern Fried Chicken

Bourbon and Praline Ham à la Epting

Garden Green Beans

Squash Casserole

Best Ever Corn Pudding

Deviled Bacon and Eggs

Clara's Pickled Peaches

Angel Biscuits

Weaver D's Cornmeal Muffins

Magnolia's Fruit Cobbler

All American Lemon Cake

Iced Tea

Lemonade

Upside Down Apple Cake

A new twist on an old favorite

Preheat oven to 350°.

Topping

3 tablespoons butter or margarine, melted
⅓ cup chopped walnuts or pecans

⅓ cup brown sugar
¼ teaspoon cinnamon
2 medium Granny Smith apples, peeled

Batter

3½ cups baking mix
⅓ cup sugar
¾ teaspoon cinnamon

2 eggs
1 cup milk
⅓ cup vegetable oil

To make topping, pour butter into a 9-inch square cake pan. Tilt pan so butter evenly covers bottom surface. Combine walnuts, brown sugar and cinnamon and sprinkle evenly over butter. Cut apples into thin rings, then cut rings in half. Arrange apples over nut mixture.

To prepare the batter, combine baking mix, sugar and cinnamon in a bowl. In a small bowl, whisk together eggs, milk and oil. Stir egg mixture into dry ingredients until just moistened. Pour batter over apples. Bake for 35 to 40 minutes or until a toothpick inserted into the center comes out clean. Run a knife around the edges of pan to loosen the cake. Carefully invert the pan onto a serving platter. Serve warm with whipped cream or ice cream.

Yield: 12 servings

Variation for Pineapple Upside Down Cake

A true classic!

1 stick butter, melted
1 cup brown sugar
1 (20-ounce) can pineapple slices, drained

5 maraschino cherries, drained and halved
½ cup chopped nuts

Pour butter into a 9-inch square cake pan. Stir in brown sugar. Arrange pineapple slices in pan. Place a cherry half, round side down, in the center of each slice. Sprinkle nuts over top. Make batter and bake as directed for Upside Down Apple Cake.

Dee's Pineapple Layer Cake

So moist, it almost melts in your mouth

Preheat oven to 325°.

Cake

2	eggs	2	cups sifted all-purpose flour
2	cups sugar	1	heaping teaspoon baking soda
2	tablespoons oil	1	teaspoon salt
1	(20-ounce) can crushed pineapple, undrained	1	cup chopped nuts
		1	teaspoon vanilla

Icing

1	(8-ounce) package cream cheese	1	(16-ounce) box powdered sugar
1	stick butter or margarine	1	teaspoon vanilla

Cream eggs, sugar and oil. Mix in undrained pineapple. In a separate bowl, combine flour, baking soda and salt. Blend dry ingredients into pineapple mixture. Fold in nuts and vanilla. Pour batter into three greased and floured 8-inch round cake pans. Bake for 25 to 30 minutes.

To make icing, combine cream cheese and butter. Mix well. Beat in sugar and vanilla until smooth. Spread icing between cake layers and stack layers on a serving platter. Spread icing on outside of cake.

Yield: 16 servings

In years past, the pineapple was so beloved that on many Southern mansions, wooden versions were carved above the front door as a symbol of hospitality.

~

Selecting a ripe pineapple is like choosing a ripe melon. You look for certain indications of ripeness and hope for the best. In general, a small compact crown usually denotes the finest type of fruit. As neither skin or fruit color indicate ripeness, a dull sound when the finger is snapped against the side of the fruit, along with protruding "eyes" and a delicious aroma, are perhaps the most reliable tests for ripeness.

A Very Chocolate Chocolate Cake

Take a bow! They will think you spent hours in the kitchen.

Preheat oven to 350°.

1 (18.5-ounce) box devil's food cake mix	¾ cup vegetable oil
4 eggs, room temperature	1 (6-ounce) package semi-sweet chocolate chips
1 cup sour cream	Powdered sugar
1 cup Kahlúa	

Combine cake mix, eggs, sour cream, Kahlúa and oil with an electric mixer on low speed. Increase to medium speed and beat 2 to 3 minutes. Add chocolate chips and beat 3 minutes longer. Pour into a greased and lightly floured Bundt pan. Bake for 55 to 60 minutes. Remove from pan and sprinkle with powdered sugar. Serve with sweetened whipped cream or vanilla ice cream.

Yield: 12 to 16 servings

Sidebar

For a light, sweet topping on rich desserts, try this:

Whipped Milk Topping

Pour ½ cup evaporated milk or evaporated skim milk into a mixing bowl. Place in freezer for 20 to 30 minutes or until soft ice crystals form. Chill electric mixer beaters in freezer at the same time. Beat with electric mixer on high speed for 2 to 3 minutes or until soft peaks form. Add 2 teaspoons lemon juice, ½ teaspoon vanilla and ⅓ cup sifted powdered sugar. Serve immediately.

Yield: 2½ cups

~

"This recipe belonged to my aunt. She would always bring this cake when she came to visit. It is an old family recipe that she gave to me a long time ago. I have shared it with my girls and I still use it at Christmas time and on other special occassions."

Gwen Griffin, wife of John E. Griffin, Vice Chairman of the Athens Academy Board of Trustees.

Brown Sugar Pound Cake

This may become your favorite pound cake.

Preheat oven to 325°.

3 sticks butter, softened	½ teaspoon baking powder
1 (16-ounce) package plus 1 cup light brown sugar	1 cup milk
5 eggs	½ teaspoon maple flavoring
3 cups sifted cake flour	1 teaspoon vanilla
½ teaspoon salt	1 cup chopped pecans, optional

Cream butter. Gradually beat in sugar until light and fluffy. Add eggs, one at a time, beating after each addition. Sift together flour, salt and baking powder in a separate bowl. Mix dry ingredients alternately with milk, maple flavoring and vanilla into creamed mixture. Stir in pecans. Pour batter into a greased and floured 10-inch tube or Bundt pan. Bake for 1 hour, 30 minutes or until a toothpick inserted into the center comes out clean. Cool on a rack for 5 minutes. Remove from pan and cool completely on rack.

Yield: 12 to 16 servings

The Quintessential Fresh Coconut Layer Cake
It's Southern, after all!

Preheat oven to 350°.

Cake

2	sticks butter, softened
2	cups sugar, sifted
4	eggs
3	cups sifted cake flour

1	tablespoon baking powder
½	teaspoon salt
1	cup milk
2	teaspoons vanilla

Icing

¾	cup sugar
3	tablespoons water
⅓	cup light corn syrup
3	egg whites

1	teaspoon vanilla
	Juice and meat from 1 large fresh coconut, or 2 small (see sidebar)

Cream butter and sugar for 10 minutes. Add eggs, one at a time, beating well after each addition. Sift together flour, baking powder and salt. Beat dry ingredients alternately with milk into creamed mixture, starting and ending with dry ingredients. Stir in vanilla. Pour batter into three greased and floured 9-inch cake pans. Bake for 30 minutes or until cake pulls away form side of pans. Cool 5 to 10 minutes in pans before inverting onto a cooling rack.

To make icing, combine sugar, water and corn syrup in a saucepan. Cover and bring to a boil. Uncover and cook until syrup mixture spins a long thread. Remove from heat. Beat egg whites in a bowl until stiff peaks form. Continue beating while slowly adding syrup mixture. Icing should hold stiff peaks. Stir in vanilla. Place a cake layer on a serving platter. Gently prick holes in top with a toothpick. Carefully drizzle about ⅓ cup coconut juice over the top. Spread icing over cake layer and sprinkle with coconut. Repeat layers and top with final cake layer. Spread icing on top and sides of cake. Cover entire cake with coconut. Carefully cover and refrigerate 24 to 48 hours. Serve at room temperature.

Yield: 16 servings

When selecting a coconut, shake it. A sloshing sound indicates the nut is fresh, and you can count on having some juice inside. To get to the juice and meat, use a hammer and a large nail to make holes in 2 of the 3 eyes of the coconut. (Two eyes are soft, 1 is very hard.) Drain coconut juice and save. Place coconut in a 200° oven until the shell cracks. Do not allow coconut to cook. Using a hammer and a sharp knife, finish cracking the shell. Remove shell and the brown peel from the white meat. Grate meat by hand, or process in a food processor along with a small amount of juice. Add any resulting juice from grating process to reserved juice.

Cecilia's Jelly Roll

Compliments of Cecilia Villaveces — Athens' premier cake baker

Good cooks know that the batter is the key to a good cake. Always let butter, cream cheese and eggs reach room temperature before using. Shortening should be soft so that it resembles whipped cream when beaten with sugar. Instead of adding flavorings last, try adding to the creamed butter and sugar. The batter absorbs the flavoring more readily this way.

Preheat oven to 350°.

⅔	cup all-purpose flour	3	tablespoons granulated sugar
3	tablespoons cornstarch		Powdered sugar
1	teaspoon baking powder		Custard or strawberries for
½	teaspoon salt		filling
8	eggs, separated		Whipped cream for topping

Line a 13x19-inch jelly-roll pan with greased wax paper. Sift together flour, cornstarch, baking powder and salt. In a separate bowl, beat egg whites until peaks form. Add egg yolks and beat 1 minute. Add sugar and beat 1 minute longer. Fold in flour mixture, a little at a time, until thoroughly combined. Pour batter into jelly-roll pan. Bake for 8 minutes. Place a damp cheesecloth on a table. Sprinkle with powdered sugar. Invert hot cake onto cheesecloth, remove wax paper, and let stand for a few minutes. Roll warm cake and cloth starting with the narrow end. Cool. Unroll and spread custard or strawberries over cake. Roll cake without towel and place on a serving platter. Cover with whipped cream and cut into 1-inch slices.

Custard for Jelly Roll

2	cups milk, divided	3	tablespoons cornstarch
¼	cup sugar	2	eggs
1	teaspoon vanilla	2	egg yolks

Combine 1½ cups milk, sugar and vanilla in a saucepan. Bring to a boil. Blend cornstarch, eggs, egg yolks and remaining ½ cup milk in a bowl. Quickly stir egg mixture into boiling mixture. Bring to a boil and remove from heat. Pour mixture into a pan and cover to prevent a film from forming on top. Refrigerate until ready to use.

Yield: 12 servings

Ambrosia

*A traditional Southern dessert that has been the
highlight of holiday dinners for generations.*

6	medium oranges, peeled and sectioned (see sidebar)
2	tablespoons sugar

Meat of 1 small coconut, or
1¼ cups frozen, flaked,
thawed

Sprinkle orange sections with sugar. Stir to mix. Place half of the sections
in a clear glass serving bowl. Cover with half of the coconut. Add
remaining orange sections and top with remaining coconut. Cover and
chill.

Yield: 6 to 8 servings

**Variation: If desired, toss all ingredients together instead of layering.
This recipe works well as a side dish, too.**

Mom's Chocolate Trifle

A big hit every time.

Preheat oven to 350°.

1	(19.8-ounce) box fudge brownie mix
½	cup Kahlúa or other coffee-flavored liqueur
3	(3.9-ounce) packages instant chocolate pudding mix

1 (12-ounce) container frozen
whipped topping, thawed
6 (1.4-ounce) toffee-flavored
candy bars, crushed

Prepare brownie mix and bake following package directions in a 9x13-inch
pan. When done, prick top of warm brownies at 1-inch intervals using a
fork; drizzle with liqueur. Let cool and crumble.

Prepare pudding mix folowing package directions. Sprinkle ⅓ of crumbled
brownies in the bottom of a 3-quart trifle dish or deep glass bowl that has
straight sides. Top with ⅓ of pudding, whipped topping and crushed candy
bars. Repeat layers twice, ending with candy. Chill 8 hours.

Yield: 16 to 18 servings

**Note: 4 tablespoons strong brewed coffee mixed with 1 teaspoon
sugar may be substituted for liqueur. For younger children,
chocolate syrup may also be substituted.**

*To section oranges,
use a sharp knife to
cut away peel. Cut
deep enough to
remove the white
membrane that covers
the pulp. Remove
sections from orange
by cutting toward the
center of the orange
along the membranes
that separate the
sections. After two or
three sections are
gently removed, the
membranes should
easily peel back,
allowing a section to
be removed by cutting
from the center out
along the membrane.*

~

**"Lamar loved his
mother's custard and
ambrosia better than
anything, and she
always served it at
Thanksgiving and
Christmas."**

*Annie Laurie Dodd,
wife of Lamar Dodd,
Regent's Professor of
Art at the University
of Georgia.*

Bavarian Cheesecake

Perfect when you need to serve a lot of people

To dress up a plain cheesecake, arrange nectarine wedges and fresh blueberries or raspberries in a decorative pattern over the top. Make an orange sauce to seal and glaze the fruit. Heat 2 cups orange juice in a saucepan. Add sugar and almond extract to taste. Thicken with cornstarch and pour over the top of the cheesecake. Garnish with mint leaves and fresh fruit around the base.

Crust

3	cups finely crushed vanilla wafers	3	tablespoons sugar
		1½	teaspoons cinnamon
1	stick butter or margarine, melted	¾	teaspoon nutmeg

Filling

3	(8-ounce) packages cream cheese, softened	3	eggs
		1	tablespoon fresh lemon juice
1	cup sugar	1	teaspoon lemon zest
		½	teaspoon vanilla

Topping

2	cups sour cream	3	tablespoons sugar
		1	teaspoon vanilla

To make crust, combine all ingredients and blend thoroughly. Press firmly and evenly into the bottom and up the sides of a greased 8-inch springform pan or two 8-inch cake pans. Chill 30 minutes.

To prepare filling, beat cream cheese and sugar together until light and fluffy. Add eggs, one at a time, beating well after each addition. Blend in lemon juice, zest and vanilla. Pour into chilled crust. Bake in pre-heated 375° oven for 45 minutes if using a springform pan, 30 minutes if using cake pans. Remove from oven and cool at room temperature for 30 minutes. Combine sour cream, sugar and vanilla for a topping. Spread carefully over cooled cake. Bake in preheated 500° oven for 10 minutes. Cool. Refrigerate overnight before serving.

Yield: 12 to 16 servings

Tiramisu

For when you really want to impress

Tiramisu

6 egg yolks
1¼ cups sugar
1¼ cups mascarpone cheese
1¾ cups heavy cream
2 (3-ounce) packages
   ladyfingers

⅓ cup coffee liqueur or
   Brandied Espresso
   Sweetened Whipped Cream
   Unsweetened cocoa or grated
   semi-sweet chocolate

Brandied Espresso

⅓ cup hot water
2 teaspoons instant coffee

1 teaspoon brandy

Sweetened Whipped Cream

½ cup heavy cream
1 tablespoon powdered sugar

¼ teaspoon vanilla

Beat egg yolks and sugar in a small mixing bowl for 1 minute or until thick and lemon-colored. Place on top of a double boiler over boiling water. Reduce heat to low and cook 8 to 10 minutes, stirring constantly. Remove from heat and beat in cheese. Whip cream in a separate bowl until stiff peaks form. Fold cream into egg mixture and set aside. Line bottom and sides of a 3-quart bowl or soufflé dish with ladyfinger halves, split sides up. Brush with coffee liqueur and spoon half of cream mixture over top. Repeat ladyfinger, liqueur and cream layers. Garnish with Sweetened Whipped Cream and cocoa. Cover and refrigerate several hours or overnight. If using Brandied Espresso, prepare by combining hot water and coffee in a small bowl. Stir until dissolved. Blend in brandy. To make Sweetened Whipped Cream, beat cream, sugar and vanilla until stiff peaks form.

Yield: 10 to 12 servings

Mascarpone Cheese: (mas kar POHN, mas kar POHN nay) A buttery-rich Italian cheese made from cow's milk. Ivory-colored, soft and delicate, it ranges in texture from light clotted cream to that of soft butter. Can be blended with other flavors or sweetened with fruit.

For a lighter version of this dessert, try the following.

Sally Foster's Tiramisu

¼ cup coffee liqueur
¼ cup espresso
1 tablespoon dark rum, Marsala or brandy
8 ounces mascarpone cheese
8 ounces fat-free ricotta cheese
¾ cup sugar
1 teaspoon almond or vanilla extract
8 ounces reduced-fat frozen whipped topping, thawed
1 fat-free sponge cake, or ladyfingers
Unsweetened cocoa

Combine liqueur, espresso and rum; set aside. In a separate bowl, mix cheeses, sugar, almond extract and whipped topping. Divide sponge cake into 3 pieces to be used as layers. Place a cake layer in a glass dish. Pour one-third of liqueur mixture over cake. Spread a third of cheese mixture on top. Repeat layers twice. Sprinkle cocoa over top layer. Refrigerate overnight.

Yield: 6 to 8 servings

Orange Creamy Custard
A light, refreshing dessert

"I have had this custard recipe since I began house-keeping in the 1950's. It was one of my mother's."
Lucy Tresp

~

Evaporated milk is nutritionally a better choice than whipping cream because it contains less fat.

Reconstitute evaporated milk by adding ½ cup water to ½ cup milk. Use this as a substitute for 1 cup milk in any recipe.

~

For a showier pecan pie, arrange pecan halves on top of filling. This makes for a nicer presentation, but it is more difficult to slice evenly.

2 egg yolks, beaten	Macaroons or ladyfingers,
⅓ cup sugar	broken (optional)
2 tablespoons cornstarch or all-	Whipped cream for topping
purpose flour	Semi-sweet or bittersweet
½ teaspoon salt	chocolate curls or chocolate
1 cup orange juice	syrup for garnish
1 cup cream or evaporated milk	

Combine egg yolks, sugar, cornstarch, salt, juice and cream in the top of a double boiler. Mix well. Cook and stir until thickened. If using, place broken macaroons in the bottom of a serving bowl or individual bowls. Pour custard filling on top. Refrigerate until cool, preferably overnight. When ready to serve, top with whipped cream. Garnish with chocolate curls or drizzle with chocolate syrup.

Yield: 5 to 6 servings

Note: This recipe is equally good with or without the macaroons or ladyfingers. If not used, it yields 5 servings.

Custard: A pudding-like dessert that is made with a sweetened mixture of eggs and milk. It can be either baked or boiled.

Never Fails Pecan Pie
It's Southern, after all!

Preheat oven to 350°.

3 eggs	1 teaspoon vanilla
1 cup sugar	¼ teaspoon salt
¾ cup light corn syrup	1 cup chopped pecans
1 stick margarine, melted	1 frozen pie crust, unbaked

Beat eggs in a medium mixing bowl. Beat in sugar, corn syrup and margarine. Stir in vanilla, salt and pecans. Mix well and pour into unbaked pie crust. Bake for about 50 minutes.

Yield: 8 servings

Spartans' Favorite Ice Cream Sandwich Dessert

Always a big hit at team dinners

1 (24-count) package ice cream sandwiches	1 (2-ounce) package chopped walnuts
2 (8-ounce) containers frozen whipped topping, thawed, divided	Caramel syrup
1 (8-ounce) package mini milk chocolate or semi-sweet chocolate chips	Maraschino cherries, sliced (optional)

Cover the bottom of a 9x13-inch glass baking dish with ice cream sandwiches. Spread with 8 ounces whipped topping. Add another layer of ice cream sandwiches, placing sandwiches in the opposite direction as the first layer. Spread remaining 8 ounces whipped topping over sandwiches. Sprinkle with chocolate chips and walnuts. Drizzle generously with caramel syrup. Garnish with cherry slices. Cover with foil and freeze at least 2 hours before serving. Cut with a sharp knife while still frozen.

Yield: 12 to 14 servings

Peggy's Easy Cherry Crunch

You won't believe something this tasty could be so easy.

Preheat oven to 350°.

1 (21-ounce) can cherry pie filling	1 stick butter or margarine, melted
1 teaspoon lemon juice	½ cup chopped nuts
1 (18-ounce) box white cake mix	Vanilla ice cream

Spread pie filling on the bottom of a 9-inch square pan. Sprinkle with lemon juice. Combine cake mix, butter and nuts. Sprinkle mixture over pie filling. Bake for 40 to 50 minutes. Serve warm with ice cream.

Yield: 9 servings

Note: Any type of fruit pie filling will work in this recipe.

No Southern cookbook would be complete without mention of two traditional summertime favorites: watermelon and homemade ice cream. Whether you prefer red or yellow meat, chilled or hot, the best way to eat watermelon is outside under a tall spreading tree. Set up a small table and cover it with plastic or newspapers. Cut the watermelon into slices. Pass the salt shaker and enjoy every sticky, sweet, juicy bite.

Homemade ice cream is best made the old time way in a hand-cranked machine, but admittedly, an electric one works just as well. The hardest part of making homemade ice cream is waiting for it to be ready. At just the right moment, the churn must be stopped, iced down, and left to season for a while. Then magically, the top is removed and cupfuls of delicious, rich, cold cream are dipped out. But be careful—too much of the cold stuff at first can give you one heck of an ice cream headache!

Seafoam Meringue

Mix 1 tablespoon cornstarch, 2 tablespoons sugar and ½ cup water in a saucepan. Cook until clear; set aside. In a mixing bowl, beat 3 egg whites and a dash of salt until stiff peaks form. Add cornstarch mixture and beat until creamy. Gradually mix in 6 tablespoons sugar, beating until creamy. Spread on pie and bake at 325° for 30 minutes or until golden brown.

~

Marshmallow Creme Meringue

In a small mixing bowl, beat 3 egg whites and a dash of salt until soft peaks form. Gradually beat in 7 ounces marshmallow creme until stiff peaks form. Spread over a cooled pie, sealing to edge of crust. Bake at 350° for 12 to 15 minutes.

Incredible Strawberry Ice Cream Pie

Very similar to the delicious strawberry ice cream pie served at the Georgia Center for Continuing Education at UGA

Preheat oven to 350°.

Crust and Filling

¼ cup egg whites	1 cup flaked coconut
½ cup sugar	¼ cup finely chopped almonds
Dash of salt	1 quart strawberry ice cream, softened

Meringue

½ cup egg whites	
1 cup sugar	Fresh or frozen strawberries, sweetened to taste

To make crust, beat egg whites, sugar and salt until stiff. Fold in coconut and almonds. Spoon into a pie pan and shape to form a crust. Bake for 8 to 10 minutes. Cool and freeze overnight. Fill frozen crust with ice cream and return to freezer.

When ice cream hardens, prepare meringue by beating egg whites and sugar until soft peaks form. Spread meringue over ice cream. Bake in preheated 425° oven for 5 minutes or until meringue is lightly browned. Immediately return pie to freezer until ready to serve. Serve with strawberries spooned over the top.

Yield: 8 servings

Meringue: A mixture of stiffly beaten egg whites and sugar that is baked until lightly browned. Used as a topping for pies and other desserts.

Frozen Almond Cream
with Rich Almond Sauce
A fabulous Latin American dessert

Frozen Cream
4	ounces blanched almonds	⅔	cup heavy cream
½	cup sugar, divided		Pinch of salt
1	cup egg substitute	½	teaspoon vanilla

Rich Almond Sauce
8	ounces blanched almonds	½	cup honey
1	cup sugar	1	teaspoon lemon zest
1	cup water	½	teaspoon cinnamon
		4	egg yolks

To make cream, bake almonds on a baking sheet at 350° for 3 to 4 minutes or until toasted a golden brown. Cool and transfer to a food processor or blender. Add ¼ cup sugar and grind as fine as possible. Beat egg substitute until frothy, then beat in remaining ¼ cup sugar. Continue beating until stiff but not dry. In a separate bowl, whip cream, salt and vanilla. Stir in all but 2 tablespoons of almond mixture. Fold in beaten egg substitute. Sprinkle reserved 2 tablespoons almond mixture into a greased 9x5-inch loaf pan. Pour egg/cream mixture into pan. Cover with foil and freeze. To serve, dip pan in hot water to loosen cream from pan. Invert onto a serving plate. Cut into slices and top with Rich Almond Sauce.

To make sauce, grind almonds and sugar in a food processor or blender until as fine as possible. Transfer to a saucepan and add water, honey, zest and cinnamon. Bring to a boil. Reduce to a simmer and cook, stirring frequently, 15 minutes or until thickened. Cool slightly. Whisk egg yolks in a small bowl. Gradually whisk in a few tablespoons of the almond mixture. Stir this back into almond mixture in saucepan. Cook over medium-high heat, stirring constantly, until mixture begins to bubble. Cool, stirring occasionally. Sauce will be the consistency of a thick custard; add water, if necessary, to thin. Serve at room temperature.

Yield: 8 servings

Note: Young children, pregnant women, the elderly and anyone with immune disorders should avoid eating raw egg.

For a simple but unique centerpiece, fill a large glass container with oranges, lemons or limes or a combination of these. Cover with water, and add long stemmed cut flowers in complementary colors.

~

A grouping of objects of similar colors or materials makes an interesting centerpiece for a table. For example, group a varied collection of blue and white vases or silver containers together on a tray or mirror and fill with flowers or greenery. Or fill small individual containers with flowers and set at each place setting.

Special Occasion Key Lime Pie

Good anytime

Crust

4   tablespoons margarine, melted
1   cup chocolate sandwich cookie crumbs

3   tablespoons sugar

Filling

1   (14-ounce) can sweetened condensed milk

2   egg yolks
½   cup fresh or bottled key lime juice
1   tablespoon lime zest

Topping

1   cup heavy cream
2   tablespoons sugar
1   tablespoon dark rum or bourbon

Chocolate shavings for garnish

To make chocolate curls for garnishes, wrap a block of chocolate in paper towels so the heat from your hand doesn't melt the chocolate. Hold a vegetable peeler against the upper edge of the chocolate at the end farthest away. Draw the blade slowly toward you. The chocolate should fall off in thin curling strips.

To make crust, combine all ingredients and press into a pie pan.

Prepare filling by mixing all ingredients together. Pour into crust and refrigerate until set.

To make topping, beat cream and sugar on high speed. Add rum and beat until peaks form. Spoon topping over individual pieces of pie and garnish with chocolate shavings.

Yield: 6 to 8 servings

Key Lime: A small, round, yellow-green lime grown in South Florida.

Black Bottom Pie

"A family Christmas Eve dessert since my childhood."

Preheat oven to 300°.

Crust
25 gingersnap cookies, crushed
5 tablespoons butter, melted

Filling
1¼ cups milk
2 eggs, well beaten
½ cup sugar
1 tablespoon cornstarch
1 ounce bitter chocolate, melted

1 teaspoon vanilla
1 tablespoon light rum
¾ cup heavy cream
½ ounce bitter chocolate, shaved or grated, for garnish

Combine cookie crumbs and butter and press evenly into a 9-inch pie pan. Bake for 10 minutes. Cool.

To make filling, scald milk in a double boiler. Slowly add eggs and blend. Combine sugar and cornstarch and stir into egg mixture. Cook, stirring occasionally, for 10 minutes or until custard coats a spoon. Transfer one-third of custard to a bowl. Add melted chocolate to bowl and stir until cool. Mix in vanilla. Stir remaining custard in double boiler until cool to avoid lumping. Mix in rum. Whip cream until peaks form. Spoon chocolate custard into prepared crust. Add rum custard and level off top. Spread whipped cream over pie and sprinkle with shaved chocolate. Refrigerate until set, preferably overnight.

Yield: 6 to 8 servings

Gingersnap: A small, very crisp ginger cookie flavored with molasses.

Bitter Chocolate: Pure chocolate that has had nothing added to it. Also known as unsweetened chocolate.

Coconut Shortcake Crust

5 tablespoons butter or margarine
3 tablespoons sugar
1 egg yolk
1 cup sifted all-purpose flour
1 cup coconut

Cream butter and sugar. Add egg yolk and blend well. Mix in flour. Stir in coconut. Press mixture into a 9-inch pie pan. Chill 30 minutes. Bake in preheated 350° oven 25 to 30 minutes or until browned. Cool and fill with cream filling of choice.

Yield: 8 servings

Makes a wonderful crust for coconut cream pie.

Patrick's Favorite Chess Pie

Taste defies description

The surprising combination of cornmeal and vinegar produces a deliciously sweet dessert.

Preheat oven to 300°.

2	eggs	1	tablespoon vinegar
1	cup sugar	1	tablespoon vanilla
1	tablespoon cornmeal	1	(9-inch) frozen pie crust,
1	stick butter or margarine		thawed

Beat eggs. Mix in sugar and cornmeal. Brown butter slightly over medium heat; add to egg mixture. Add vinegar and vanilla and mix well. Pour mixture into pie crust. Bake for 35 to 40 minutes or until center is firm.

Yield: 8 servings

Sour Cream Apple Pie

"Really easy and really good."

Preheat oven to 400°.

Pie

2	tablespoons all-purpose flour	1	egg, beaten
¼	teaspoon salt	1	cup sour cream
¾	cup sugar	1	teaspoon vanilla
¼	teaspoon nutmeg	3	cups peeled and sliced apples
		1	pie crust, unbaked

Topping

⅓	cup sugar	2	teaspoons cinnamon
⅓	cup all-purpose flour	2	tablespoons butter, softened

Combine flour, salt, sugar, nutmeg, egg, sour cream, vanilla and apples. Pour into unbaked pie crust. Bake for 15 minutes. Reduce heat to 350° and cook 30 minutes longer. To make topping, combine all ingredients and mix well until crumbly. Sprinkle over hot pie. Bake 10 minutes more.

Yield: 8 servings

Variation: For added crunch, add ¼ cup chopped pecans to topping mixture.

Low Country Sweet Potato Pie
with White Chocolate and Bourbon Sauce

Sweet potato pie never tasted so good!

Preheat oven to 350°.

Pie

1½ pounds sweet potatoes,
   baked
1¼ cups plus 3 tablespoons light
   brown sugar, divided
1   egg
¼   cup milk

½   teaspoon cinnamon
¼   teaspoon nutmeg
1   tablespoon vanilla
1   cup white chocolate chips or
    chunks
1   (10-inch) deep dish pie crust

Bourbon Sauce

2   sticks butter, diced
1   cup plus 2 tablespoons
    brown sugar

½   cup heavy cream
¼   cup bourbon
    Whipped cream

Cool, peel and mash sweet potatoes. Measure 2½ cups potatoes into a mixing bowl. Add 1¼ cups brown sugar and mix until smooth. Blend in egg. Add milk, cinnamon, nutmeg and vanilla. Mix well. Fold in chocolate. Pour filling into crust. Sprinkle remaining 3 tablespoons brown sugar over filling. Place on a baking sheet on the bottom rack of the oven. Bake for 20 minutes. Move baking sheet with pie to the middle rack and bake 30 to 40 minutes or until crust is golden and filling is slightly puffed.

To make sauce, melt butter in a saucepan over medium heat. Add sugar and stir until completely dissolved. Slowly whisk in cream and then bourbon. Use immediately or store for up to one week in the refrigerator. To serve, place 2 to 3 tablespoons Bourbon Sauce on an individual plate. Top with a slice of pie. Top with whipped cream.

Yield: 8 servings

Powdered sugar is sugar that has been processed to a very fine consistency. The number of X's indicates the degree of fineness: 4X is fine, 6X is very fine, 10X is extremely fine. Measure powdered sugar like flour. Sift first, add to a measuring cup being careful not to pack down and level off with a spatula.

"My mother made the best fresh whipped cream ever. She would make a bowl just for me."

Coach Bill Hartman, University of Georgia football letterman, former kicking coach of the Georgia Bulldogs, National Football Foundation Hall of Famer

Buckhead Diner's Famous
White Chocolate-Banana Cream Pie

A specialty of the Buckhead Diner in Atlanta, Georgia

"My favorite food group is puddings. Bread and rice puddings like the ones I recall from boyhood Depression days are infrequently found or matched today. Another favorite is a seasonal, chilled liver pudding my dad made from his mother's recipe. At the top of the list is Betty's heavenly banana pudding, set apart not just by the best fruit, wafers and meringue, but by a carefully prepared custard, lovingly — to paraphrase James Bond—stirred, not shaken. The gods should be so lucky as to have some."

—Bill Simpson,
a local public relations professional whose wife, Betty, is a former teacher at Athens Academy.

1	(4-ounce) bar white chocolate, finely chopped, divided	2	tablespoons white crème de cacao liqueur
1	cup milk	2	tablespoons crème de banane liqueur
½	vanilla bean		
3	tablespoons sugar	2-3	bananas, sliced
2	tablespoons cornstarch	3	tablespoons lemon juice
3	egg yolks, beaten	1	(9-inch) pie crust, baked
1	tablespoon butter or margarine		Unsweetened cocoa and fresh strawberries for garnish
1	cup heavy cream		

Place half of white chocolate in the top of a double boiler over boiling water. Cook until melted, stirring often. Pour onto a foil-lined baking sheet. Let stand at room temperature until chocolate cools and feels slightly tacky. (If chocolate is too hard, curls will break; if too soft, chocolate will not curl.) Pull a cheese cutter across chocolate until a curl forms. Repeat until all chocolate is curled. Refrigerate curls. Combine milk and vanilla bean in a small saucepan. Bring to a boil. Discard vanilla bean; set milk aside. Combine sugar, cornstarch and egg yolks in a heavy saucepan. Gradually stir in hot milk. Bring to a boil over medium heat, stirring constantly. Boil 1 minute. Remove from heat and add butter and remaining white chocolate. Stir until chocolate melts. Place plastic wrap directly on surface of chocolate mixture and cool. Beat cream until soft peaks form. Fold cream into chocolate mixture. Stir in liqueurs. Coat banana slices with lemon juice; drain. Pat slices dry with paper towels. Gently stir slices into chocolate mixture. Spoon into baked pie crust. Top with chocolate curls. Dust lightly with cocoa and garnish with strawberries. Refrigerate until ready to serve.

Yield: 8 servings

Crème de cacao: A dark chocolate flavored liqueur with a hint of vanilla. White crème de cacao is a white form of the same liqueur.

Crème de banane: A sweet liqueur with a full ripe banana taste.

Georgia Peach Delight Pie

It's Southern, after all!

Preheat oven to 350°.

2 cups sliced fresh peaches	1 stick butter, softened
1 9-inch pie crust, unbaked	3 tablespoons all-purpose flour
1 cup plus 6 tablespoons sugar, divided	3 eggs, separated

Spread peach slices evenly over pie crust. Set aside. Combine 1 cup sugar, butter, flour and egg yolks in a bowl. Beat until smooth. Spread mixture over peaches. Bake for 35 to 40 minutes or until brown and firm. If necessary, cover lightly with foil during final 10 minutes of baking to prevent overbrowning. Beat egg whites until soft peaks form. Add remaining 6 tablespoons sugar and beat until stiff peaks form. Spread meringue over hot pie. Bake at 400° for 10 minutes or until lightly browned.

Yield: 6 to 8 servings

Everybody's Favorite Lemon Pie

"We always ask Elizabeth to bring this pie to every covered dish function." Louise Simpson

Preheat oven to 300°.

1 cup sugar, divided	1 tablespoon butter or margarine, melted
3 tablespoons cornstarch	1 tablespoon lemon flavoring
4 eggs, separated	1 (9-inch) deep-dish pie crust, baked
Juice of 2 large lemons	
Pinch of salt	
1 cup boiling water	

Combine ¾ cup sugar and cornstarch. Add egg yolks and cream thoroughly. Add lemon juice and salt and mix well. Set aside. Add boiling water and butter to the top of a double boiler. Stir in creamed mixture and cook, stirring constantly, until thick. Beat egg whites, gradually adding remaining ¼ cup sugar until stiff peaks form. Fold lemon flavoring and half of egg white mixture into creamed mixture. Pour into baked pie crust. Top with remaining egg white mixture. Bake until top is lightly browned.

Yield: 8 servings

When making a two-crust pie, double the ingredients. Make the bottom crust larger than the top. Dampen the rim of the bottom crust before placing the top crust over it; then seal the two together. Be careful not to stretch crusts so they will stay together when baked.

~

To make a crispy pie crust, brush a little beaten egg over the crust and freeze for 10 minutes before baking.

~

To prevent overbrowning, cover the edges of the crust with foil before baking. The edges will still brown even though they are covered.

Magnolia's Fruit Cobbler

A Charleston favorite

Preheat oven to 350°.

Filling

6 cups fresh blueberries	1 tablespoon lemon juice
3 cups fresh strawberries	½ cup all-purpose flour
1½ cups sugar	½ teaspoon salt

Topping

1½ cups all-purpose flour	6 tablespoons cold unsalted
½ cup sugar	butter, diced
½ teaspoon baking powder	⅓ cup buttermilk
½ teaspoon salt	

Combine all filling ingredients in a bowl. Stir gently until berries are coated. Pour mixture into a 9x13-inch baking dish.

To make topping, combine flour, sugar, baking powder and salt. Stir to mix well. Cut butter into flour until mixture appears crumbly. Add buttermilk, a little at a time, until dough starts to hold together. The mixture should be very crumbly, but not sticky. It should not form into a firm ball, as a pie crust dough would. Sprinkle topping over filling. Bake for 60 minutes or until topping is a light golden color and the filling is bubbling up around the sides. Serve with ice cream or whipped topping.

Yield: 8 to 10 servings

Japanese Fruit Pie

An old Virginia favorite

Preheat oven to 350°.

2 sticks butter, melted	1 cup raisins
2 cups sugar	1 cup chopped nuts
4 eggs, beaten	1 (3½-ounce) can coconut
2 teaspoons vanilla	2 (9-inch) frozen pie crusts,
2 teaspoons vinegar	unbaked

Combine butter, sugar, eggs, vanilla and vinegar. Stir in raisins, nuts and coconut. Divide mixture between 2 pie crusts. Bake for 35 to 40 minutes. Serve topped with ice cream or whipped cream.

Yield: 16 servings

Mother's Fried Apple Pies

*"My dad's absolute favorite dessert. Mother packed one
in his lunchbox every day. He never tired of them."*

1½ cups sliced dried apples	2 cups all-purpose flour
2 cups water	½ teaspoon salt
1 tablespoon butter or margarine	½ cup shortening
½ cup sugar	¼-½ cup milk
¾ teaspoon cinnamon	Vegetable oil
½ teaspoon nutmeg	Sifted powdered sugar

Combine apples and water in a medium saucepan. Bring to a boil. Reduce
heat and simmer 30 minutes or until apples are soft and liquid evaporates.
Mash apples with a fork. Stir in butter, sugar, cinnamon and nutmeg. Set aside.
Combine flour and salt in a bowl. Cut in shortening until mixture is crumbly.
Sprinkle milk, 1 tablespoon at a time, over surface. Stir with a fork until dry
ingredients are moistened. Divide pastry dough into 6 portions. Roll each
portion to ⅛-inch thickness on a lightly floured surface. Cut each into a 6-inch
diameter circle. Divide apple mixture among circles, placing mixture on half
of each circle. Moisten edges with water and fold dough over apple mixture.
Press edges to seal, then crimp with a fork. Heat vegetable oil, ½-inch deep, in
a large heavy skillet over medium-high heat. Fry pies, turning once, until
golden brown. Drain on brown paper bags. Dust with powdered sugar.

Yield: 6 servings

Note: Any dried fruit will work in this recipe.

*Fried pies are
quintessentially
Southern, the
filling reflecting
regional specialties.
To enhance their
appearance, dust
lightly with
powdered sugar.*

~

*One pound dried
apples equals 3½
to 4 pounds fresh.*

~

*Store dried fruit
tightly covered in a
cool, dark place.
Under most
household conditions,
the shelf life is
several months.*

~

*Dried fruits are
easier to snip, slice or
chop if placed in the
freezer for a few
minutes. It also helps
to coat the knife or
kitchen shears with
nonstick cooking
spray.*

Too much flour used in mixing can make cookies tough. To reduce the amount of flour needed to roll dough out, chill dough in the refrigerator for ten minutes. Use powdered sugar rather than flour on rolling pin and cutting surface. For thin rolled cookies, roll dough directly onto a prepared cookie sheet. Cut out as desired and remove excess dough between cookies.

Best Cookies on Earth

"These cookies have never lasted longer than 12 waking hours at my house."

Preheat oven to 350°.

2 sticks butter or margarine	1½ cups oatmeal
¾ cup light brown sugar	1 cup semi-sweet chocolate chips
¾ cup granulated sugar	
1 egg	1 cup chopped dried cranberries
1 teaspoon vanilla	
1½ cups self-rising flour	1 (7.5-ounce) package toffee bits

Cream butter and sugars. Add egg and vanilla, mixing well. Blend in flour, oatmeal, chocolate chips, cranberries and toffee bits. Drop by teaspoonfuls onto a greased baking sheet. Bake for 10 minutes. Cool slightly before transferring from pan to a wire rack.

Yield: 3 dozen cookies

Boyfriend Cookies

If you don't have a boyfriend already, this is guaranteed to get you one!

Preheat oven to 375°.

1½ cups granulated sugar	1½ cups all-purpose flour
1½ cups brown sugar	1 teaspoon baking soda
2 sticks butter or margarine	3 cups oatmeal
1 cup peanut butter	1 (6-ounce) package semi-sweet chocolate chips
2 eggs	

Cream sugars, butter and peanut butter. Stir in eggs, one at a time. Add flour and baking soda. Mix well. Stir in oatmeal and chocolate chips. Drop by rounded teaspoonfuls onto an ungreased baking sheet. Bake for 10 minutes or until golden brown. Cool slightly before transferring from pan to a wire rack. Cool completely.

Yield: 9 dozen cookies

Macadamia Nut and White Chocolate Cookies

Just like Mrs. Field's

Preheat oven to 325°.

2 sticks butter	1 teaspoon baking soda
1½ cups granulated sugar	1 teaspoon salt
½ cup brown sugar	12 ounces white chocolate,
2 eggs	coarsely chopped
3¼ cups all-purpose flour	6 ounces macadamia nuts

Cream butter and sugars until light and fluffy. Add eggs and mix well. In a separate bowl, combine flour, baking soda and salt. Stir dry ingredients into creamed mixture. Blend well. Add extra flour, if needed, to make dough slightly stiff. Stir in chocolate and nuts. Drop by heaping teaspoonfuls, 2 inches apart, onto an ungreased baking sheet. Flatten slightly. Bake for 13 to 15 minutes. Cool slightly before transferring from pan to a wire rack.

Yield: 4 to 5 dozen cookies

Mary Jo's Cookies

Varied flavor — Great taste

Preheat oven to 375°.

2 sticks butter, softened	½ teaspoon baking powder
1 cup granulated sugar	1 teaspoon salt
1 cup brown sugar	2 cups corn flakes
2 eggs	2 cups oatmeal
1 teaspoon vanilla	1 cup chopped nuts
2 cups all-purpose flour	1 cup chopped dates
1 teaspoon baking soda	2 cups chocolate chips

Cream butter. Cream in sugars. Stir in eggs and vanilla until smooth. In a separate bowl, sift together flour, baking soda, baking powder and salt. Blend dry ingredients into creamed mixture. Stir in corn flakes, oatmeal, nuts, dates and chocolate chips. Mixture will be coarse. Roll into small balls and place on a greased baking sheet. Flatten with a fork. Bake for 10 minutes.

Yield: 80 cookies

By altering the ingredients in some recipes, you can dramatically change the texture and taste of the cookie. For a crispy, thin cookie, use an all-butter dough. The dough spreads as it cooks because butter melts faster than shortening. For a fatter, puffier cookie, use shortening as it keeps the dough from spreading. For a softer cookie, use only brown sugar as a sweetener. Combine brown sugar with granulated sugar for a crispier version.

Chocolate Chip Toffee Cookies

The toffee adds crunch as well as flavor.

Preheat oven to 375°.

2 (12-ounce) packages snack-
      size chocolate-covered
      toffee candy bars
2 (26.3-ounce) packages
      chocolate chip cookie mix

2 eggs
6 tablespoons water
⅔ cup vegetable oil
1 cup chopped pecans or
      walnuts

Chop candy bars in a food processor. Prepare cookie mix according to package directions, using eggs, water and oil as listed above. Fold in nuts and candy. Drop by rounded teaspoonfuls, about 3-inches apart, onto a greased baking sheet. Bake for 8 to 10 minutes.

Yield: 8 dozen cookies

Almond Macaroons

A true classic

Preheat oven to 325°.

3 egg whites
⅛ teaspoon cream of tartar
¼ teaspoon almond extract

1 cup sugar
1¾ cups ground almonds

Line 2 baking sheets with parchment paper. Beat egg whites and cream of tartar until soft peaks form. Beat in almond extract. Slowly add sugar, one spoonful at a time, beating about 10 minutes or until stiff and glossy. Fold in ground almonds in 2 batches. Drop by teaspoonfuls, 2 inches apart, onto prepared baking sheets. Bake for 10 to 15 minutes. Cool on a wire rack.

Yield: 5 dozen cookies

Note: Use a food processor to grind almonds.

Cream of Tartar: Added to candy and frosting mixtures for a creamier consistency; added to egg whites before beating to improve stability and volume.

Southerners are partial to pecans and are likely to use them in any recipe that calls for nuts. Though shelled pecans are readily available in most grocery stores, pecan trees are so plentiful that this versatile nut may be as close as the back yard. Cracking the nut and picking out the meat is time consuming but well worth the effort. Soaking whole nuts overnight in salty water will help to keep the fruit from breaking when shelled. Never store pecans at room temperature. They may be kept in the refrigerator for up to 3 months if shelled. For longer periods of time, freeze in freezer-safe containers or screw top glass jars.

Forgotten Cookies

These cookies melt in your mouth.

Preheat oven to 350°.

6 **egg whites**	1 **(6-ounce) bag semi-sweet**
½ **teaspoon cream of tartar**	**chocolate chips**
1½ **cups sugar**	1 **cup chopped pecans or**
	walnuts

Beat egg whites and cream of tartar using an electric mixer at high speed until foamy. Add sugar, 2 tablespoons at a time, beating constantly until sugar is dissolved. (To test, rub a little between your thumb and forefinger to see if all has dissolved.) Continue to beat until mixture is glossy and soft peaks form. Carefully fold in chocolate chips and pecans. Drop by rounded teaspoonfuls onto a baking sheet lined with parchment paper. Turn oven off. Immediately put baking sheets into oven and leave overnight or until dry and crisp.

Yield: 9 dozen cookies

Parchment Paper: A heavy, grease and moisture resistant paper commonly used to keep baked goods from sticking to pans.

No Bake Granola Bars

Great for team snacks and school parties

2½ **cups crispy rice cereal**	½ **cup light corn syrup**
2 **cups quick oats**	½ **cup peanut butter**
½ **cup raisins**	1 **teaspoon vanilla**
½ **cup brown sugar**	½ **cup milk chocolate chips**

Combine cereal, oats and raisins in a large bowl. In a small saucepan, bring brown sugar and corn syrup to a boil, stirring constantly over medium heat. Remove from heat and stir in peanut butter and vanilla. Pour peanut butter mixture over cereal mixture. Stir until coated. Let stand 10 minutes. Stir in chocolate chips. Press mixture into a 9x13-inch pan. Cool on a wire rack. Cut into bars when cool.

Yield: 3 dozen bars

Many recipes are difficult to prepare successfully in hot, humid weather, including divinity candy, seven minute icing and meringue-type cookies or desserts. These are best left for cooler days later in the year.

~

An 8x8x2-inch pan will yield 16 (2-inch square) bar cookies. A 9x13x2 pan will yield 32 to 40 bar cookies, depending on size desired.

Because chocolate contains cocoa butter, it may develop a gray film called "bloom" when stored at temperatures that fluctuate between hot and cold. This film, which is caused by the cocoa butter rising to the surface, does not affect the taste and may be eliminated by melting.

Cherry Logs
Very easy

Preheat oven to 325°.

Crust

1	cup all-purpose flour
1	stick butter, softened

3   tablespoons powdered sugar

Topping

2   eggs
1   cup sugar
¼   cup all-purpose flour
½   teaspoon baking powder
1   teaspoon vanilla

¾   cup chopped pecans
½   cup maraschino cherries, coarsely chopped
½   cup coconut

Combine flour, butter and powdered sugar to make a soft dough. Press evenly into an 8-inch square pan. Bake for 25 minutes. Combine all topping ingredients in a separate bowl. Mix well. Pour topping over baked crust and bake 25 minutes longer. Cool and cut into squares.

Yield: 16 squares

Cracker Candy
No one will believe these are saltines!

Preheat oven to 350°.

¼   (16-ounce) box saltine crackers (1 sleeve)
2   sticks butter
½   cup sugar

1   (12-ounce) bag chocolate chips
1   cup chopped pecans or walnuts

Line a jelly-roll pan with foil; grease the foil. Layer bottom of pan with crackers, sides touching. Combine butter and sugar in a saucepan. Bring to a boil and cook 3 minutes. Pour mixture over crackers. Bake for 10 to 12 minutes. Cool 2 minutes. Sprinkle chocolate chips over crackers. As chocolate melts, spread to cover. Sprinkle nuts on top. Refrigerate until cool. Break into bite-size pieces.

Yield: 10 servings

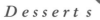

Rugelach

*This Eastern European pastry is often
served at Jewish holiday celebrations.*

Preheat oven to 350°.

Dough

1 cup sour cream	2 cups all-purpose flour
2 sticks butter, softened	

Nut Filling

⅓ cup sugar	½ cup chopped walnuts or
1 tablespoon cinnamon	pecans

Chocolate Filling

⅓ cup sugar	½ cup grated semi-sweet
1 tablespoon cinnamon	chocolate

Fruit Fillings

Raspberry jam or preserves	Apricot jam or preserves

Combine sour cream, butter and flour to make a dough; do not over-work. Wrap in plastic and refrigerate at least 2 hours or overnight.

To prepare nut filling, combine sugar, cinnamon and walnuts. To make chocolate filling, mix together sugar, cinnamon and chocolate. For the fruit fillings, use the jams straight from the jar.

To assemble, roll chilled dough into a ball. Cut into 4 sections. Use one section at a time, refrigerating others until needed. Roll dough into a 10-inch circle. Spread one of the fillings on the circle and cut pizza-style into 16 narrow wedges. Starting at the widest end, roll up each wedge like a crescent roll. Place on an ungreased baking sheet. Repeat with remaining dough and fillings. Bake for 25 minutes or until golden.

Yield: 64 rugelach

If you forget to take the butter out of the refrigerator to soften, grate it with a hand grater, using the tablespoon markings on the wrapper as your measurement guide.

~

Cloyde's Tea Cakes

1 egg
1 cup sugar
½ cup vegetable shortening
¼ cup buttermilk
1 teaspoon baking soda
1 teaspoon vanilla or lemon flavored extract

Combine all ingredients. Roll out dough until very thin. Cut with a cookie cutter and place on an ungreased baking sheet. Bake in pre-heated 400° oven for 9 minutes. Remove from oven and immediately loosen with a spatula.

Yield: 4 dozen

Creamy Southern Pralines

It's Southern, after all!

1½ cups granulated sugar	½ stick butter or margarine
1½ cups brown sugar	2 cups pecan halves
1 cup evaporated milk	1 teaspoon vanilla

Combine sugars and milk in a heavy skillet or Dutch oven. Bring to a boil, stirring constantly. Cook over medium heat, stirring frequently, until mixture reaches 228° on a candy thermometer. Add butter and pecans and continue cooking, stirring constantly, until mixture reaches 236° (soft-ball stage). Remove from heat and add vanilla. Beat vigorously with a wooden spoon until mixture starts to thicken. Quickly drop by rounded tablespoonfuls onto greased wax paper. Cool until firm.

Yield: 3 dozen

Variations: Add ½ cup semi-sweet chocolate chips and ¼ cup creamy peanut butter before cooking. For a uniquely different taste, substitute 1½ tablespoons instant coffee granules for the peanut butter.

Chocolate Covered Peppermint Patties

Just like York's!

1 (16-ounce) box powdered sugar	½ teaspoon vanilla
	¼ cup evaporated milk
3 tablespoons butter or margarine, softened	1 (12-ounce) package semi-sweet chocolate chips
2-3 teaspoons peppermint extract	2 tablespoons shortening

Combine sugar, butter, extract and vanilla. Add milk and mix well. Roll into 1-inch balls and place on a wax paper-lined baking sheet. Refrigerate 20 minutes. Flatten with the bottom of a glass to ¼-inch thick. Chill 30 minutes longer. In a double boiler or microwave, melt chocolate chips and shortening. Dip patties in chocolate mixture and place on wax paper or a rack until chocolate hardens.

Yield: 5 dozen

"My grandmother enjoyed making homemade candies. She had a special candy jar; that was the first spot we went when we visited her! Pralines were one of our favorite candies."

~

Don't be afraid to try your hand at making pralines! There are many ways to use the "mistakes". If the pralines don't harden, scrape the gooey mixture off and fold into vanilla ice cream for Praline Ice Cream. Or, roll into balls and cover with chocolate for Praline Chocolate Truffles. If the praline mixture becomes too hard, break into pieces and sprinkle over a commercial cheesecake for Praline Cheesecake.

Microwave Peanut Brittle

It's Southern, after all!

1½ cups raw shelled peanuts	1 teaspoon butter
1 cup sugar	1 teaspoon vanilla
½ cup light corn syrup	1 teaspoon baking soda
⅛ teaspoon salt	

In a 1½-quart casserole dish, stir together peanuts, sugar, syrup and salt. Cook in a microwave on high power for 8 minutes, stirring well halfway through. Stir in butter and vanilla. Microwave on high 2 minutes longer. Add baking soda and quickly stir until light and foamy. Immediately pour onto a greased baking sheet and spread into a thin layer. When cool, break into small pieces. Store in an airtight container.

Yield: about 1 pound

Chocolate Covered Cherries

You can't buy them this good.

1 stick margarine	1 (10-ounce) jar maraschino cherries, drained well
½ cup sweetened condensed milk	1 (6-ounce) package milk chocolate chips
1 (16-ounce) box powdered sugar	2 (1-ounce) squares semi-sweet chocolate
1 teaspoon vanilla	1 (1-inch) square paraffin wax

Melt margarine. Mix in milk, sugar and vanilla. Roll into small balls and flatten into circles. Blot cherries dry on paper towel and remove stems. Add 1 cherry to each circle and mold mixture around cherry. Chill thoroughly. Melt chocolates and wax together in top of a double boiler. Using a toothpick, dip cherry balls into chocolate mixture. Chill. If needed, dip a second time to cover. Fill toothpick hole with a small drop of chocolate.

Yield: 45 to 50 candies

Sweetened Condensed Milk: A mixture of whole milk and sugar, heated until 60% of water evaporates. The resulting mixture is very sticky and sweet.

Peppermint Puffs

2 egg whites
⅛ teaspoon cream of tartar
⅛ teaspoon salt
¾ cup sugar
8-10 drops red food coloring
3 tablespoons crushed peppermint candy
1 cup semi-sweet chocolate chips
1 cup chopped pecans

Beat egg whites until foamy. Add cream of tartar and salt. Add sugar slowly, beating until stiff. Mix in food coloring. Fold in peppermint, chocolate chips and pecans. Drop by teaspoonfuls onto baking sheets lined with brown paper bags. Bake in preheated 350° oven on center rack for 1 minute. Turn oven off and leave pans inside oven overnight. Do not open oven door until the oven has completely cooled.

Yield: 50 puffs

Rocky Road Clusters
Crunchy and chewy all in one

2   cups semi-sweet chocolate
    chips
¾   cup golden raisins

16 large marshmallows, cut into
    pieces
1½ cups chopped walnuts

Melt chocolate over warm water, stirring until smooth. Add raisins, marshmallows and walnuts and mix well. Drop by teaspoonfuls onto wax paper. Cool.

Yield: 3 dozen

Three Chocolates Fudge
Everybody's favorite

3⅓ cups granulated sugar
1   cup dark brown sugar
2   sticks butter or margarine
1   (12-ounce) can evaporated
    milk
32 large marshmallows, halved
1   (12-ounce) package semi-
    sweet chocolate chips

2   (7-ounce) milk chocolate
    candy bars, broken into
    pieces
2   (1-ounce) squares semi-sweet
    baking chocolate, chopped
1   teaspoon vanilla
2   cups chopped pecans

Combine sugars, butter and milk in a saucepan. Cook over medium heat, stirring until sugar dissolves. Bring to a rapid boil and cook 5 minutes, stirring constantly. Remove from heat and stir in marshmallows until melted. Add chocolate chips and stir until melted. Add chocolate bars and baking chocolate pieces and stir until melted. Fold in vanilla and pecans and mix well. Pour into a greased 10x15x1-inch pan. Chill until firm. Cut into small squares.

Yield: 5½ pounds

To keep fudge from becoming grainy, coat the saucepan with butter before adding ingredients or cover the pan with a lid for a few minutes once the ingredients come to a boil.

Sherried Strawberries

Two summertime favorites, strawberries and ice cream,
come together for this refreshing dessert.

1 quart fresh strawberries, hulled and halved lengthwise	2 tablespoons orange juice
	2 teaspoons freshly squeezed lemon juice
3 tablespoons sherry	2 tablespoons sugar
1 teaspoon orange zest	1 (10-ounce) package frozen raspberries, thawed
½ teaspoon lemon zest	Premium vanilla ice cream

Combine strawberries, sherry, orange and lemon zests, juices and sugar. Cover and chill 60 minutes or longer. Purée raspberries in a blender or food processor. Strain to remove seeds. Chill. To serve, combine strawberry mixture and raspberry sauce. Scoop vanilla ice cream into individual chilled sherbet dishes. Spoon strawberry sauce over the top.

Yield: 6 servings

Variation: *Any almond-flavored, brickle or praline ice cream may be used.*

Georgia Peaches with Raspberry Sauce

It's Southern, after all!

6 ripe peaches, peeled and halved	1 teaspoon cornstarch
Sugar	2 tablespoons freshly squeezed lemon juice
¼ cup sweet sherry	1 quart pistachio ice cream
2 (10-ounce) packages frozen raspberries, thawed	

Place peaches in a casserole dish and sprinkle with a little sugar. Drizzle sherry over fruit and let stand 30 minutes. Purée raspberries in a blender or food processor. Strain to remove seeds. Put into a saucepan and bring to a boil. Dissolve cornstarch in lemon juice and add to saucepan. Cook until slightly thickened. Cool and chill. To serve, place 2 peach halves in each of 6 sherbet dishes. Add a scoop of ice cream and spoon raspberry sauce over top.

Yield: 6 servings

Southerners love their peaches. We grow and eat a lot of them. Peach varieties fall into one of two categories: freestone and clingstone, terms descriptive of how easily the flesh separates from the pit. Most peaches sold fresh are freestone. They are generally juicier and easier to eat. Most canned peaches are clingstone because they are firmer.

~

To peel peaches, plums or nectarines, blanch them for 30 to 60 seconds in boiling water. Lift out with a slotted spoon and cool in ice water. Slip the skins off with your fingers or rub them off with the back of a knife.

Chocolate Fudge Sauce

½ cup unsweetened cocoa
1 cup light corn syrup
1 cup sugar
½ cup half-and-half

3 tablespoons butter or
   margarine
¼ teaspoon salt
1 teaspoon vanilla

Combine all ingredients, except vanilla, in a saucepan. Bring to a boil and cook 5 minutes. Remove from heat and stir in vanilla.

Yield: 2 cups

Low-Fat Chocolate Sauce

¾ cup sugar
¼ cup unsweetened cocoa
1 tablespoon plus 1 teaspoon
    cornstarch

½ cup evaporated skim milk
1 teaspoon vanilla

Mix sugar, cocoa and cornstarch in a small saucepan. Slowly add milk, stirring constantly. Cook over medium heat until thickened. Continue to cook and stir 2 minutes. Remove from heat and add vanilla.

Rum Sundae Sauce

¾ cup brown sugar
⅓ cup water
⅓ cup light corn syrup

2 tablespoons butter or margarine
⅛ teaspoon salt
½ teaspoon rum extract

Combine all ingredients, except rum extract, in a saucepan. Cook and stir over medium heat until sugar dissolves. Reduce to low and cook, without stirring, until mixture reaches 230°. Remove from heat and cool slightly. Stir in rum extract.

Yield: 1 cup

When the menu calls for an elegant dessert, but time is short, try one of these quick and easy toppings.

Toffee Topping

Chill 6 chocolate covered toffee bars and crush. In a chilled bowl, beat 2 cups heavy cream with ½ cup powdered sugar until stiff. Fold in candy pieces. Use to frost a store-bought angel food cake. Chill 1 to 2 hours before serving.

~

Almond Fluff

In a chilled bowl, beat 2 cups heavy cream until stiff. Gently fold in ½ cup white crème de cacao. Serve on slices of angel food cake and garnish with toasted sliced almonds.

If desired, omit crème de cacao and instead gradually add ½ cup instant sweetened chocolate drink mix to the cream as it is beaten.

~

Cherry Topping

Chill 1 can cherry pie filling. In a chilled bowl, beat ¾ cup chilled heavy cream, ½ teaspoon almond extract and 3 tablespoons powdered sugar until stiff. Fold in pie filling. Serve over slices of store-bought pound cake.

Toffee Fudge Sauce

1 (14-ounce) bag caramels   ¼ cup strong coffee
½ cup chocolate chips   ¼ cup milk

Combine all ingredients. Cook over medium heat, stirring occasionally, until melted.

Yield: 2 cups

Peanut-Butter Sundae Sauce

⅔ cup light brown sugar   1 tablespoon honey
½ cup half-and-half   ¾ cup peanut butter

Combine brown sugar, half-and-half and honey. Bring to a boil, stirring constantly. Remove from heat and stir in peanut butter until smooth. Serve warm.

Yield: 1½ cups

Blueberry Sauce

2   cups fresh blueberries   ⅓   cup water
⅓   cup sugar

Combine all ingredients in a medium saucepan. Mix well and bring to a boil. Reduce heat and simmer 4 minutes, stirring occasionally. Serve warm.

Yield: 2 cups

One Minute Liqueur Desserts

Fill a champagne glass with large, ripe strawberries. Sprinkle with toasted almonds. Pour 2 to 3 tablespoons amaretto liqueur over the top and serve with Amaretti cookies.

~

Fill a parfait glass with chocolate ice cream. Drizzle with 2 to 3 tablespoons Irish cream liqueur. Top with whipped cream and grated chocolate.

~

Fill a sherbet dish with lemon sherbet. Drizzle with 2 to 3 tablespoons green crème de menthe liqueur. Garnish with a mint leaf.

~

Place a thin slice of pound cake on a dessert plate. Top with thin slices of kiwi and a scoop of vanilla ice cream. Drizzle with 2 to 3 tablespoons Drambuie liqueur.

Contributors

A book of this type would not be possible without the help of countless volunteers. To those who contributed recipes and memories, we offer a big thank you. A cookbook is only as good as its recipes, and we have some of the best. We regret that we were not able to include all that we received due to space limitations and duplications. Know that your submissions were appreciated and contributed greatly to the overall quality of the book. To those who spent numerous hours testing and evaluating recipes, copying, writing, editing, compiling, marketing, selling and, in many cases, simply listening to our labor pains, our heartfelt thanks. Thanks as well to those whose efforts are yet to come as this book continues to be read and enjoyed. To anyone whose name we have inadvertently omitted, please accept our sincere apologies. Lastly, to our families who have so patiently waited with us for this book to become a reality, a very special thank you.

Francine Adair
Mary Adams
Lee Albright
Marianne Rogers Alias
Lucy Allen
Glenda Anderson
Evelyn Anthony
Jeane Argo
Mimi Argo-Laney
Kim Arnold
ATHENS COUNTRY CLUB
Sue Austin
Donna Avans
THE BASIL PRESS
Terry Barker
Emma Barnes
Sally Barnes
Kathy Barrow
Ruth Bauerle
Cindy Beck
Mary Beisswenger
Amanda Bell
Kay Bennett
Angie Bentley
Nancy Bethmann
Sally Bingham
Andrea Blaesing
Delores Blanton
Dottie Blitch
Cindy Boerma
Ceil Bone
Denise Bonner
Annie Booth
Jackie Booth
Nina Borremans
Tina Boswell
Mary Jean Bouton
Sara Bowen
Jenny Broadnax
Jan Brooks
Sharon Broun
Barbi Brown
Nancy Brudney
Susan Buchanan
Alice Bullock
Anita Bunn
Jeanie Burbage
Deveraux Burch
Cindy Calandra
Myra Callaway
Claire Callaway

Sarah Callaway
Betsy Canfield
Jacqueline Canupp
Winnie Carey
Candy Carillo
Libby Carson
Gayle Carswell
Bobbie Carter
Stephanie Cartwright
Jerry Caskin
SALLY ANN CAUTHEN–
    DELIGHTFUL BITEFULS
Nell Chambers
Alex Chambers
Dene Channell
CHARLIE WILLIAMS
    PINECREST LODGE
Elizabeth Chastain
Suzanne Chastain
Clara Childers
Linda Childers
Carol Clack
Mrs. H. H. Cobb
Terry Coffey
Alice Ann Colley
Geneva Colley
Arnelle Combs
Linda Cook
Deanna Cook
Deborah Cornelison
Ellen Coulliard
Amy Cowsert
Paula Crosby
Susie Cross
Ellen Cunningham
Elizabeth Dalton
Debbie Darracott
Natalie Darracott
Janet Darvill
Gautum DasGupta
Anne Dattilo
Bobbi Davis
Rosemary Davis
Carol Deaton
Terry DeMeo
Mrs. George Denegre
DE PALMA'S
Betty DeVore
Vicki Dickens
Lynn Dicks
Mary Donnan

Melody Dorfman
Laurie Douglas
Meg Downs
Becky Duncan
John Dunleavy
Bess Durham
Anna Dyer
EAST WEST BISTRO
Deena Eberhardt
Milton Eisenberg
Sheri Eldridge
Judith Ellis
Betsy Ellison
Marsha Elsberry
Chad Erwin
Lee Erwin
Sissy Erwin-Toro
Flora Faircloth
Leon Farmer, Jr.
Gayle Felchlin
Julie Finleyson
Jan Firth
FIVE STAR CAFE
Jennifer Foster
Sally Foster
Valerie Franklin
Vicki Gaines
Jane Galis
Carol Gardner
Karen Gardner
Henry Garrard
Carolyn Garrard
Terry Gautreaux
Ken Gaver
Carolyn Gazda
Em Gibson
Kay Giese
Cheryl Goldsleger
Joyce Green
Helen Gregory
Gwen Griffin
Pat Gritton
DeDe Guest
Diana Guest
Frances Guest
Beth Haggard
Allison Hale
Catherine Hardman
Mary Ann Hardman

HARRY BISSETT'S
  NEW ORLEANS CAFÉ
  AND OYSTER BAR
Terry Hastings
Beth Hawk
Julie Hayes
Alison Hays
Jayne Henson
Lee Herrin
Nina Herrington
Jeanne Higbee
Bert Hill
Lyn Hill
Joanna Hill
Mary Ella Hill
Sally Hillard
Suzette Hodge
Ann Holcombe
Jana Hollingsworth
Rita Hollingsworth
Melanie Hollis
Anne Holmes
Paula Hooper
Warren Horn
Anne Howard
Patsy Huban
Lisa Huggins
Donna Hulsey
Zanne Hunt
Nancy Hunter
Jane Inscoe
Cathy Jackson
Sandy Jarrett
Lance F. Jeffers, Jr.
Mary Jenkins
JENNINGS MILL
  COUNTRY CLUB
Susie Jerkins
Valerie Johnson
Charlotte Johnson
Anne Jones
Debbie Jones
Bonnie Jones
Marianne Jordan
Elaine Kalber
Patty Keith
Marty Keller
Marty Kemp
Thelma Kenney
Karen Kimbaris
Sheryl Kimbrough
Suzanne King
Teresa Kittle
Brenda Klein
Tina Kukanza
Carol Kurtz
Ruth Ann Lariscy
THE LAST RESORT
Elizabeth Latimer
LEE EPTING CATERING
Mary Ann Lewis
Charlie Lewis
Mrs. Tommy Lewis
Margaret Liedberg
Sharon Lindell
Robbie Link
Katie Lloyd

Kathy Lober
Mary Long
John Lough
Lee Lyons
Kim Maddox
Stacy Mallet
Rosemary Malone
Sue Marion
Sherry Martin
Marion Marvel
Diana Maxwell
Patricia Maxwell
Julie Maynard
Christopher McCook
Mary McCutchen
Paula McDonald
Cindy McFadden
Frank McKinley
Sheri McLeod
Shari Messer
Karen Middendorf
Larry Millard
Mary Miller
Gilbert Milner
Wanda Moon
Susan Moore
Winnie Moore
Laura Morang
Frances Morang
Becky Morang
Anne Moreman
Marietta Morris
Jane Mullins
Melissa Murray
Susan Myers
Pam NeSmith
Gayla Nickerson
Anne Nielson
Terry Noel
Vicki Noffke
Wilma Nozza
Amy O'Neill
Robin O'Rear
Claudia O'Steen
Omayma Obeidin
Crysty Odom
Becky Padgett
Mary Padgett
Josephine Paine
Toni Parr
Milton Parr
Beth Petrie
Jean Petrovs
Nancy Pettee
Beverly Phares
Debra Pigage
Melissa Poland
Bob Poss, Sr.
Kathy Pruett
Alice Pruitt
Mary Ellen Quinn
Diane Rankin
Lisa Ransom
Mayson Ransom
Peggy Reigle
Sharon Reinking
Jan Rhodes

Mrs. Melvin Richoux
Caroline Ridlehuber
Sue Roalman
Eileen Robb
Tudy Roberts
Margaret Robinson
Carol Robinson
Lili Rogers
Lisa Roper
Barbara Rose
Kathy Rowan
Tricia Ruppersburg
Sandy Sanders
Jan Satterfield
Beth Saye
Marty Shaw
Sally Shealy
Louise Simpson
Leslie Sinyard
Betty Sisk
Christa Slaughter
Beverly Sligh
Michelle Sligh
Gwen Smith
Judy Smith
Vicki Smith
Margie Spalding
Wendy Steiner
Robin Stewart
Jerri Stracener
Virginia Stutsman
Susanne Sweat
Mary Anna Terrell
Andree Terry
Ruby Tillman
Gina Tillman
Kelley Tison
Linda Todd
Juan Toro
Lucy Tresp
Charlotte Trice
Christina Van Fleet
Linda VanSickle
Lauren Venditto
Reggie Vipperman
CECILIA VILLAVECES
  CAKES
Jody Vrana
Patty Walker
Buck Walters
Laura Wayson
WEAVER D'S
Geneva Wedgeworth
Carroll Wellman
Susan West
Nick White
Marlo Wiggans
Anne Wilfong
Ellen Wilkins
John Wilkins
Lovat Wilkins
Paula Williams
Mary Wimberly
Gwen Wines
Nita Woodruff
Katherine Youngquist
ZIM'S BAGEL BAKERY

249

Index

Index

Index

Index

Index

Index

Index

Under the Magnolias

A Tasteful Tour of Athens

Athens' Newest Community Cookbook

Over 400 tested recipes from Athens' finest cooks are complemented by sidebars full of food facts and fancy — all intended to enhance your "tasteful tour of Athens." Whether you are looking for something quick and easy to make between the board meeting and the soccer game, or an elegant dessert for your holiday table, *Under the Magnolias* delivers.

Please send me _____ copies
    of *Under the Magnolias, A Tasteful Tour of Athens*   @ $ 18.95 each
Shipping and Handling   @ $ 3.50 each
Gift Wrapping   @ $ 1.00 each
                  Total Payment $_____

Name_____

Address_____

City_____ State _____ Zip _____

Send order form and payment to:

Under the Magnolias

c/o Athens Academy PSO • P.O. Box 6548 • Athens, Georgia 30604

Please enclose check payable to Athens Academy PSO Cookbook.
For more information or credit card orders, in Athens call (706) 549-9225 or
www.athensacademy.org

Under the Magnolias

A Tasteful Tour of Athens

Athens' Newest Community Cookbook

Over 400 tested recipes from Athens' finest cooks are complemented by sidebars full of food facts and fancy — all intended to enhance your "tasteful tour of Athens." Whether you are looking for something quick and easy to make between the board meeting and the soccer game, or an elegant dessert for your holiday table, *Under the Magnolias* delivers.

Please send me _____ copies
    of *Under the Magnolias, A Tasteful Tour of Athens*   @ $ 18.95 each
Shipping and Handling   @ $ 3.50 each
Gift Wrapping   @ $ 1.00 each
                  Total Payment $_____

Name_____

Address_____

City_____ State _____ Zip _____

Send order form and payment to:

Under the Magnolias

c/o Athens Academy PSO • P.O. Box 6548 • Athens, Georgia 30604

Please enclose check payable to Athens Academy PSO Cookbook.
For more information or credit card orders, in Athens call (706) 549-9225 or
www.athensacademy.org